FINDING SCRIPTURE VERSES MADE EASY

FINDING SCRIPTURE VERSES MADE EASY

'Thy word have I hid in mine heart.'

M. G. Barr

AMBASSADOR INTERNATIONAL
GREENVILLE, SOUTH CAROLINA & BELFAST, NORTHERN IRELAND

www.ambassador-international.com

Finding Scripture Verses Made Easy

'Thy word have I hid in mine heart.'

ISBN: 978-1-935507-36-9

Designed and Printed by Bethel Solutions

Ambassador International
Emerald House
427 Wade Hampton Blvd
Greenville, SC 29609, USA

Ambassador Books and Media
The Mount
2 Woodstock Link
Belfast, BT6 8DD, Northern Ireland, UK

www.ambassador-international.com

"Thy word have I hid in mine heart, that I might not sin against thee."

Psalm 119 v 11

Dedicated to SermonAudio, which provides the world with sound doctrinal teaching.

www.sermonaudio.com

Special thanks to Mr Sam Lowry, publisher of Ambassador Publications, for agreeing to publish my unusual book.

Special thanks to Mr Mark Linton, of Bethel Solutions, for so painstakingly working on a very difficult manuscript.

Also special thanks to my proofreader, friend and mentor, Miss Mary McKendry who spent hours tirelessly scrutinizing the manuscript.

CONTENTS

FOREWARD

As I read this book I am genuinely intrigued by the unique way in which the author has developed the idea of:

(Bible verse location by association).

Through her persistence and passion for scripture, she has been successful in the production of a work, which to the best of my knowledge has never been attempted before.

She has conscientiously approached each Bible reference with a genuine desire to be of assistance to those who wish to locate scripture verses, and this has been carried out in an unusual and sometimes humorous way.

My knowledge of scripture has certainly been enhanced by the memorization of certain sections, and the references to parallel verses have been most informative.

Mary Mc Kendry B.A. (Hons) D.A.S.E.

INTRODUCTION

This book is all about mnemonics, i.e. forming associations to enable you to find verses of Scripture. It has always been my intention to be able to locate well-known Scripture verses, and although I remembered which page and the position on the page, I was unable to remember book and chapter.

However, I have discovered an excellent way to be able to locate verses quickly. Using this method I am able to locate any verse that I choose. It is not necessary to memorize the verse, just the book and chapter. This is a lighter load for the mind. If you can identify the book and chapter it is not difficult to find the verse.

You may have to think some of the associations through, as these are my associations, and not everyone comprehends a concept in the same way. However it will be well worth the effort and you can then learn to form your own associations for the verses you want to find.

If you are not familiar with forming associations then I will offer you some advice concerning them.

Always take time to make sure the association is understood and that it is fixed in your mind in accordance with the verse or verses which you want to memorize the location of. Do not try to memorize more than three each day. Before starting to memorize additional locations always check that you still remember the ones you have already learned.

This is not a teaching book, so when I form associations they are only aids to help in memorizing where to find verses of Scripture.

N.B. When I add an extra word to the Scripture text I am not adding to the word of God. It is either to inform you who is being referred to, or it is used to form an association. The word of God is always witten in *italics* to differentiate it, e.g. *But his* (Lot's) *wife looked back from behind him, and she became a pillar of salt.* The word 'Lot's' is used to tell you who is being referred to.

And Jacob (**supplanter**) *was left alone; and there wrestled a man with him until the breaking of the day.* The word 'supplanter' is used to form an association, so it is written in bold.

How To Use This Book

When forming associations, in order to remember which chapter the verses are in, I sometimes count the number of letters in a phrase and at other times I count the number of words.

The letters or words that need to be **counted** are always printed in **BOLD CAPITALS**, e.g. *And Abraham lifted up his eyes (**ABRAHAM LIFTED UP HIS EYES**), and looked, and behold behind [him] a ram caught in a thicket by his horns: and Abraham went and took the ram, and offered him up for a burnt offering in the stead of his son.* Genesis 22:13.

ABRAHAM LIFTED UP HIS EYES – **22** letters, so this verse is in chapter **22**.

*The fire shall ever be burning (**THE FIRE SHALL EVER BE BURNING**) upon the altar; it shall never go out.* Leviticus 6:13.

THE FIRE SHALL EVER BE BURNING – **6** words, so this verse is in chapter **6**.

As you can see from the above examples a verse could be in either one of two chapters. The first example could be in chapter 22 or chapter 5 and the second example could be in chapter 25 or chapter 6. This shouldn't present a significant problem as it narrows the chapters down to two, so if it is not in one of the chapters then it is in the other. In the course of time you will memorize whether to count letters or words.

Occasionally it is not possible to use the actual words of Scripture for determining the chapter, so I form a sentence, which is related to the words in the verse/verses of Scripture, e.g. *The name of the LORD [is] a strong tower **(strong tower)**: the righteous runneth into it, and is safe.* Proverbs 18:10.

WE HAVE A STRONG TOWER – **18** letters, so this verse is in chapter **18**.

In the following example I am **not counting** the letters or words to determine which chapter the verse is in, so the words are printed in **bold lower case**.

*And Jacob said, Sell me this day thy birthright **(birthright)**.* Genesis 25:31.

December **25th** is when we specially remember our Saviour's **birth**, so it is in chapter **25**.

Occasionally I have to use a slightly different method to arrive at the correct number for the chapter – e.g. *Come unto me, all [ye] that labour **(labour)** and are heavy laden **(laden)**, and I will give you rest.* Matthew 11:28.

The first letter of **l**abour and **l**aden is **l**, put the two letters together **ll** and it looks like number **11**, so this verse is in chapter **11**.

There are other methods used but I will always explain how to work them out.

As you progress through this book you will notice that I use frequent repetition with some consecutive associations. You will also notice that I use the words 'for the purpose of association' throughout the book. This is necessary as each association is a separate item.

I am convinced that memorizing the number of chapters in each book of the Bible is a great advantage to Bible study. Matthew has

28 chapters and if one knows that the story of the crucifixion is near the end of the book then he/she knows that it is somewhere around chapter 26 - 28. If the number of chapters is not known then it is impossible to know which chapter it is in.

Matthew has 28 chapters and the story of the crucifixion is in chapter 27.
Mark has 16 chapters and the story of the crucifixion is in chapter 15.
Luke has 24 chapters and the story of the crucifixion is in chapter 23.
John has 21 chapters and the story of the crucifixion is in chapter 19.

I know from experience that memorizing the number of chapters in each book of the Bible is helpful in many ways when studying the Bible. I suggest that you start this book by doing just that.

39 BOOKS OF THE OLD TESTAMENT

Genesis **50**, Exodus **40**, Leviticus **27**, Numbers **36**, Deuteronomy **34**, Joshua **24**, Judges **21**, Ruth **4**, 1st Samuel **31**, 2nd Samuel **24**, 1st Kings **22**, 2nd Kings **25**, 1st Chronicles **29**, 2nd Chronicles **36**, Ezra **10**, Nehemiah **13**, Esther **10**, Job **42**, Psalms **150**, Proverbs **31**, Ecclesiastes **12**, Song of Solomon **8**, Isaiah **66**, Jeremiah **52**, Lamentations **5**, Ezekiel **48**, Daniel **12**, Hosea **14**, Joel **3**, Amos **9**, Obadiah **1**, Jonah **4**, Micah **7**, Nahum **3**, Habakkuk **3**, Zephaniah **3**, Haggai **2**, Zechariah **14**, Malachi **4**.

27 BOOKS OF THE NEW TESTAMENT

Matthew **28**, Mark **16**, Luke **24**, John **21**, Acts **28**, Romans **16**, 1st Corinthians **16**, 2nd Corinthians **13**, Galatians **6**, Ephesians **6**, Philippians **4**, Colossians **4**, 1st Thessalonians **5**, 2nd Thessalonians **3**, 1st Timothy **6**, 2nd Timothy **4**, Titus **3**, Philemon **1**, Hebrews **13**, James **5**, 1st Peter **5**, 2nd Peter **3**, 1st John **5**, 2nd John **1**, 3rd John **1**, Jude **1**, Revelation **22**.

Some Other Details To Memorize Before Starting To Form Associations

If you are not familiar with the following details then I would suggest that you take your Bible and read the relevant chapters.

The book of Exodus starts with a list of the children of Israel, i.e. the twelve tribes, who came into Egypt. Abram (Abraham) was the Great grandfather of the twelve tribes, so he was before this time; therefore the narratives about (Abram) Abraham are in the book of Genesis. The last chapter of the book of Exodus, i.e. chapter 40, is about the setting up of the tabernacle. The last five verses are about the cloud covering the tabernacle and the glory of the LORD filling it.

The last chapter of the book of Deuteronomy, i.e. chapter 34, records the death of Moses. Joshua was Moses' minister, and after the death of Moses he took over the task of leading the Israelites into Canaan. So the book of Joshua follows the book of Deuteronomy. Joshua's death is recorded in the last chapter of the book of Joshua.

The book of Judges follows the book of Joshua and records the history of the Israelites under the rule of the judges. The Israelites had no king as yet, so God raised up the judges to deliver them from their enemies.

The book of 1st Samuel is about Samuel, Saul and David. The book of 1st Samuel contains the narrative of the anointing of the first king of Israel, (a good association: 1st Samuel, 1st king). His name was Saul and the prophet Samuel anointed him. The book of 1st Samuel also contains the narrative of the prophet Samuel anointing David to be king after Saul. The book of 1st Samuel chapter 31, i.e. the last chapter, records the death of Saul.

The book of 2nd Samuel 2:4 informs us that the men of Judah anointed David king over the house of Judah. The book of 2nd Samuel 5:3 informs us that the elders of Israel anointed David king over Israel. The book of 2nd Samuel is about David when he is king.

The book of 1st Kings chapter 2 records the death of David. The book of 1st Kings 2:12 to the end, and the book of 2nd Kings in its entirety contain the narratives about the kings of Israel and Judah beginning with Solomon. The last chapter of the book of 1st Kings, i.e. chapter 22 records the deaths of king Jehoshaphat the 4th king of Judah and king Ahab the 7th king of Israel. The book of 1st Kings also contains the narratives about Elijah.

The book of 2nd Kings 2:11 tells us that Elijah went up by a whirlwind into heaven. The book of 2nd Kings also contains the narratives about Elisha.

The book of Ezra is about the building of the temple of the LORD.

The book of Nehemiah is about the building of the walls of Jerusalem.

The 10 commandments are known as The Moral Law.
The book of Deuteronomy is known as The Second Law.
The Jews called the book of Deuteronomy 'These are the words' or 'Words.'

Psalm 119 is the longest chapter in the Bible.
Psalm 117 is the shortest chapter in the Bible.

The longest verse in the Bible is Esther 8:9: *Then the king's scribes were called at that time, in the third month Sivan, on the twenty-third day of the month; and it was written according to all that Mordecai commanded to the Jews, and to the satraps, and the governors and princes of the provinces which are from India to Ethiopia, one hundred twenty-seven provinces, to every province according to its writing, and to every people in their language, and to the Jews in their writing, and in their language.*

The shortest verse in the Bible is John 11:35: *Jesus wept.*

The seven 'I am's' of Jesus are found in the gospel of John.

I am the Bread of life. John chapter 6.
I am the Light of the world. John chapter 8.
I am the Door. John chapter 10.
I am the Good Shepherd. John chapter 10.
I am the Resurrection and the Life. This verse is found in the narrative of the death of Lazarus. John chapter 11.

I am the way, the Truth and the Life. John chapter 14.
I am the True Vine. John chapter 15.

I will form associations for these later. Just remember that they are in the gospel of John, and that will be helpful when the associations are being formed.

The book of Matthew portrays Jesus as the King.
The book of Mark portrays Jesus as the Servant.
The book of Luke portrays Jesus as the Son of man.
The book of John portrays Jesus as the Son of God.
The book of Acts is about the early church.

Chapter 1 records the details of our Lord's ascension into Heaven, and also the choosing of an apostle to replace Judas Iscariot.

Chapter 2 is about the coming of the Holy Spirit on the day of Pentecost.

Any sermons or orations by the disciples, or miracles that God performed through the disciples are recorded in the book of Acts.
Any manifestations from Heaven to the disciples when Jesus is not present are recorded in the book of Acts.
The choosing of the seven deacons is recorded in the book of Acts.
Paul's missionary journeys are recorded in the book of Acts.
The spread of the gospel is recorded in the book of Acts.

But ye shall receive power, after that the Holy Ghost is come upon you: and ye shall be witnesses unto me both in Jerusalem, and in all Judaea, and in Samaria, and unto the uttermost part of the earth. Acts 1:8.

The phrases 'Barnabas and Saul', 'Paul and Barnabas', 'Barnabas and Paul' and 'Paul and Silas' are only found in the book of Acts.
The church at Philippi was the first church in Europe.

I have used some numbers when forming associations, as numbers have great significance in Scripture.

3 is the number of divine perfection.
4 is the number of creation.

5 is the number of grace.
6 is the number of man.
7 is the number of spiritual perfection.
9 is the number of finality or judgment.
10 is the number of divine order.
11 is the number of disorder and imperfection.
12 is the number of perfect government.
13 is the number of rebellion, apostasy and corruption.

Ezekiel is called the son of man 93 times.
Daniel is called the son of man 1 time.
Jesus is called the Son of man 44 times in Matthew, 2 times in Mark, 26 times in Luke and 13 times in John.

If you arrange the gospels in order of how many chapters each has, starting with the highest number it looks like this.

Matthew has	28 chapters.	44 times.
Luke has	24 chapters.	26 times.
John has	21 chapters.	13 times.
Mark has	16 chapters.	2 times.

Notice that the above two lists start with the highest number and continue to the lowest number. Matthew has two ts in it and 44 has two fours in it, so that is a good association. Then notice that there is 26, 13 and 2. 13x2 =26. So that is another good association.

Now all you have to do is remember 44 and 13x2=26 and write out both lists starting with the highest number.

I would suggest that you memorize the names of the kings of Judah and Israel. This will be a great help when you are studying the Old Testament, as there is so much detail about the kings recorded in it.

Saul was the first king of Israel.
David was the second king of Israel.

After Saul's death, his son Ishbosheth was made king by Abner, who is described in Scripture as the captain of Saul's host. The tribe of Judah rejected Ishbosheth, choosing David as their king, as he was of their tribe, had a great record of success, and the LORD had chosen him to be king. During Ishbosheth's two years as king, there was constant strife between Israel and Judah, and throughout this period Judah grew stronger and Israel weaker.

Solomon (David's son) was the third king of Israel and the second king of the House of David. Rehoboam (Solomon's son) was the fourth king of Israel and the third king of the House of David. During his reign the kingdom was divided into Judah and Israel.

KINGS OF JUDAH OF THE DIVIDED KINGDOM

(1) Rehoboam,
(2) Abijah, also known as Abijam,
(3) Asa,
(4) Jehoshaphat,
(5) Joram, also known as Jehoram,
(6) Ahaziah, also known as Jehoahaz and Azariah,
(7) Athaliah was a queen,
(8) Joash, also known as Jehoash,
(9) Amaziah,
(10) Azariah, also known as Uzziah,
(11) Jotham,
(12) Ahaz,
(13) Hezekiah,
(14) Manasseh,
(15) Amon,
(16) Josiah,
(17) Jehoahaz, also known as Shallum,
(18) Jehoiakim, also known as Eliakim,
(19) Jehoiachin, also known as Jeconiah, Coniah and Jechonias,
(20) Zedekiah. also known as Mattaniah.

KINGS OF ISRAEL OF THE DIVIDED KINGDOM

(1) Jeroboam,
(2) Nadab,
(3) Baasha,
(4) Elah,

(5) Zimri,
(6) Omri,
(7) Ahab,
(8) Ahaziah,
(9) Joram, also known as Jehoram,
(10) Jehu,
(11) Jehoahaz,
(12) Jehoash, also known as Joash
(13) Jeroboam II,
(14) Zachariah,
(15) Shallum,
(16) Menahem,
(17) Pekahiah,
(18) Pekah,
(19) Hoshea.

This may seem like a lot to memorize but I can assure you it is worth the effort. It is also helpful to know what age each king was when he began to reign and how many years he reigned. Some of the kings were very young when they began to reign. Joash (Jehoash) king of Judah was seven years old, Azariah, (Uzziah) king of Judah was sixteen years old, Josiah king of Judah was eight years old, Manasseh king of Judah was twelve years old and Jehoiachin king of Judah was eight years old.

This book is written to help and encourage all who love the Bible, and desire to study it, and also for those who have not yet discovered the joy and benefits of Bible study.

Forming Associations

GENESIS

No. 1
And the LORD God formed man (i.e. his physical **body**) *[of] the dust of the ground, and breathed into his nostrils the breath of life; and man became a living soul* (his **soul**). Genesis 2:7.

Genesis means **beginning**. This verse is about the **beginning** of mankind, so it is in the book of Genesis. This verse speaks of **2** parts of man: **body** and **soul**, so it is in chapter **2**.

No. 2
And the LORD God said unto the serpent, Because thou hast done this, thou [art] cursed above all cattle, and above every beast of the field; upon thy belly shalt thou go, and dust shalt thou eat all the days of thy life:
And I will put enmity between thee and the woman, and between thy seed and her **(HER)** *seed; it shall bruise thy head, and thou shalt bruise his heel.* Genesis 3:14-15.

God spoke these words to the serpent in the Garden of Eden, so these verses concern the **beginning** of mankind. Genesis means **beginning**, so they are in the book of Genesis.

HER – **3** letters, so these verses are in chapter **3**.

No. 3
Unto the woman **(EVE)** *he said, I will greatly multiply thy sorrow and thy conception; in sorrow thou shalt bring forth children; and thy desire [shall be] to thy husband, and he shall rule over thee.* Genesis 3:16.

This verse is about the **beginning** of mankind. Genesis means **beginning,** so it is in the book of Genesis.

EVE – **3** letters, so this verse is in chapter **3**.

No. 4
In the sweat of thy face shalt thou eat bread, till thou return unto the ground; for out of it wast thou (Adam) *taken: for dust thou [art]* **(DUST THOU [ART])**, *and unto dust shalt thou return.*
Genesis 3:19.

God spoke these words to Adam, so this verse concerns the **beginning** of mankind. Genesis means **beginning**, so it is in the book of Genesis.

DUST THOU ART – **3** words, so this verse is in chapter **3**.

No. 5
And Cain talked with Abel his brother: and it came to pass, when they were in the field, that Cain rose up against Abel his brother, and slew **(SLEW)** *him.* Genesis 4:8.

Cain and Abel were Adam and Eve's sons, so this verse is about a time near the **beginning** of mankind. Genesis means **beginning**, so it is in the book of Genesis.

SLEW - **4** letters, so this verse is in chapter **4**.

No. 6
But Noah **(a man)** *found grace in the eyes of the LORD.*
Genesis 6:8.

Genesis means **beginning**. Noah and his family were the **beginning** of the population following the flood, so this verse is in the book of Genesis.
Noah was a **man** but he found grace in the eyes of the LORD.

6 is the number of **man**, so this verse is in chapter **6**.

No. 7
*And it came to pass at the end of forty days, that Noah (**Noah**) opened the window of the ark which he had made:*
*And he sent forth a raven, which went forth to and fro (**TO AND FRO**), until the waters were dried up from off the earth.*
Genesis 8:6-7.

Genesis means **beginning**. **Noah** and his family were the **beginning** of the population following the flood, so these verses are in the book of Genesis.

TO AND FRO – 8 letters, so they are in chapter **8**.

No. 8
*While the earth remaineth, seedtime (**seedtime**) and harvest (**harvest**), and cold (**cold**) and heat (**heat**), and summer (**summer**) and winter (**winter**), and day (**day**) and night (**night**) shall not cease.*
Genesis 8:22.

Genesis means **beginning**. God spoke these words to Noah. Noah and his family were the **beginning** of the population following the flood, so this verse is in the book of Genesis.

(1) seedtime
(2) harvest
(3) cold
(4) heat
(5) summer
(6) winter
(7) day
(8) night

The above verse is in chapter **8**.

No. 9
Therefore is the name of it called Babel; because the LORD did there confound (**to throw into confusion or a state of disorder**) *the language of all the earth: and from thence did the LORD scatter them abroad upon the face of all the earth.* Genesis 11:9.

This was the **beginning** of people being scattered over the earth and Genesis means **beginning**, so this verse is in the book of Genesis.

11 is the number of **disorder**, so it is in chapter **11**.

No. 10
*Now the LORD had said unto Abram **(Abram)**, Get thee out of thy country, and from thy kindred, and from thy father's house **(and from thy father's house)**, unto a land that I will shew thee:*
And I will make of thee a great nation, and I will bless thee, and make thy name great; and thou shalt be a blessing:
And I will bless them that bless thee, and curse him that curseth thee: and in thee shall all families of the earth be blessed. Genesis 12:1-3.

Remember I stated at the beginning of this book that Exodus starts with a list of the children of Israel, i.e. the twelve tribes who came into Egypt. **Abram** was the Great grandfather of the twelve tribes; therefore he was before this time, so these verses are in the book of Genesis. For the purpose of association, think that **God separated Abram from his father's house** to be the progenitor of the **12** tribes of Israel.

12 tribes – so these verses are in chapter **12**.

No. 11
*Neither shall thy name any more be called Abram **(ABRAM)**, but thy name shall be Abraham **(ABRAHAM)**; for a father* **(BEGAT)** *of many nations have I made thee.* Genesis 17:5.

Remember I stated at the beginning of this book that Exodus begins with a list of the children of Israel, i.e. the twelve tribes who came into Egypt. Abraham was the Great grandfather of the twelve tribes; therefore he was before this time. Abraham's name is mentioned in many books of the Bible, but any narratives that record incidents during the lifetime of Abraham are in the book of Genesis.

ABRAM ABRAHAM BEGAT – **17** letters, so this verse is in chapter **17**.

No. 12
*And it came to pass, when they had brought them forth abroad, that he said, Escape for thy life; look not behind thee, neither stay thou in all the plain; escape to the mountain (**ESCAPE TO THE MOUNTAIN**), lest thou be consumed.* Genesis 19:17.

But his (Lot's) wife looked back from behind him, and she became a pillar of salt. Genesis 19:26.

His wife looked back. For the purpose of association, think of looking back as looking back to the **beginning,** and Genesis means **beginning,** so these verses are in the book of Genesis.

In verse seventeen Lot and his family are advised to **ESCAPE TO THE MOUNTAIN** – **19** letters, so these verses are in chapter **19**.

No. 13
And the LORD visited Sarah as he had said, and the LORD did unto Sarah as he had spoken.
For Sarah conceived, and bare Abraham a son in his old age, at the set time of which God had spoken to him.
*And Abraham called the name of his son that was born unto him, whom Sarah bare to him, Isaac **(Isaac)**.* Genesis 21:1-3.

See association number 11 for details concerning Abraham.

ABRAHAM CALLED HIM ISAAC - 21 letters, so these verses are in chapter **21**.

No. 14
*And Abraham lifted up his eyes (**ABRAHAM LIFTED UP HIS EYES**), and looked, and behold behind [him] a ram caught in a thicket by his horns: and Abraham went and took the ram, and offered him up for a burnt offering in the stead of his son.* Genesis 22:13.

See association number 11 for details concerning Abraham.

ABRAHAM LIFTED UP HIS EYES – **22** letters, so this verse is in chapter **22**.

No. 15
*And after this, Abraham buried Sarah **(buried Sarah)** his wife in the cave of the field of Machpelah **(Machpelah)** before Mamre: the same [is] Hebron in the land of Canaan.* Genesis 23:19.

See association number 11 for details concerning Abraham.

SARAH'S TOMB IS AT MACHPELAH – **23** letters, so this verse is in chapter **23**.

No. 16
*And they called Rebekah **(Rebekah)**, and said unto her, Wilt thou go with this man? And she said, I will go.* Genesis 24:58.

This was the **beginning** of a new life for **Rebekah**, and Genesis means **beginning**, so this verse is in the book of Genesis.

REBEKAH COMMENCES A NEW LIFE – **24** letters, so it is in chapter **24**.

No. 17
And these [are] the days of the years of Abraham's life which he lived, an hundred threescore and fifteen years.
*Then Abraham gave up the ghost **(THEN ABRAHAM GAVE UP THE GHOST)**, and died in a good old age, an old man, and full [of years]; and was gathered to his people.*
And his sons Isaac and Ishmael buried him in the cave of Machpelah, in the field of Ephron the son of Zohar the Hittite, which [is] before Mamre; Genesis 25:7-9.

See association number 11 for details concerning Abraham.

THEN ABRAHAM GAVE UP THE GHOST – **25** letters, so these verses are in chapter **25**.

No. 18
*And Jacob said, Sell me this day thy birthright **(birth**right).*
Genesis 25:31.

Birth is at the **beginning** of life, and Genesis means **beginning**, so this verse is in the book of Genesis.

December **25**th is when we specially remember our Saviour's **birth**, so it is in chapter **25**.

No. 19
*And Jacob (**Jacob**) said unto his father (**father**), I [am] Esau thy firstborn; I have done according as thou badest me: arise, I pray thee, sit and eat of my venison, that thy soul may bless me.* Genesis 27:19.

Remember I stated at the beginning of this book that Exodus begins with a list of the children of Israel (Jacob), i.e. the twelve tribes who came into Egypt. Jacob was the father of the twelve tribes and he has no children as yet, so this verse is in the book of Genesis.

JACOB DECEIVES HIS FATHER ISAAC – **27** letters, so it is in chapter **27.**

No. 20
*And he (Jacob) dreamed, and behold a ladder set up on the earth (**earth**), and the top of it reached to heaven (**AND THE TOP OF IT REACHED TO HEAVEN**): and behold the angels of God ascending and descending on it.* Genesis 28:12.

Genesis means **beginning**, and for the purpose of association, think of the **beginning** of the ladder, i.e. the bottom of it, being on **earth**, so this verse is in the book of Genesis.

AND THE TOP OF IT REACHED TO HEAVEN – **28** letters, so it is in chapter **28.**

No. 21
*And Jacob (**Jacob**) (**supplanter**) was left alone; and there wrestled a man with him until the breaking of the day.*
And when he saw that he prevailed not against him, he touched the hollow of his thigh; and the hollow of Jacob's thigh was out of joint, as he wrestled with him.

And he said, Let me go, for the day breaketh. And he said, I will not let thee go, except thou bless me.

And he said unto him, What [is] thy name? And he said, Jacob.

And he said, Thy name shall be called no more Jacob, but Israel **(Thy name shall be called no more Jacob, but Israel)***: for as a prince hast thou power with God and with men, and hast prevailed.*

Genesis 32:24-28.

Remember I stated at the beginning of this book that Exodus begins with a list of the children of Israel (Jacob), i.e. the twelve tribes who came into Egypt. Jacob was the father of the twelve tribes and he has no children as yet, so these verses are in the book of Genesis.

JACOB THE SUPPLANTER NOW HAS A NEW NAME – 32 letters so they are in chapter **32**.

No. 22

Now the sons of Jacob (Israel) *were twelve:*

The sons of Leah **(THE SONS OF LEAH)***; Reuben, Jacob's firstborn, and Simeon, and Levi, and Judah, and Issachar, and Zebulun:*

The sons of Rachel **(RACHEL)***; Joseph, and Benjamin:*

And the sons of Bilhah **(BILHAH)***, Rachel's handmaid; Dan, and Naphtali:*

And the sons of Zilpah **(ZILPAH)***, Leah's handmaid; Gad, and Asher: these [are] the sons of Jacob, which were born to him in Padan-aram.* Genesis 35:22-26.

Remember I stated at the beginning of this book that Exodus begins with a list of the children of Israel (Jacob), i.e. the twelve tribes who came into Egypt. These verses record the names of Jacob's (Israel's) children who were born to him in Padanaram, so they are in the book of Genesis.

I would suggest that you memorize the following names, and also the mother of each individual, as they are referred to throughout the Bible. See also Genesis 29, 30 and 35.

The association for determining the chapter is different this time. I trust you can remember it.

THE SONS OF LEAH RACHEL BILHAH ZILPAH – 31 letters.
4 different women bore these sons - **31+4=35**, so these verses are in chapter **35.**

Leah	Rachel	Bilhah	Zilpah
Reuben	Joseph	Dan	Gad
Simeon	Benjamin	Naphtali	Asher
Levi			
Judah			
Issachar			
Zebulun			

No. 23
Now Israel (Jacob) *loved Joseph more than all his children, because he [was] the son of his old age: and he made him a coat of [many] colours* (**coat of [many] colours**).
And when his brethren saw that their father loved him more than all his brethren, they hated him, and could not speak peaceably unto him.
Genesis 37:3-4.

Remember I stated at the beginning of this book that Exodus begins with a list of the children of Israel (Jacob), i.e. the twelve tribes who came into Egypt. These verses concern a time before they came into Egypt, so they are in the book of Genesis.

THE COAT OF MANY COLOURS CAUSED SOME TROUBLE – 37 letters, so these verses are in chapter **37.**

No. 24
And the Midianites sold him (**Joseph**) *into Egypt* (**Egypt**) *unto Potiphar* (**Potiphar**), *an officer of Pharaoh's, [and] captain of the guard.*
Genesis 37:36.

See association number 23 for details concerning the children of Israel. Joseph is one of the children of Israel, and this verse tells of him being sold into Egypt. The other members of the family are not in Egypt yet, so this verse is in the book of Genesis.

JOSEPH IS TAKEN TO EGYPT AND SOLD TO POTIPHAR

– **37** letters, so it is in chapter **37**.

No. 25
*And it came to pass about this time, that [Joseph] (**[JOSEPH]**) went into the house to do his business; and [there was] none of the men of the house there within.*
And she (Potiphar's wife) *caught him by his garment, saying, Lie with me: and he left his garment (**LEFT HIS GARMENT**) in her hand, and fled, and got him out (**AND FLED, AND GOT HIM OUT**). Genesis 39:11-12.*

For details of the children of Israel see association 23. Joseph is in Egypt, but the other members of the family are not there yet, so these verses are in the book of Genesis.

JOSEPH LEFT HIS GARMENT AND FLED AND GOT HIM OUT – **39** letters, so they are in chapter **39**.

No. 26
I suggest that you read Genesis chapter 41 in its entirety.

And Joseph said unto Pharaoh, The dream of Pharaoh [is] one: God hath shewed Pharaoh what he [is] about to do.
The seven good kine [are] seven years; and the seven good ears [are] seven years: the dream [is] one. Genesis 41:25-26.

See association number 25 for details concerning Joseph.
I am using a different type of association for these verses.
There are 7 good kine and 7 good ears of corn mentioned in verse 26. 7+7= **14**.

For the purpose of association, think that when Joseph interpreted Pharaoh's dream, he **changed** the 7 good kine into 7 years, and the 7 good ears of corn into 7 years. If **14** is changed into **41** that gives the number of this chapter.

EXODUS

No. 1
And the child grew, and she brought him unto Pharaoh's daughter, and he became her son. And she called his name Moses: and she said, Because I (I) drew him (him) out (out) of the water. Exodus 2:10.

Exodus can be defined as going **out**. Moses means drawn **out** of the water, so this verse is in the book of Exodus.

I **(I)** drew him **(him)** out of the water. 'I' and 'him' – 2 people, so it is in chapter **2**.

No. 2
*And he said, Draw not nigh hither (**Draw not nigh hither**): put off thy shoes from off thy feet (**put off thy shoes from off thy feet**), for the place whereon thou standest [is] holy ground (**for the place whereon thou standest [is] holy ground**).* Exodus 3:5.

Exodus can be defined as a **departure**. Moses was not allowed to draw too near to the burning bush. For the purpose of association, think of Moses as having to **depart** from the bush, so this verse is in the book of Exodus.

(1) Draw not nigh hither:
(2) put off thy shoes from off thy feet,
(3) for the place whereon thou standest [is] holy ground.
3 directives from God, so this verse is in chapter **3**.

No. 3
Moses said unto God, Behold, [when] I come unto the children of Israel, and shall say unto them, The God of your fathers hath sent

me unto you; and they shall say to me, What [is] his name? what shall I say unto them?

*And God said unto Moses, I AM THAT I AM: Thus shalt thou say unto the children of Israel, I AM **(I AM)** hath sent me unto you.*
Exodus 3:13-14.

These verses concern the time when God told Moses that he would deliver the children of Israel **out** of Egypt. Exodus means to come **out**, so these verses are in the book of Exodus.

I AM – **3** letters, so they are in chapter 3.

No. 4

*Your lamb shall be without blemish **(Your lamb shall be without blemish)**, a male of the first year: ye shall take [it] out from the sheep, or from the goats:*

And ye shall keep it up until the fourteenth day of the same month: and the whole assembly of the congregation of Israel shall kill it in the evening.

*And they shall take of the blood, and strike [it] on the two side posts **(TWO SIDE POSTS)** and on the upper door post of the houses, wherein they shall eat it.* Exodus 12:5-7.

The above verses refer to the time of the last plague, which God brought upon Pharaoh, while the children of Israel were still in Egypt. The children of Israel came **out** of Egypt after this plague. For the purpose of association, think that Exodus means to come **out** so these verses are in the book of Exodus.

TWO SIDE POSTS – **12** letters, so they are in chapter **12**.

In the book of 1st Peter 1:18-19 the following words are recorded:
Forasmuch as ye know that ye were not redeemed with corruptible things, [as] silver and gold, from your vain conversation [received] by tradition from your fathers;

*But with the precious blood of Christ, as of a lamb without blemish **(a lamb without blemish)** and without spot.*

No. 5
And the blood shall be to you for a token upon the houses where ye [are]: and when I see the blood (I SEE THE BLOOD), I will pass over you, and the plague shall not be upon you to destroy [you], when I smite the land of Egypt. Exodus 12:13.

This verse is part of the narrative concerning the children of Israel being brought **out** of Egypt. Exodus means to come **out**, so this verse is in the book of Exodus.

I SEE THE BLOOD - **12** letters, so it is in chapter **12**.

No. 6
And Moses took the bones of Joseph (BONES OF JOSEPH) with him: for he had straitly sworn the children of Israel, saying, God will surely visit you; and ye shall carry up my bones away hence with you. Exodus 13:19.

Moses took the bones of Joseph with him when the Israelites came **out** of Egypt. Exodus means to come **out**, so this verse is in the book of Exodus.

BONES OF JOSEPH - **13** letters, so it is in chapter **13**.

No. 7
And the LORD went before them by day in a pillar of a cloud, to lead them the way; and by night in a pillar of fire (A PILLAR OF FIRE), to give them light; to go by day and night:
He took not away the pillar of the cloud by day, nor the pillar of fire by night, [from] before the people. Exodus 13:21-22.

This is the first time a pillar of a cloud and a pillar of fire are mentioned in Scripture, so these verses are about the Israelites just after they came **out** of Egypt. Exodus means to come **out**, so these verses are in the book of Exodus.

A PILLAR OF FIRE – **13** letters, so they are in chapter **13**.

No. 8

And Moses stretched out his hand over the sea; and the LORD caused the sea to go [back] by a strong east wind (STRONG EAST WIND) all that night, and made the sea dry [land], and the waters were divided.

And the children of Israel went into the midst of the sea upon the dry [ground]: and the waters [were] a wall unto them on their right hand, and on their left. Exodus 14:21-22.

These verses are part of the narrative concerning the children of Israel being brought **out** of Egypt. Exodus means to come **out**, so these verses are in the book of Exodus.

STRONG EAST WIND - 14 letters, so they are in chapter **14**.

No. 9

Behold, I will stand before thee there upon the rock in Horeb; and thou shalt smite the rock, and there shall come water out of it, that the people may drink (THE PEOPLE MAY DRINK). And Moses did so in the sight of the elders of Israel. Exodus 17:6.

This verse concerns the journeying of the children of Israel after the came **out** of Egypt. They have pitched in Rephidim, and there is no water to drink. Exodus means to come **out**, so this verse is in Exodus.

THE PEOPLE MAY DRINK - 17 letters, so it is in chapter **17**.

No. 10

And God spake all these words, saying,

I [am] the LORD thy God, which have brought thee out of the land of Egypt, out of the house of bondage.

Thou shalt have no other gods before me.

Thou shalt not make unto thee any graven image, or any likeness [of any thing] that [is] in heaven above, or that [is] in the earth beneath, or that [is] in the water under the earth:

Thou shalt not bow down thyself to them, nor serve them: for I the LORD thy God [am] a jealous God, visiting the iniquity of the fathers upon the children unto the third and fourth [generation] of them that hate me;

And shewing mercy unto thousands of them that love me, and keep my commandments.

Thou shalt not take the name of the LORD thy God in vain; for the LORD will not hold him guiltless that taketh his name in vain.

Remember the sabbath day, to keep it holy.

Six days shalt thou labour, and do all thy work:

But the seventh day [is] the sabbath of the LORD thy God: [in it] thou shalt not do any work, thou, nor thy son, nor thy daughter, thy manservant, nor thy maidservant, nor thy cattle, nor thy stranger that [is] within thy gates:

For [in] six days the LORD made heaven and earth, the sea, and all that in them [is], and rested the seventh day: wherefore the LORD blessed the sabbath day, and hallowed it.

Honour thy father and thy mother: that thy days may be long upon the land which the LORD thy God giveth thee.

Thou shalt not kill.

Thou shalt not commit adultery

Thou shalt not steal.

Thou shalt not bear false witness against thy neighbour.

Thou shalt not covet thy neighbour's house, thou shalt not covet thy neighbour's wife, nor his manservant, nor his maidservant, nor his ox, nor his ass, nor any thing that [is] thy neighbour's. Exodus 20 1:17.

For the purpose of association, think of Moses as going **out** from the Israelites when he went to mount Sinai where he received the Ten Commandments. Exodus means to go **out**, so the Ten Commandments are in the book of Exodus.

Moses broke the first two tables. *And it came to pass, as soon as he came nigh unto the camp, that he saw the calf, and the dancing: and Moses' anger waxed hot, and he cast the tables out of his hands, and brake them beneath the mount.* Exodus 32:19.

Two more tables had to be written upon by the finger of God. There were **10** commandments on the first two tables and **10** commandments on the second two tables – **10+10=20**, so the Ten Commandments are in chapter **20**.

The Ten Commandments are also in the book of Deuteronomy, but not exactly the same words as the book of Exodus. For the purpose of association, think that Deuteronomy is the **5**th book of the Pentateuch, or the **5**th book of the Old Testament, so they are in chapter **5**.

No. 11

And the LORD said unto Moses, Come up to me into the mount (**And the LORD said unto Moses, Come up to me into the mount**), *and be there: and I will give thee tables of stone, and a law, and commandments which I have written; that thou mayest teach them.* Exodus 24:12.

For the purpose of association, think of Moses as going **out** from the Israelites to go to Mount Sinai where he received the Ten Commandments. Exodus means to go **out**, so this verse is in the book of Exodus.

MOSES GOES UP TO MEET WITH GOD – **24** letters, so it is in chapter **24**.

No. 12

And look that thou make [them] after their pattern (**MAKE [THEM] AFTER THEIR PATTERN**), *which was shewed thee in the mount.* Exodus 25:40.

This verse refers to the instructions God gave to Moses upon Mount Sinai concerning the erection and furnishing of the tabernacle. Exodus means to come **out**, and the Israelites have come **out** of Egypt, so this verse is in the book of Exodus.

MAKE THEM AFTER THEIR PATTERN - **25** letters, so it is in chapter **25**.

No. 13

And thou shalt make a vail [of] blue, and purple, and scarlet, and fine twined linen of cunning work: with cherubims shall it be made:
And thou shalt hang it upon four pillars of shittim [wood] overlaid with gold: their hooks [shall be of] gold, upon the four sockets of silver.
And thou shalt hang up the vail under the taches, that thou mayest

bring in thither within the vail the ark of the testimony: and the vail shall divide unto you between the holy [place] and the most holy (THE HOLY [PLACE] AND THE MOST HOLY).

And thou shalt put the mercy seat upon the ark of the testimony in the most holy [place]. Exodus 26:31-34.

This is an account of the instructions God gave to Moses upon Mount Sinai concerning the erection and furnishing of the tabernacle. Exodus means to come **out**, and the Israelites have come **out** of Egypt, so these verses are in the book of Exodus.

THE HOLY PLACE AND THE MOST HOLY - 26 letters, so they are in chapter **26**.

No. 14
And take thou unto thee Aaron thy brother, and his sons with him, from among the children of Israel, that he may minister unto me in the priest's office, [even] Aaron, Nadab and Abihu, Eleazar and Ithamar, Aaron's sons.

And thou shalt make holy garments (AND THOU SHALT MAKE HOLY GARMENTS) for Aaron thy brother for glory and for beauty. Exodus 28:1-2.

This is part of God's instructions to Moses after the Israelites came **out** of Egypt. Exodus means to come **out**, so these verses are in the book of Exodus.

AND THOU SHALT MAKE HOLY GARMENTS – 28 letters, so they are in chapter **28**.

No. 15
And thou shalt take two onyx stones (ONYX STONES), and grave on them the names of the children of Israel:
Six of their names on one stone, and [the other] six names of the rest on the other stone, according to their birth. Exodus 28:9-10.

And thou shalt put in the breastplate of judgment the Urim (URIM) and the Thummim (THUMMIM); and they shall be upon Aaron's heart, when he goeth in before the LORD: and Aaron shall bear the judgment of the children of Israel upon his heart before the LORD continually. Genesis 28:30.

This is part of God's instructions to Moses after the Israelites came **out** of Egypt. Exodus means to come **out**, so these verses are in the book of Exodus.

ONYX STONES WITH URIM AND THUMMIM – 28 letters, so they are in chapter **28**.

No. 16

*And thou shalt make a plate [of] pure gold, and grave upon it, [like] the engravings of a signet, HOLINESS TO THE LORD (**HOLINESS TO THE LORD**).*
*And thou shalt put it on a blue lace (**ON A BLUE LACE**), that it may be upon the mitre; upon the forefront of the mitre it shall be.*
And it shall be upon Aaron's forehead, that Aaron may bear the iniquity of the holy things, which the children of Israel shall hallow in all their holy gifts; and it shall be always upon his forehead, that they may be accepted before the LORD. Exodus 28:36-38.

These verses contain a portion of God's instructions to Moses after the Israelites came **out** of Egypt. Exodus means to come **out**, so these verses are in the book of Exodus.

HOLINESS TO THE LORD   ON A BLUE LACE – 28 letters, so they are in chapter **28**.

No. 17

*And he gave (**HE GAVE**) unto Moses (**MOSES**), when he had made an end of communing with him upon mount Sinai, two tables of testimony (**TWO TABLES OF TESTIMONY**), tables of stone, written with the finger of God.* Exodus 31:18.

Exodus means to go **out**. For the purpose of association, think of Moses as going **out** from the people when he went to Mount Sinai, so this verse is in the book of Exodus.

HE GAVE MOSES TWO TABLES OF TESTIMONY – 31 letters, so it is in chapter **31**.

36

No. 18

*And when the people saw that Moses delayed to come down out of the mount, the people gathered themselves together unto Aaron, and said unto him, Up, make us gods, which shall go before us (**UP, MAKE US GODS, WHICH SHALL GO BEFORE US**); for [as for] this Moses, the man that brought us up out of the land of Egypt, we wot not what is become of him.*

And Aaron said unto them, Break off the golden earrings, which [are] in the ears of your wives, of your sons, and of your daughters, and bring [them] unto me.

And all the people brake off the golden earrings which [were] in their ears, and brought [them] unto Aaron.

And he received [them] at their hand, and fashioned it with a graving tool, after he had made it a molten calf: and they said, These [be] thy gods, O Israel, which brought thee up out of the land of Egypt.
Exodus 32:1-4.

Moses is still on Mount Sinai. For the purpose of association, think of Moses as going **out** from the Israelites to go to Mount Sinai where he received the Ten Commandments. Exodus means to go **out**, so these verses are in the book of Exodus.

UP MAKE US GODS WHICH SHALL GO BEFORE US – 32 letters, so they are in chapter **32**.

No. 19

*And the LORD said unto Moses, Hew thee two tables of stone (**Hew thee two tables of stone**) like unto the first: and I will write upon [these] tables the words that were in the first tables, which thou brakest.*

And be ready in the morning, and come up in the morning unto Mount Sinai, and present thyself there to me in the top of the mount.
Exodus 34:1-2.

For the purpose of association, think of Moses as going **out** from the Israelites when he went to Mount Sinai. Exodus means to go **out**, so these verses are in the book of Exodus.

GOD TELLS MOSES TO HEW TWO TABLES OF STONE – 34 letters, so they are in chapter **34**.

The parallel narrative is in the 10th chapter of the book of Deuteronomy.

No. 20
And the LORD spake unto Moses, saying,
On the first day of the first month shalt thou set up the tabernacle of the tent of the congregation.
*And thou shalt put therein the ark of the testimony (**And thou shalt put therein the ark of the testimony**), and cover the ark with the vail.* Exodus 40:1-3.

These verses contain a portion of God's instructions to Moses after the Israelites came **out** of Egypt. Exodus means to come **out**, so these verses are in the book of Exodus.

GOD TELLS MOSES TO PUT IN THE ARK OF THE TESTI-MONY – 40 letters, so they are in chapter **40**.

No. 21
And he reared up the court round about the tabernacle and the altar, and set up the hanging of the court gate. So Moses finished the work.
Then a cloud covered the tent of the congregation, and the glory of the LORD filled the tabernacle.
And Moses was not able to enter into the tent of the congregation, because the cloud abode thereon, and the glory of the LORD filled the tabernacle.
*And when the cloud was taken up from over the tabernacle, the children of Israel went onward in all their journeys (**And when the cloud was taken up from over the tabernacle, the children of Israel went onward in all their journeys**):*
But if the cloud were not taken up, then they journeyed not till the day that it was taken up.
For the cloud of the LORD [was] upon the tabernacle by day, and fire was on it by night, in the sight of all the house of Israel, throughout all their journeys. Exodus 40:34-38.

Moses has just completed all the instructions that God gave to him after the Israelites came **out** of Egypt. Exodus means to come **out**, so these verses are in the book of Exodus.

THE ISRAELITES MOVED WHEN THE CLOUD WAS TAKEN UP – **40** letters, so they are in chapter **40**.

LEVITICUS

No. 1

And the LORD called unto Moses, and spake unto him out of the tabernacle of the congregation, saying,

Speak unto the children of Israel, and say unto them, If any man of you bring an offering unto the LORD, ye shall bring your offering of the cattle, [even] of the herd, and of the flock.

If his offering [be] a burnt sacrifice **(sacrifice)** *of the herd, let him offer a male without blemish: he shall offer it of his own voluntary will at the door of the tabernacle of the congregation before the LORD.*

And he shall put his hand upon the head of the burnt offering; and it shall be accepted for him to make atonement for him.

And he shall kill the bullock before the LORD: and the priests, Aaron's sons, shall bring the blood, and sprinkle the blood round about upon the altar that [is by] the door of the tabernacle of the congregation.

And he shall flay the burnt offering, and cut it into his pieces.

And the sons of Aaron the priest shall put fire upon the altar, and lay the wood in order upon the fire:

And the priests, Aaron's sons, shall lay the parts, the head, and the fat, in order upon the wood that [is] on the fire which [is] upon the altar:

But his inwards and his legs shall he wash in water: and the priest shall burn all on the altar, [to be] a burnt sacrifice, an offering made by fire, of a sweet savour unto the LORD. Leviticus 1:1-9.

These verses are about a **sacrifice.** Sacrifices are mentioned in many books of Scripture, but all of the verses in this publication, which are recorded in the Old Testament and mention **Aaron**, **Aaron's sons** or the **priest**, are taken from the book of Leviticus.

In Exodus 40 i.e. the last chapter, the tabernacle is set up and verse 34 tells us that the glory of the LORD filled the tabernacle. The above verses are a continuation of the narrative in Exodus, so they are in chapter 1.

No. 2
*And the fire upon the altar shall be burning in it; it shall not be put out: and the priest (**priest**) shall burn wood on it every morning, and lay the burnt offering in order upon it; and he shall burn thereon the fat of the peace offerings.*

*The fire shall ever be burning (**THE FIRE SHALL EVER BE BURN-ING**) upon the altar; it shall never go out.* Leviticus 6:12-13.

See explanation at association number 1.

THE FIRE SHALL EVER BE BURNING – 6 words, so these verses are in chapter **6**.

No. 3
*And Aaron (**Aaron**) lifted up his hand toward the people, and blessed them, and came down from offering of the sin offering, and the burnt offering, and peace offerings.*

And Moses and Aaron went into the tabernacle, and came out, and blessed the people: and the glory of the LORD appeared unto all the people.

*And there came a fire out from before the LORD (**THERE CAME A FIRE OUT FROM BEFORE THE LORD**), and consumed upon the altar the burnt offering and the fat: [which] when all the people saw, they shouted, and fell on their faces.* Leviticus 9:22-24.

See explanation at association number 1.

THERE CAME A FIRE OUT FROM BEFORE THE LORD – 9 words, so these verses are in chapter **9**.

No. 4
*And Nadab (**NADAB**) and Abihu (**ABIHU**), the sons of Aaron (**Sons of Aaron**), took either of them his censer, and put fire (**fire**)*

therein, and put incense thereon, and offered strange fire before the LORD, which he commanded them not.

And there went out fire from the LORD, and devoured them, and they died before the LORD. Leviticus 10:1-2.

Fire is used for sacrifices. Sacrifices are mentioned in many books of Scripture, but all of the verses in this publication, which are recorded in the Old Testament and mention **Aaron, Aaron's sons** or the **priest**, are taken from the book of Leviticus.

NADAB ABIHU - 10 letters, so these verses are in chapter **10**.

No. 5
And he (Aaron) *shall take the two goats, and present them before the LORD [at] the door of the tabernacle of the congregation.*

And Aaron shall cast lots upon the two goats; one lot for the LORD, and the other lot for the scapegoat.

And Aaron **(Aaron)** *shall bring the goat upon which the LORD'S lot fell, and offer him [for] a sin offering.*

But the goat, on which the lot fell to be the scapegoat **(TO BE THE SCAPEGOAT)**, *shall be presented alive before the LORD, to make an atonement with him, [and] to let him go for a scapegoat into the wilderness.* Leviticus 16:7-10.

See explanation at association number 1.

TO BE THE SCAPEGOAT – 16 letters, so these verses are in chapter **16**.

No. 6
For the life of the flesh [is] in the blood: and I have given it to you upon the altar **(altar)** *to make an atonement* **(TO MAKE AN ATONEMENT)** *for your souls: for it [is] the blood [that] maketh an atonement for the soul.* Leviticus 17:11.

Sacrifices are mentioned in many books of Scripture, but all of the verses in this publication, which are recorded in the Old Testament and mention **Aaron, Aaron's sons** or the **priest**, are taken from the book of Leviticus.

For the purpose of association, think that the **priest** offered the sacrifice upon the **altar**, so this verse is in Leviticus.

TO MAKE AN ATONEMENT - **17** letters, so this verse is in chapter **17**.

This is the only place in Scripture where the words *'it [is] the blood [that] maketh an atonement for the soul'* are recorded.

No. 7
*Speak unto Aaron (**Aaron**), and to his sons, and unto all the children of Israel, and say unto them, Whatsoever [he be] of the house of Israel, or of the strangers in Israel, that will offer his oblation for all his vows, and for all his freewill offerings, which they will offer unto the LORD for a burnt offering;*
[Ye shall offer] at your own will a male without blemish, of the beeves, of the sheep, or of the goats.
*[But] whatsoever hath a blemish (**WHATSOEVER HATH A BLEMISH**), [that] shall ye not offer: for it shall not be acceptable for you.* Leviticus 22:18-20.

See explanation at association number 1.

WHATSOEVER HATH A BLEMISH – **22** letters, so these verses are in chapter **22**.

No. 8
*A jubile (**jubile**) shall that fiftieth year be unto you: ye shall not sow, neither reap that which groweth of itself in it, nor gather [the grapes] in it of thy vine undressed.* Leviticus 25:11.

The word **jubile** occurs 21 times in the book of Leviticus.

The only other place where it occurs is in Numbers 36:4. *And when the **jubile** of the children of Israel shall be, then shall their inheritance be put unto the inheritance of the tribe whereunto they are received: so shall their inheritance be taken away from the inheritance of the tribe of our fathers.*

Since the word jubile only occurs once in the book of Numbers and 21 times in Leviticus then for the purpose of association, I will call the book of Leviticus the book of jubile.

To help you remember that it is Leviticus, think that the first two letters of **Le**viticus are the same as the last two letters of jubi**le**.

DON'T FORGET THE YEAR OF JUBILE – 25 letters, so this verse is in chapter **25**.

In some King James editions of the Bible Jubile is written Jubilee.

NUMBERS

No. 1
And the LORD spake unto Moses, saying,
Speak unto Aaron and unto his sons, saying, On this wise ye shall bless the children of Israel, saying unto them,
The LORD bless thee, and keep thee:
The LORD make his face shine upon thee, and be gracious unto thee:
The LORD lift up his countenance upon thee, and give thee peace.
And they shall put my name upon the children of Israel; and I will bless them. Numbers 6:22-27.

(1) The LORD bless thee, and keep thee:
(2) The LORD make his face shine upon thee, and be gracious unto thee:
(3) The LORD lift up his countenance upon thee, and give thee peace.

This association is a little different.
For the purpose of association, think of Aaron and his sons saying **'the LORD'** 3 times. **3** is a **number**, so these verses are in the book of **Numbers**.

(1) The LORD bless thee
(2) and keep thee:
(3) The LORD make his face shine upon thee,
(4) and be gracious unto thee:
(5) The LORD lift up his countenance upon thee,
(6) and give thee peace.

The above verses are in chapter **6**.

To enable you to remember that the number **3** is the association for the book and the number **6** is the association for the chapter, and not vice versa, just think that the book of Numbers remains the same and the chapters change each time. e.g. Numbers chapter 1, Numbers chapter 2. The above list of **3** remains the same i.e. (1) The LORD, (2) The LORD, (3) The LORD. The above list of **6** changes each time i.e. (1) The Lord bless thee, (2) and keep thee etc.

No. 2
And the LORD spake unto Moses, saying,
Make thee two trumpets of silver; of a whole piece **(WHOLE PIECE)** *shalt thou make them: that thou mayest use them for the calling of the assembly, and for the journeying of the camps.*
And when they shall blow with them, all the assembly shall assemble themselves to thee at the door of the tabernacle of the congregation.
And if they blow [but] with one **(one)** *[trumpet], then the princes, [which are] heads of the thousands of Israel, shall gather themselves unto thee.*
When ye blow an alarm, then the camps that lie on the east parts shall go forward.
When ye blow an alarm the second time, then the camps that lie on the south side shall take their journey: they shall blow an alarm for their journeys.
But when the congregation is to be gathered together, ye shall blow, but ye shall not sound an alarm. Numbers 10:1-7.

For the purpose of association, think that **one** is a **number**, so these verses are in the book of **Numbers**.

WHOLE PIECE – **10** letters, so they are in chapter **10**.

No. 3
(Now the man Moses (MOSES) [was] very meek (MEEK), above all the men which [were] upon the face of the earth.) Numbers 12:3.
When you read this verse think immediately of Matthew 5:5.
Blessed [are] the meek (MEEK): for they shall inherit the earth.

When the Lord Jesus said *"Blessed [are] the meek: for they shall inherit the earth."* He was referring to a **number** of people. For the purpose of association, think that the word **'meek'** in Matthew 5:5 refers to a **number** of people, so the verse about Moses being **meek** is in the book of **Numbers**.

MOSES WAS MEEK – **12** letters, so this verse is in chapter **12**.

No. 4
And the LORD spake unto Moses, saying,
Send thou men, that they may search the land of Canaan, which I give unto the children of Israel: of every tribe of their fathers shall ye send a man, every one a ruler among them. Numbers 13:1-2.

And they came unto the brook of Eshcol (BROOK OF ESHCOL), and cut down from thence a branch with one (one) cluster of grapes, and they bare it between two (two) upon a staff; and [they brought] of the pomegranates, and of the figs.
The place was called the brook Eshcol, because of the cluster of grapes which the children of Israel cut down from thence.
And they returned from searching of the land after forty days.
Numbers 13:23-25.

For the purpose of association, think that **one** and **two** are numbers, so these verses are in the book of **Numbers**.

BROOK OF ESHCOL – **13** letters, so they are in chapter **13**.

No. 5
And it came to pass, that on the morrow Moses went into the tabernacle of witness; and, behold, the rod (rod) of Aaron for the house of Levi was budded, and brought forth buds, and bloomed blossoms, and yielded almonds (AND YIELDED ALMONDS). Numbers 17:8.

For the purpose of association, think of what we read in Proverbs 23:13. *Withhold not correction from the child: for [if] thou beatest him with the rod (**rod**), he shall not die.*

Associate **rod** with child. Also for the purpose of association, think that a child needs to learn **numbers** as part of his/her education, so this verse is in the book of **Numbers**.

AND YIELDED ALMONDS – 17 letters, so it is in chapter **17**.

No. 6

*And Moses lifted up his hand (**MOSES LIFTED UP HIS HAND**), and with his rod he smote the rock twice (**twice**): and the water came out abundantly, and the congregation drank, and their beasts [also].*
And the LORD spake unto Moses and Aaron, Because ye believed me not, to sanctify me in the eyes of the children of Israel, therefore ye shall not bring this congregation into the land which I have given them. Numbers 20:11-12.

He smote the rock **twice**, i.e. **2** times. For the purpose of association, think that **2** is a **number**, so these verses are in the book of **Numbers**.

MOSES LIFTED UP HIS HAND – **20** letters, so they are in chapter **20**.

No. 7

*And the LORD said unto Moses, Make thee a fiery serpent (**MAKE THEE A FIERY SERPENT**), and set it upon a pole: and it shall come to pass, that every one that is bitten, when he looketh upon it, shall live.*
And Moses made a serpent of brass, and put it upon a pole, and it came to pass, that if a serpent had bitten any man, when he beheld the serpent of brass, he lived. Numbers 21:8-9.

For the purpose of association, think that there were a **number** of people preserved by looking upon the serpent, so these verses are in the book of **Numbers**.

MAKE THEE A FIERY SERPENT – **21** letters, so they are in chapter **21**.

No. 8
Then the LORD opened the eyes of Balaam, and he saw the angel of the LORD standing in the way, and his sword drawn in his hand ***(HIS SWORD DRAWN IN HIS HAND)***: *and he bowed down his head, and fell flat on his face.*
And the angel of the LORD said unto him, Wherefore hast thou smitten thine ass these three ***(3)*** *times? behold, I went out to withstand thee, because [thy] way is perverse before me:*
And the ass saw me, and turned from me these three times: unless she had turned from me, surely now also I had slain thee, and saved her alive. Numbers 22:31-33.

For the purpose of association, think that **3** is a **number**, so these verses are in the book of **Numbers**.

HIS SWORD DRAWN IN HIS HAND – **22** letters, so they are in chapter **22**.

No. 9
Surely none of the men that came up out of Egypt, from twenty ***(20)*** *years old and upward, shall see the land which I sware unto Abraham, unto Isaac, and unto Jacob; because they have not wholly followed me:*
Save Caleb the son of Jephunneh the Kenezite, and Joshua the son of Nun: for they have wholly followed the LORD ***(FOR THEY HAVE WHOLLY FOLLOWED THE LORD)***. Numbers 32:11-12.

For the purpose of association, think that **20** is a **number**, so these verses are in the book of **Numbers**.

FOR THEY HAVE WHOLLY FOLLOWED THE LORD – **32** letters, so they are in chapter **32**.

DEUTERONOMY

No. 1
*For the LORD thy God [is] a consuming fire **(FIRE) (consuming fire)** [even] a jealous God.* Deuteronomy 4:24.

The end of Deuter**onomy** rhymes with the end of ec**onomy**. For the purpose of association, think of **consumer economy (consuming fire)** so this verse is in the book of Deuteronomy.

FIRE – **4** letters, so it is in chapter **4**.

No. 2
*Hear, O Israel **(ISRAEL)**: The LORD our God [is] one LORD:*
And thou shalt love the LORD thy God with all thine heart, and with all thy soul, and with all thy might. Deuteronomy 6:4-5.

Verse 5 is a **command** of God. For the purpose of association, think that the 10 **command**ments are known as the Moral **law**, and the book of Deuteronomy is known as the second **law**, so these verses are in the book of Deuteronomy.

ISRAEL – **6** letters, so they are in chapter **6**.

The following words are also in the gospel of Mark.

And Jesus answered him, The first of all the commandments [is], Hear, O Israel; The Lord our God is one Lord:
And thou shalt love the Lord thy God with all thy heart, and with all thy soul, and with all thy mind, and with all thy strength: this [is] the first commandment. Mark 12:29-30.

Deuteronomy chapter 6, and Mark chapter 12 are the only chapters in Scripture where the words *'The LORD our God [is] one LORD'* are recorded.

No. 3

For the LORD thy God bringeth thee into a good land, a land of brooks of water, of fountains and depths that spring out of valleys and hills;

A land of wheat, and barley, and vines, and fig trees, and pomegranates; a land of oil olive, and honey;

A land wherein thou shalt eat bread without scarceness, thou shalt not lack any [thing] in it; a land whose stones [are] iron, and out of whose hills thou mayest dig brass.

When thou hast eaten and art full, then thou shalt bless the LORD thy God for the good land which he hath given thee.

Beware that thou forget not the LORD thy God, in not keeping his commandments, and his judgments, and his statutes, which I command thee this day:

Lest [when] thou hast eaten and art full, and hast built goodly houses, and dwelt [therein];

And [when] thy herds and thy flocks multiply, and thy silver and thy gold is multiplied, and all that thou hast is multiplied;

Then thine heart be lifted up **(LIFTED UP)***, and thou forget the LORD thy God* **(forget the LORD thy God,)** *which brought thee forth out of the land of Egypt, from the house of bondage;*

Deuteronomy 8:7-14.

The above verses record the words of Moses as he describes the land to which the Israelites are going. Moses described the land, but he didn't lead the children of Israel into it. Joshua led them into it.

The book of Joshua follows the book of Deuteronomy, and in the first chapter of Joshua we read the following words: *Now after the death of Moses the servant of the LORD it came to pass, that the LORD spake unto Joshua the son of Nun, Moses' minister, saying,*

Moses my servant is dead; now therefore arise, go over this Jordan, thou, and all this people, unto the land which I do give to them, [even] to the children of Israel. Therefore the above eight verses are in the book of Deuteronomy.

LIFTED UP – **8** letters, so these verses are in chapter **8**.

The words **'forget the LORD'** and **'forget the LORD thy God'** are only found in the book of Deuteronomy. The words 'forget the LORD thy God' are in chapter 8 and verse 14 as you can see from the above portion of Scripture. The words 'forget the LORD thy God' are also in verse 19 of this chapter. *And it shall be, if thou do at all (forget the LORD thy God), and walk after other gods, and serve them, and worship them, I testify against you this day that ye shall surely perish.*

The words 'forget the LORD' are in chapter 6 and verse 12. *[Then] beware (BEWARE) lest thou (forget the LORD), which brought thee forth out of the land of Egypt, from the house of bondage.* Deuteronomy 6:12.

BEWARE – **6** letters, so this verse is in chapter **6**.

No. 4
When a prophet speaketh in the name of the LORD (IN THE NAME OF THE LORD), if the thing follow not, nor come to pass, that [is] the thing which the LORD hath not spoken, [but] the prophet hath spoken it presumptuously: thou shalt not be afraid of him. Deuteronomy 18:22.

For the purpose of association, think that The Jews called Deuteronomy **'words,'** and prophets speak **words**, so this verse is in the book of Deuteronomy.

IN THE NAME OF THE LORD – **18** letters, so it is in chapter **18**.

No. 5
The eternal God (God) [is thy] refuge (refuge), and underneath [are] the everlasting arms (underneath [are] the everlasting arms): and he shall thrust out the enemy (enemy) from before thee; and shall say, Destroy [them]. Deuteronomy 33:27.

This is a different type of association.

Deuteronomy is the **fifth** book of the Old Testament. For the purpose of association, think that there are **five** nouns (**God, refuge, 2 arms and enemy**) in this verse, so it is in the book of Deuteronomy.

THE EVERLASTING ARMS ARE UNDERNEATH US – 33 letters, so this verse is in chapter **33**.

No. 6
And Moses went up from the plains of Moab unto the mountain of Nebo, to the top of Pisgah, that [is] over against Jericho. And the LORD shewed him all the land of Gilead, unto Dan,
And all Naphtali, and the land of Ephraim, and Manasseh, and all the land of Judah, unto the utmost sea,
And the south, and the plain of the valley of Jericho, the city of palm trees, unto Zoar.
And the LORD said unto him, This [is] the land which I sware unto Abraham, unto Isaac, and unto Jacob, saying, I will give it unto thy seed: I have caused thee to see [it] with thine eyes, but thou shalt not go over thither.
So Moses the servant of the LORD died there in the land of Moab, according to the word of the LORD.
And he buried him in a valley in the land of Moab, over against Bethpeor: but no man knoweth of his sepulchre unto this day.
And Moses [was] an hundred and twenty years old when he died: his eye was not dim, nor his natural force abated. Deuteronomy 34:1-7.

Remember I stated at the beginning of this book that the death of Moses is recorded in the last chapter of the book of Deuteronomy i.e. chapter 34.

JOSHUA

No. 1

*Now after the death of Moses the servant of the LORD it came to pass, that the LORD spake unto Joshua **(Joshua)** the son of Nun, Moses' minister, saying,*

*Moses my servant is dead; now therefore arise, go over this Jordan **(go over this Jordan)**, thou, and all this people, unto the land which I do give to them, [even] to the children of Israel.*

Every place that the sole of your foot shall tread upon, that have I given unto you, as I said unto Moses.

From the wilderness and this Lebanon even unto the great river, the river Euphrates, all the land of the Hittites, and unto the great sea toward the going down of the sun, shall be your coast.

There shall not any man be able to stand before thee all the days of thy life: as I was with Moses, [so] I will be with thee: I will not fail thee, nor forsake thee.

Be strong and of a good courage: for unto this people shalt thou divide for an inheritance the land, which I sware unto their fathers to give them.

Only be thou strong and very courageous, that thou mayest observe to do according to all the law, which Moses my servant commanded thee: turn not from it [to] the right hand or [to] the left, that thou mayest prosper whithersoever thou goest.

This book of the law shall not depart out of thy mouth; but thou shalt meditate therein day and night, that thou mayest observe to do according to all that is written therein: for then thou shalt make thy way prosperous, and then thou shalt have good success.

Have not I commanded thee? Be strong and of a good courage; be not afraid, neither be thou dismayed: for the LORD thy God [is] with thee whithersoever thou goest. Joshua 1:1-9.

These verses are in the first chapter of the book of **Joshua** as God commands him to **go over the Jordan**.

No. 2

*And Joshua **(Joshua)** the son of Nun sent out of Shittim two men to spy secretly, saying, Go view the land, even Jericho. And they went, and came into an harlot's house **(HARLOT'S HOUSE)**, named Rahab, and lodged there.* Joshua 2:1.

This verse is obviously in the book of **Joshua**.

HARLOT'S HOUSE – **2** words, so it is in chapter **2**.

No. 3

*And Joshua **(Joshua)** said unto the children of Israel, Come hither, and hear the words of the LORD your God.*

And Joshua said, Hereby ye shall know that the living God [is] among you, and [that] he will without fail drive out from before you the Canaanites, and the Hittites, and the Hivites, and the Perizzites, and the Girgashites, and the Amorites, and the Jebusites.

Behold, the ark of the covenant of the Lord of all the earth passeth over before you into Jordan.

Now therefore take you twelve men out of the tribes of Israel, out of every tribe a man.

And it shall come to pass, as soon as the soles of the feet of the priests that bear the ark of the LORD, the Lord of all the earth, shall rest in the waters of Jordan, [that] the waters of Jordan shall be cut off [from] the waters that come down from above; and they shall stand upon an heap.

And it came to pass, when the people removed from their tents, to pass over Jordan, and the priests bearing the ark of the covenant before the people;

And as they that bare the ark were come unto Jordan, and the feet of the priests that bare the ark were dipped in the brim of the water, (for Jordan overfloweth all his banks all the time of harvest,)

That the waters which came down from above stood [and] rose up upon an heap very far from the city Adam, that [is] beside Zaretan: and those that came down toward the sea of the plain, [even] the salt sea, failed, [and] were cut off: and the people passed over right against Jericho.

*And the priests that bare the ark of the covenant of the LORD stood firm on dry ground in the midst of Jordan, and all the Israelites passed over on dry **(DRY)** ground, until all the people were passed clean over Jordan.* Joshua 3:9-17.

These verses are obviously in the book of **Joshua**.

DRY - **3** letters, so they are in chapter **3**.

No. 4
*Joshua **(Joshua)** therefore commanded the priests, saying, Come ye up out of Jordan.*

*And it came to pass, when the priests that bare the ark of the covenant of the LORD were come up out of the midst of Jordan, [and] the soles of the priests' feet were lifted up unto the dry land, that the waters of Jordan **(THE WATERS OF JORDAN)** returned unto their place, and flowed over all his banks, as [they did] before.* Joshua 4:17-18.

These verses are obviously in the book of **Joshua**.

THE WATERS OF JORDAN – **4** words, so they are in chapter **4**.

No. 5
And it came to pass, when all the kings of the Amorites, which [were] on the side of Jordan westward, and all the kings of the Canaanites, which [were] by the sea, heard that the LORD had dried up the waters of Jordan from before the children of Israel, until we were passed over, that their heart melted, neither was there spirit in them any more, because of the children of Israel.

*At that time the LORD said unto Joshua, Make thee sharp **(SHARP)** knives, and circumcise again the children of Israel the second time.*

*And Joshua **(Joshua)** made him sharp knives, and circumcised the children of Israel at the hill of the foreskins.*

And this [is] the cause why Joshua did circumcise: All the people that came out of Egypt, [that were] males, [even] all the men of war, died in the wilderness by the way, after they came out of Egypt.
Joshua 5:1-4.

These verses are obviously in the book of **Joshua**.

SHARP – **5** letters, so they are in chapter **5**.

No. 6

*And the LORD said unto Joshua (**Joshua**), See, I have given into thine hand Jericho, and the king thereof, [and] the mighty men of valour.*

*And ye shall compass the city, all [ye] men of war, [and] go round about the city once. Thus shalt thou do six days (**THUS SHALT THOU DO SIX DAYS**).* Joshua 6:2-3.

These verses are obviously in the book of **Joshua**.

THUS SHALT THOU DO SIX DAYS – **6** words, so they are in chapter **6**.

No. 7

*And Achan answered Joshua (**Joshua**), and said, Indeed I have sinned against the LORD God of Israel, and thus and thus have I done:*

*When I saw among the spoils a goodly Babylonish garment (**GARMENT**), and two hundred shekels of silver, and a wedge of gold of fifty shekels weight, then I coveted them, and took them; and, behold, they [are] hid in the earth in the midst of my tent, and the silver under it.* Joshua 7:20-21.

Joshua is speaking in these verses, so they are in the book of Joshua.

GARMENT – **7** letters, so these verses are in chapter **7**.

No. 8

*And if it seem evil unto you to serve the LORD, choose you this day whom ye will serve; whether the gods which your fathers served that [were] on the other side of the flood, or the gods of the Amorites, in whose land ye dwell (**dwell**): but as for me and my house, we will serve the LORD (**we will serve the LORD**).* Joshua 24:15.

The Israelites are now **dwelling** in the land of the Amorites and Joshua brought them there, so this verse is in the book of Joshua.

WE SERVE THE LORD IN OUR HOUSE – **24** letters, so it is in chapter **24**.

No. 9
*And it came to pass after these things, that Joshua the son of Nun,
the servant of the LORD, died, [being] an hundred and ten years old.*
*And they buried him in the border of his inheritance in Timnath-
serah, which [is] in mount Ephraim, on the north side of the hill of
Gaash. Joshua 24:29-30.*

This is part of the last chapter of the book of Joshua and it records
Joshua's death.

JUDGES

Below are the names of the Judges of Israel. There are two more
judges mentioned in 1st Samuel, namely Samuel and Eli. All of the
names on my list are mentioned in the book of Judges.

Othniel, Ehud, Shamgar, Deborah, Gideon, Abimelech, (Abimelech usurped power and some people don't consider him a
judge). Tola, Jair, Jephthah, Ibzan, Elon, Abdon, Samson.

No. 1
*Now after the death of Joshua (**Now after the death of Joshua**) it
came to pass, that the children of Israel asked the LORD, saying, Who
shall go up for us against the Canaanites first, to fight against them?*
*And the LORD said, Judah shall go up: behold, I have delivered the
land into his hand.*
*And Judah said unto Simeon his brother, Come up with me into my
lot, that we may fight against the Canaanites; and I likewise will go
with thee into thy lot. So Simeon went with him.*
*And Judah went up; and the LORD delivered the Canaanites and
the Perizzites into their hand: and they slew of them in Bezek ten
thousand men.*

And they found Adonibezek in Bezek: and they fought against him, and they slew the Canaanites and the Perizzites.

But Adonibezek fled; and they pursued after him, and caught him, and cut off his thumbs and his great toes.

And Adonibezek (Adonibezek) said, Threescore and ten kings, having their thumbs and their great toes cut off, gathered [their meat] under my table: as I have done, so God hath requited me. And they brought him to Jerusalem, and there he died. Judges 1:1-7.

The book of Judges follows the book of Joshua. If you read verse one of this narrative you will see that it says **after the death of Joshua**. Joshua's death is recorded at the end of the book of Joshua, so these verses are in the book of Judges.

Adonai means Lord and there is only **1** Lord, so they are in chapter **1**.

No. 2

And when the children of Israel cried unto the LORD, the LORD raised up a deliverer (judge) to the children of Israel, who delivered them, [even] Othniel (Othniel) the son of Kenaz, Caleb's younger brother (CALEB'S YOUNGER BROTHER).

And the Spirit of the LORD came upon him, and he judged Israel, and went out to war: and the LORD delivered Chushanrishathaim king of Mesopotamia into his hand; and his hand prevailed against Chushanrishathaim.

And the land had rest forty years. And Othniel the son of Kenaz died. Judges 3:9-11.

Verse nine: *the LORD raised up a deliverer (judge) to the children of Israel, who delivered them, [even] Othniel (Othniel) the son of Kenaz, Caleb's younger brother.*

Othniel was the first judge, so these verses are in the book of Judges.

CALEB'S YOUNGER BROTHER - **3** words, so they are in chapter **3**.

No. 3

*And Gideon (**Gideon**) said unto God, If thou wilt save Israel by mine hand, as thou hast said,*

*Behold, I will put a fleece (**FLEECE**) of wool in the floor; [and] if the dew be on the fleece only, and [it be] dry upon all the earth*

[beside], then shall I know that thou wilt save Israel by mine hand, as thou hast said.

And it was so: for he rose up early on the morrow, and thrust the fleece together, and wringed the dew out of the fleece, a bowl full of water. Judges 6:36-38.

Gideon was a judge, so these verses are in the book of Judges.

FLEECE – 6 letters, so they are in chapter **6.**

No. 4

*And Manoah said unto his wife, We shall surely die, because we have seen God (**WE HAVE SEEN GOD**).*

But his wife said unto him, If the LORD were pleased to kill us, he would not have received a burnt offering and a meat offering at our hands, neither would he have shewed us all these [things], nor would as at this time have told us [such things] as these.

*And the woman bare a son, and called his name Samson (**Samson**): and the child grew, and the LORD blessed him.*

And the Spirit of the LORD began to move him at times in the camp of Dan between Zorah and Eshtaol. Judges 13:22-25.

These verses are obviously in the book of Judges because verse twenty-four records the birth of **Samson** and Samson was a judge.

WE HAVE SEEN GOD – 13 letters, so they are in chapter **13.**

No. 5

*[And] when he (**Samson**) came unto Lehi, the Philistines shouted against him: and the Spirit of the LORD came mightily upon him, and the cords that [were] upon his arms became as flax that was burnt with fire, and his bands loosed from off his hands.*

*And he found a new jawbone of an ass, and put forth his hand, and took it, and slew a thousand (**and slew a thousand**) men therewith.* Judges 15:14-15.

Samson was a **judge**, so these verses are in the book of **Judges**.

SAMSON SLAYS 1,000 – **15** letters and figures, so they are in chapter **15**.

RUTH

No. 1
And Ruth (Ruth) said, Intreat me not to leave thee, [or] to return from following after thee: for whither thou goest, I (I) will go; and where thou lodgest, I (I) will lodge: thy people [shall be] my people, and thy God my God:
Where thou diest, will I (I) die, and there will I (I) be buried: the LORD do so to me, and more also, [if ought] but death part thee and me. Ruth 1:16-17.

These verses are about **Ruth**, so they are in the book of Ruth.

If you read through these two verses you will find that they are all about **I**. I looks similar to **1**, so they are in chapter **1**.

No. 2
So Boaz took Ruth (Ruth), and she was his wife: and when he went in unto her, the LORD gave her conception, and she bare a son.
And the women said unto Naomi, Blessed [be] the LORD, which hath not left thee this day without a kinsman, that his name may be famous in Israel.
And he shall be unto thee a restorer of [thy] life, and a nourisher of thine old age: for thy daughter in law, which loveth thee, which is better to thee than seven sons, hath born him.
And Naomi took the child, and laid it in her bosom, and became nurse unto it.
And the women her neighbours gave it a name, saying, There is a son born to Naomi; and they called his name Obed (OBED): he [is] the father of Jesse, the father of David. Ruth 4:13-17.

These verses are about **Ruth**, so they are in the book of Ruth.

OBED – **4** letters, so these verses are in chapter **4**.

1ST SAMUEL

No. 1

And the LORD came, and stood, and called as at other times, Samuel, Samuel. Then Samuel answered, Speak; for thy servant heareth. 1st Samuel 3:10.

The Lord spoke **4** times to Samuel i.e. **1+3 = 4**, so this verse is in the book of **1**st Samuel and chapter **3**.

No. 2

*And it came to pass, when he (a man of Benjamin) made mention of the ark of God, that he (Eli) fell from off the seat backward by the side of the gate, and his neck brake, and he died (**DIED**): for he was an old man, and heavy. And he had judged Israel forty years.*
And his daughter in law, Phinehas' wife, was with child, [near] to be delivered: and when she heard the tidings that the ark of God was taken, and that her father in law and her husband were dead, she bowed herself and travailed; for her pains came upon her.
And about the time of her death the women that stood by her said unto her, Fear not; for thou hast born a son. But she answered not, neither did she regard [it].
*And she named the child I-chabod (**I-chabod**), saying, The glory is departed from Israel: because the ark of God was taken, and because of her father in law and her husband.*
And she said, The glory is departed from Israel: for the ark of God is taken. 1st Samuel 4:18.22.

Just remember that Samuel was brought up with Eli, so these verses are in some book of Samuel.

If you look at how I-chabod is written you will see that the 'I' is separated from the rest of the letters. 'I' looks similar to **1**, so these verses are in the book of **1**st Samuel.

DIED – **4** letters, so they are in chapter **4**.

No. 3
And when they arose early on the morrow morning, behold, Dagon (DAGON) [was] fallen upon his face to the ground before the ark of the LORD; and the head of Dagon and both the palms (palms) of his hands [were] cut off upon the threshold; only [the stump of] Dagon was left to him. 1st Samuel 5:4.

For the purpose of association, think that the first syllable of **Sam**uel rhymes with the first four letters of **palm**s, so this verse is in some book of Samuel.

Also for the purpose of association, think that the **1st** thing the Philistines did was to bring the ark of God into the house of Dagon, so this verse is in the book of **1st** Samuel.

DAGON – **5** letters, so it is in chapter **5**.

No. 4
Then Samuel took a vial of oil (A VIAL OF OIL), and poured [it] upon his (Saul's) head, and kissed him, and said, [Is it] not because the LORD hath anointed thee [to be] captain over his inheritance? 1st Samuel 10:1.

Saul and **Sa**muel both start with **Sa**, so this verse is in some book of Samuel.

Or simply think that **Samuel** anointed Saul, so it is in some book of **Samuel**.

Remember I stated at the beginning of this book that **Saul's death** is recorded in the **last** chapter of **1st** Samuel, i.e. chapter 31, so this verse is in the book of **1st** Samuel.

A VIAL OF OIL – **10** letters, so it is in chapter **10**.

No. 5

*And Saul said unto Samuel, Yea, I have obeyed the voice of the LORD, and have gone the way which the LORD sent me, and have brought Agag the king of Amalek **(THE KING OF AMALEK)**, and have utterly destroyed the Amalekites.*

But the people took of the spoil, sheep and oxen, the chief of the things which should have been utterly destroyed, to sacrifice unto the LORD thy God in Gilgal.

*And Samuel **(Samuel)** said, Hath the LORD [as great] delight in burnt offerings and sacrifices, as in obeying the voice **(OBEYING THE VOICE)** of the LORD? Behold, to obey [is] better than sacrifice, [and] to hearken than the fat of rams.* 1st Samuel 15:20-22.

These verses are obviously in some book of **Samuel**.

Remember I stated at the beginning of this publication that the book of 1st Samuel is about Samuel, Saul and David, so these verses are in the book of 1st Samuel.

OBEYING THE VOICE – **15** letters, so they are in chapter **15**.

Or – **THE KING OF AMALEK** – **15** letters.

No. 6

And Samuel said unto Jesse, Are here all [thy] children? And he said, There remaineth yet the youngest, and, behold, he keepeth the sheep. And Samuel said unto Jesse, Send and fetch him: for we will not sit down till he come hither.

And he sent, and brought him in. Now he [was] ruddy, [and] withal of a beautiful countenance, and goodly to look to. And the LORD said, Arise, anoint him: for this [is] he.

*Then Samuel took the horn of oil, and anointed him in the midst of his brethren **(THEN SAMUEL TOOK THE HORN OF OIL, AND ANOINTED HIM IN THE MIDST OF HIS BRETHREN)**: and the Spirit of the LORD came upon David from that day forward. So Samuel rose up, and went to Ramah.* 1st Samuel 16:11-13.

The narratives concerning David are in 1st and 2nd Samuel. David's death is recorded in 1st Kings chapter 2 and in 1st Chronicles chapter 29, which is the last chapter. David was still young when he was anointed king, so these verses are in the book of 1st Samuel.

THEN SAMUEL TOOK THE HORN OF OIL, AND ANOINTED HIM IN THE MIDST OF HIS BRETHREN - 16 words, so they are in chapter **16**.

No. 7
*And David (**David**) put his hand in his bag, and took thence a stone, and slang [it], and smote the Philistine in his forehead, that the stone sunk into his forehead; and he fell upon his face to the earth.* 1st Samuel 17:49.

The narratives concerning David are in the books of 1st and 2nd Samuel.

David was still young when he slew Goliath the Philistine, so this verse is in the book of 1st Samuel.

DAVID SLAYS GOLIATH - 17 letters, so it is in chapter **17**.

No. 8
*And Saul disguised himself, and put on other raiment, and he went, and two men with him, and they came to the woman by night (**AND THEY CAME TO THE WOMAN BY NIGHT**): and he said, I pray thee, divine unto me by the familiar spirit, and bring me [him] (**Samuel**) up, whom I shall name unto thee.* 1st Samuel 28:8.

Saul desired to have **Samuel** brought up, so this verse is in some book of **Samuel**.

For the purpose of association, think that there is only **1** visit to En-dor mentioned, so this verse is in the book of **1**st Samuel.

AND THEY CAME TO THE WOMAN BY NIGHT – 28 letters, so it is in chapter **28**.

2ND SAMUEL

No. 1

*And they set the ark of God upon a new cart, and brought it out of the house of Abinadab that [was] in Gibeah: and Uzzah **(Uzzah)** and Ahio **(Ahio)**, the sons of Abinadab, drave the new cart.*

And they brought it out of the house of Abinadab which [was] at Gibeah, accompanying the ark of God: and Ahio went before the ark.

And David and all the house of Israel played before the LORD on all manner of [instruments made of] fir wood, even on harps, and on psalteries, and on timbrels, and on cornets, and on cymbals.

*And when they came to Nachon's **(Nachon's)** threshingfloor, Uzzah put forth [his hand] to the ark of God, and took hold of it; for the oxen shook [it].*

And the anger of the LORD was kindled against Uzzah; and God smote him there for [his] error; and there he died by the ark of God.
2nd Samuel 6:3-7.

Just remember that the narratives about David are in the books of 1st and 2nd Samuel, so these verses are in some book of Samuel.

For the purpose of association, think that Uzzah and Ahio (**2** men) drove the new cart, so they are in **2**nd Samuel.

It was at the threshingfloor of **NACHON** that Uzzah took hold of the Ark of God.

NACHON – **6** letters, so these verses are in chapter **6**.

The parallel narrative is in the book of 1st Chronicles chapter 13.

No. 2

*So Mephibosheth dwelt in Jerusalem: for he did eat continually at the king's table; and was lame (**lame**) on both his feet.* 2nd Samuel 9:13.

Remember I stated at the beginning of this book that king Saul's death is recorded in the last chapter of 1st Samuel. Mephibosheth was king Saul's grandson, so this verse is in the book of 2nd Samuel.

HE WAS LAME – 9 letters, so it is in chapter **9**.

No. 3

*And it came to pass in an eveningtide (**EVENINGTIDE**), that David arose from off his bed, and walked upon the roof of the king's house (**walked upon the roof of the king's house**): and from the roof (**FROM THE ROOF**) he saw a woman washing herself; and the woman [was] very beautiful to look upon.* 2nd Samuel 11:2.

Remember I stated at the beginning of this publication that the narratives about David are in the books of 1st and 2nd Samuel.

I also stated that in the book of 2nd Samuel the men of Judah anointed David king over the house of Judah, and later the elders of Israel anointed him king over Israel. The above verse concerns David when he was **king**, so it is in the book of 2nd Samuel.

EVENINGTIDE - 11 letters, so this verse is in chapter **11**.

Or - **FROM THE ROOF – 11** letters.

No. 4

And the LORD sent Nathan unto David. And he came unto him, and said unto him, There were two men in one city; the one rich, and the other poor.

The rich [man] had exceeding many flocks and herds:

But the poor [man] had nothing, save one little ewe lamb, which he had bought and nourished up: and it grew up together with him, and with his children; it did eat of his own meat, and drank of his own cup, and lay in his bosom, and was unto him as a daughter.

And there came a traveller unto the rich man, and he spared to take of his own flock and of his own herd, to dress for the wayfaring man that was come unto him; but took the poor man's lamb (**POOR MAN'S LAMB**), and dressed it for the man that was come to him.

And David's anger was greatly kindled against the man; and he said to Nathan, [As] the LORD liveth, the man that hath done this [thing] shall surely die:

And he shall restore the lamb fourfold, because he did this thing, and because he had no pity.

And Nathan said to David, Thou [art] the man. Thus saith the LORD God of Israel, I anointed thee king over Israel, and I delivered thee out of the hand of Saul; 2nd Samuel 12:1-7.

Just remember that the narratives about David are in the books of 1st and 2nd Samuel, so these verses are in some book of Samuel.

2 men are having a conversation in these verses, so they are in the book of **2**nd Samuel.

POOR MAN'S LAMB - **12** letters, so these verses are in chapter **12**.

No. 5

*And Nathan departed unto his house. And the LORD struck the child that Uriah's wife bare unto David, and it was very sick (**it was very sick**).* 2nd Samuel 12:15.

Remember I stated at the beginning of this publication that in the book of 2nd Samuel the men of Judah anointed David king over the house of Judah, and later the elders of Israel anointed him king over Israel. The above verse concerns David when he was **king**, so it is in the book of 2nd Samuel.

VERY ILL CHILD – **12** letters, so this verse is in chapter **12**.

1ST KINGS

No. 1
*In Gibeon the LORD appeared to Solomon in a dream by night: and God said, Ask **(ASK)** what I shall give thee.* 1st Kings 3:5.

Give therefore thy servant an understanding heart to judge thy people, that I may discern between good and bad: for who is able to judge this thy so great a people? 1st Kings 3:9.

The book of 1st Kings 2:12 to the end, and the book of 2nd Kings in its entirety contain the narratives about the kings of Israel and Judah beginning with Solomon, so these verses are in the book of 1st Kings.

ASK - **3** letters, so they are in chapter **3**.

The narrative chapter is in the book of 2nd Chronicles chapter 1.

No. 2
Then came there two women, [that were] harlots, unto the king (Solomon), and stood before him.
And the one woman said, O my lord, I and this woman dwell in one house; and I was delivered of a child with her in the house.
And it came to pass the third day after that I was delivered, that this woman was delivered also: and we [were] together; [there was] no stranger with us in the house, save we two in the house.
And this woman's child died in the night; because she overlaid it.
And she arose at midnight, and took my son from beside me, while thine handmaid slept, and laid it in her bosom, and laid her dead

child in my bosom. 1st Kings 3:16-20.
And the king said, Bring me a sword. And they brought a sword before the king.
And the king said, Divide the living child in two, and give half to the one, and half to the other. 1st Kings 3:24-25.

See association number 1 for details concerning Solomon.

There are **3** people mentioned in these verses: Solomon and the two harlots, so they are in chapter **3**.

No. 3
*And it came to pass, when the priests were come out of the holy [place], that the cloud filled the house **(THE HOUSE)** of the LORD **(THE CLOUD FILLED THE HOUSE OF THE LORD)**,*
So that the priests could not stand to minister because of the cloud: for the glory of the LORD had filled the house of the LORD.
Then spake Solomon, The LORD said that he would dwell in the thick darkness.
I have surely built thee an house to dwell in, a settled place for thee to abide in for ever. 1st Kings 8:10-13.

These verses are about the dedication of the temple, which king Solomon built. See association number 1 for details concerning Solomon.

THE HOUSE - **8** letters, so they are in chapter **8**.

Or - **THE CLOUD FILLED THE HOUSE OF THE LORD – 8** words.

No. 4
*And when the queen **(QUEEN)** of Sheba **(SHEBA)** heard of the fame of Solomon **(Solomon)** concerning the name of the LORD, she came to prove him with hard questions.* 1st Kings 10:1.

Remember that the narratives about king **Solomon** during his lifetime are in the book of 1st Kings, so this verse is in the book of 1st Kings.

QUEEN SHEBA – **10** letters, so it is in chapter **10**.
The parallel chapter is in the book of 2nd Chronicles chapter 9.

No. 5
*And Elijah the Tishbite (**ELIJAH THE TISHBITE**), [who was] of the inhabitants of Gilead, said unto Ahab, [As] the LORD God of Israel liveth, before whom I stand, there shall not be dew nor rain these years, but according to my word.* 1st Kings 17:1.

Remember that the book of 2nd Kings chapter 2 informs us that **Elijah** was taken up to Heaven by a whirlwind, so this verse is in the book of 1st Kings.

ELIJAH THE TISHBITE – **17** letters, so it is in chapter **17**.

No. 6
*[And] the barrel of meal wasted not (**meal wasted not**), neither did the cruse of oil fail (**neither did the cruse of oil fail**), according to the word of the LORD, which he spake by Elijah (**Elijah**).* 1st Kings 17:16.

For details concerning **Elijah** see association number 5.

MEAL AND OIL ENDURED – **17** letters, so this verse is in chapter **17**.

No. 7
*And it came to pass after these things, [that] the son of the woman, the mistress of the house, fell sick; and his sickness was so sore, that there was no breath left in him (**NO BREATH LEFT IN HIM**).
And she said unto Elijah (**Elijah**), What have I to do with thee, O thou man of God? art thou come unto me to call my sin to remembrance, and to slay my son?* 1st Kings 17:17-18.

For details concerning **Elijah** see association number 5.

NO BREATH LEFT IN HIM – **17** letters, so these verses are in chapter **17**.

No. 8
And it came to pass [after] many days, that the word of the LORD came to Elijah in the third year, saying, Go, shew thyself unto Ahab; and I will send rain upon the earth. 1st Kings 18:1.

And now thou sayest, Go, tell thy lord, Behold, Elijah [is here] **(BEHOLD, ELIJAH [IS HERE])**: *and he shall slay me* (Obadiah).
And Elijah said, [As] the LORD of hosts liveth, before whom I stand, I will surely shew myself unto him to day.
So Obadiah went to meet Ahab, and told him: and Ahab went to meet Elijah.
And it came to pass, when Ahab saw Elijah, that Ahab said unto him, [Art] thou he that troubleth Israel?
And he answered, I have not troubled Israel; but thou,
and thy father's house, in that ye have forsaken the commandments of the LORD, and thou hast followed Baalim. 1st Kings 18:14-18.

For details concerning **Elijah** see association number 5.

BEHOLD ELIJAH IS HERE – **18** letters, so these verses are in chapter **18**.

No. 9
And it came to pass at [the time of] the offering of the [evening] sacrifice, that Elijah **(Elijah)** *the prophet came near, and said, LORD God of Abraham, Isaac, and of Israel, let it be known this day that thou [art] God in Israel* **(THOU ART GOD IN ISRAEL),** *and [that] I [am] thy servant, and [that] I have done all these things at thy word.*
Hear me, O LORD, hear me, that this people may know that thou [art] the LORD God, and [that] thou hast turned their heart back again.
Then the fire of the LORD fell, and consumed the burnt sacrifice, and the wood, and the stones, and the dust, and licked up the water that [was] in the trench.
And when all the people saw [it], they fell on their faces: and they said, The LORD, he [is] the God; the LORD, he [is] the God.
1st Kings 18:36-39.

For details concerning **Elijah** see association number 5.

THOU ART GOD IN ISRAEL – 18 letters, so these verses are in chapter **18**.

No. 10
*Then Jezebel sent a messenger unto Elijah **(Elijah)**, saying, So let the gods do [to me], and more also, if I make not thy life as the life of one of them by to morrow about this time.*

And when he saw [that], he arose, and went for his life, and came to Beersheba, which [belongeth] to Judah, and left his servant there.

*But he himself went a day's journey into the wilderness, and came and sat down under a juniper tree: and he requested for himself that he might die; and said, It is enough; now, O LORD, take away my life **(O LORD TAKE AWAY MY LIFE)**; for I [am] not better than my fathers. 1st Kings 19:2-4.*

For details concerning **Elijah** see association number 5.

O LORD TAKE AWAY MY LIFE – 19 letters, so these verses are in chapter **19**.

No. 11
*So he **(Elijah)** departed thence, and found Elisha the son of Shaphat, who [was] plowing [with] twelve yoke [of oxen] before him, and he with the twelfth **(AND HE WITH THE TWELFTH)**: and Elijah passed by him, and cast his mantle upon him. 1st Kings 19:19.*

For details concerning **Elijah** see association number 5.

AND HE WITH THE TWELFTH – 19 letters, so this verse is in chapter **19**.

No. 12
*And Ahab spake unto Naboth, saying, Give me thy vineyard, that I may have it for a garden of herbs, because it [is] near unto my house: and I will give thee for it a better vineyard than it **(A BETTER VINEYARD THAN IT)**; [or], if it seem good to thee, I will give thee the worth of it in money. 1st Kings 21:2.*

For the purpose of association, think that this verse is about Ahab and he was a **king**, so it is in some book of **Kings**. Also for the purpose of association, think that '**A**' is the **1st** letter of the alphabet, and '**A**' is the **1st** letter of Ahab, so this verse is in the book of **1st** Kings.

A BETTER VINEYARD THAN IT – **21** letters,
so it is in chapter **21**.

2ND KINGS

No. 1
So she went from him (**Elisha**)*, and shut the door upon her and upon her sons, who brought [the vessels] to her; and she poured out.*
*And it came to pass, when the vessels were full, that she said unto her son, Bring me yet a vessel. And he said unto her, [There is] not a vessel more. And the oil stayed (**AND THE OIL STAYED**).*
2nd Kings 4:5-6.

Remember I stated at the beginning of this publication that the book of 2nd Kings contains the narratives of **Elisha**, so these verses are in the book of 2nd Kings.

AND THE OIL STAYED – **4** words, so they are in chapter **4**.

No. 2
And the woman conceived, and bare a son at that season that Elisha had said unto her, according to the time of life.
And when the child was grown, it fell on a day, that he went out to his father to the reapers.
*And he said unto his father, My head, my head (**MY HEAD, MY HEAD**). And he said to a lad, Carry him to his mother.*
2nd Kings 4:17-19.

Then he (**Elisha**) *returned, and walked in the house to and fro;*

*and went up, and stretched himself upon him: and the child sneezed (**sneezed**) seven times, and the child opened his eyes.* 2nd Kings 4:35.

For details concerning **Elisha** see association number 1.

MY, HEAD MY HEAD – 4 words, so these verses are in chapter **4**. In the past I had difficulty remembering whether it was Elijah or Elisha who performed this miracle. Now I remember it was Elisha because verse thirty-five says *and the child sneezed* (**sneezed**) *seven times.* When one sneezes it sounds like a**tish**oo, and the second syllable of a**tish**oo rhymes with the second syllable of E**lish**a.

No. 3
*Now Naaman, captain of the host of the king of Syria, was a great man with his master, and honourable, because by him the LORD had given deliverance unto Syria: he was also a mighty man in valour, [but he was] a leper (**BUT HE WAS A LEPER**).*
And the Syrians had gone out by companies, and had brought away captive out of the land of Israel a little maid; and she waited on Naaman's wife.
And she said unto her mistress, Would God my lord [were] with the prophet (**Elisha**) *that [is] in Samaria! for he would recover him of his leprosy.* 2nd Kings 5:1-3.

For details concerning **Elisha** see association number 1.

BUT HE WAS A LEPER – 5 words,
so these verses are in chapter **5**.

No. 4
*But Gehazi, the servant of Elisha (**Elisha**) the man of God, said, Behold, my master hath spared Naaman this Syrian, in not receiving at his hands that which he brought: but, [as] the LORD liveth, I will run after him (**I WILL RUN AFTER HIM**), and take somewhat of him.* 2nd Kings 5:20.

For details concerning **Elisha** see association number 1.

I WILL RUN AFTER HIM – 5 words, so this verse is in chapter **5**.

No. 5

*And the LORD said unto Jehu **(Jehu)**, Because thou hast done well in executing [that which is] right in mine eyes, [and] hast done unto the house of Ahab **(Ahab)** according to all that [was] in mine heart, thy children of the fourth [generation] **(GENERATION)** shall sit on the throne of Israel.* 2nd Kings 10:30.

For the purpose of association, think that **Jehu** and **Ahab** were kings, so this verse is in some book of Kings.

JEHU AHAB – **2** kings, so it is in the book of **2**nd Kings.
GENERATION – **10** letters, so this verse is in chapter **10**.

No. 6

And when Athaliah the mother of Ahaziah saw that her son was dead, she arose and destroyed all the seed royal.
*But Jehosheba, the daughter of king Joram, sister of Ahaziah, took Joash **(Joash)** the son of Ahaziah, and stole him from among the king's sons [which were] slain; and they hid him, [even] him and his nurse, in the bedchamber from Athaliah, so that he was not slain.*
And he was with her hid in the house of the LORD six years. And Athaliah did reign over the land. 2nd Kings 11:1-3.

And when she looked, behold, the king stood by a pillar, as the manner [was], and the princes and the trumpeters by the king, and all the people of the land rejoiced, and blew with trumpets: and Athaliah rent her clothes, and cried, Treason, Treason.
*But Jehoiada the priest commanded the captains of the hundreds, the officers of the host, and said unto them, Have her forth without the ranges: and him that followeth her kill with the sword. For the priest had said, Let her not be slain in the house of the LORD **(LET HER NOT BE SLAIN IN THE HOUSE OF THE LORD)**.*
2nd Kings 11:14-15.

Remember I stated at the beginning of this publication that the last chapter of the book of 1st kings, i.e. chapter 22 records the deaths of king Jehoshaphat the 4th king of Judah and king Ahab the 7th king of Israel.

These verses are about king **Joash** (Jehoash) the 8th monarch of

Judah. I say monarch because one of them was a queen. So they are in the book of 2nd kings.

LET HER NOT BE SLAIN IN THE HOUSE OF THE LORD – **11** words, so these verses are in chapter **11**.

The parallel chapter is in the book of 2nd Chronicles chapter 22.

No. 7
And Elisha died (AND ELISHA DIED), and they buried him. And the bands of the Moabites invaded the land at the coming in of the year.
And it came to pass, as they were burying a man, that, behold, they spied a band [of men]; and they cast the man into the sepulchre of Elisha (BONES OF ELISHA), and when the man was let down, and touched the bones of Elisha (BONES OF ELISHA), he revived, and stood up on his feet. 2nd Kings 13:20-21.

For details concerning **Elisha** see association number 1.

AND ELISHA DIED – 13 letters, so these verses are in chapter **13**.

Or - **BONES OF ELISHA – 13** letters.

No. 8
In those days was Hezekiah (Hezekiah) sick unto death. And the prophet Isaiah the son of Amoz came to him, and said unto him, Thus saith the LORD, Set thine house in order (SET THINE HOUSE IN ORDER); for thou shalt die, and not live. 2nd Kings 20:1.

Hezekiah was the **thirteenth** monarch of Judah. I say monarch because one of them was a queen. There were twenty monarchs of Judah. Hezekiah was the thirteenth; therefore any narrative concerning him during his lifetime is in the book of 2nd Kings, so this verse is in the book of 2nd Kings.

SET THINE HOUSE IN ORDER – 20 letters,
so it is in chapter **20**.

1ST CHRONICLES

No. 1

Then David the king stood up upon his feet, and said, Hear me, my brethren, and my people: [As for me], I [had] in mine heart to build an house of rest for the ark of the covenant of the LORD, and for the footstool of our God, and had made ready for the building:

But God said unto me, Thou shalt not build an house for my name, because thou [hast been] a man of war (BECAUSE THOU [HAST BEEN] A MAN OF WAR), and hast shed blood.

Howbeit the LORD God of Israel chose (chose) me before all the house of my father to be king over Israel for ever: for he hath chosen (chosen) Judah [to be] the ruler; and of the house of Judah, the house of my father; and among the sons of my father he liked me to make [me] king over all Israel:

And of all my sons, (for the LORD hath given me many sons,) he hath chosen (chosen) Solomon my son to sit upon the throne of the kingdom of the LORD over Israel.

And he said unto me, Solomon thy son, he shall build my house and my courts: for I have chosen (chosen) him [to be] my son, and I will be his father. 1st Chronicles 28:2-6.

For the purpose of association think of God's **chosen** ones having their names **recorded/chronicled** in Heaven, so these verses are in some book of Chronicles.

Also for the purpose of association, think that **1** house was being built, so they are in the book of **1**st Chronicles.

BECAUSE THOU HAST BEEN A MAN OF WAR – 28 letters, so these verses are in chapter **28**.

No. 2

*And thou, Solomon my son, know thou the God of thy father, and serve him with a perfect heart and with a willing mind: for the LORD searcheth all hearts **(FOR THE LORD SEARCHETH ALL HEARTS)**, and understandeth all the imaginations of the thoughts: if thou seek him, he will be found of thee; but if thou forsake him, he will cast thee off for ever.*

*Take heed now; for the LORD hath chosen **(chosen)** thee to build an house for the sanctuary: be strong, and do [it].*

1st Chronicles 28:9-10.

For the purpose of association, think of God's **chosen** ones having their names **recorded/chronicled** in Heaven, so these verses are in some book of **Chronicles**.

Also for the purpose of association, think that **1** house was being built, so they are in the book of **1**st Chronicles.

FOR THE LORD SEARCHETH ALL HEARTS – **28** letters, so these verses are in chapter **28**.

2ND CHRONICLES

No. 1

*And Solomon **(Solomon)** sent to Huram **(Huram)** the king of Tyre, saying, As thou didst deal with David my father, and didst send him cedars to build him an house to dwell therein, [even so deal with me].*

*Behold, I build an house **(AN HOUSE)** to the name of the LORD my God, to dedicate [it] to him, [and] to burn before him sweet incense, and for the continual shewbread, and for the burnt offerings morning and evening, on the sabbaths, and on the new moons, and on the solemn feasts of the LORD our God. This [is an ordinance] for ever to Israel.*

And the house which I build [is] great: for great [is] our God above all gods.

*But who is able to build him an house **(an house)**, seeing the heaven and heaven of heavens cannot contain him? who [am] I then, that I should build him an house **(an house)**, save only to burn sacrifice before him?*

Send me now therefore a man cunning to work in gold, and in silver, and in brass, and in iron, and in purple, and crimson, and blue, and that can skill to grave with the cunning men that [are] with me in Judah and in Jerusalem, whom David my father did provide.

Send me also cedar trees, fir trees, and algum trees, out of Lebanon: for I know that thy servants can skill to cut timber in Lebanon; and, behold, my servants [shall be] with thy servants,

Even to prepare me timber in abundance: for the house which I am about to build [shall be] wonderful great.

And, behold, I will give to thy servants, the hewers that cut timber, twenty thousand measures of beaten wheat, and twenty thousand measures of barley, and twenty thousand baths of wine, and twenty thousand baths of oil.

*Then Huram the king of Tyre answered in writing **(writing)**, which he sent to Solomon, Because the LORD hath loved his people **(his people)**, he hath made thee king over them.* 2nd Chronicles 2:3-11.

For the purpose of association, think of the LORD'S **people** having their names **written/chronicled** in Heaven, so these verses are in some book of **Chronicles**.

Also for the purpose of association, think that these verses are about **2** people: **Solomon** and **Huram**, so they are in the book of 2nd Chronicles.

An house is the subject of these verses.

AN HOUSE – **2** words, so they are in chapter **2**.

No. 2
*If my people **(my people)**, which are called by my name, shall humble themselves **(humble themselves)**, and pray **(pray)**, and seek my face **(seek my face)**, and turn from their wicked ways **(turn from their wicked ways)**; then will I hear from heaven **(then will I hear from heaven)**, and will forgive their sin **(forgive their sin)**, and will heal their land **(heal their land)**.* 2nd Chronicles 7:14.

For the purpose of association, think of **God's people** having their names **recorded/chronicled** in Heaven, so this verse is in some book of **Chronicles.**

(1) *forgive their sin*
(2) *heal their land*

2 promises, so this verse is in the book of **2**nd Chronicles.

(1) *humble themselves*
(2) *pray*
(3) *seek my face*
(4) *turn from their wicked ways*
(5) *then will I hear from heaven*
(6) *will forgive their sin*
(7) *will heal their land*

The above verse is in chapter **7.**

EZRA

No. 1
Now in the first year (1st) of Cyrus king of Persia, that the word of the LORD by the mouth of Jeremiah might be fulfilled, the LORD stirred up the spirit of Cyrus king of Persia, that he made a proclamation throughout all his kingdom, and [put it] also in writing, saying,

Thus saith Cyrus king of Persia, The LORD God of heaven hath given me all the kingdoms of the earth; and he hath charged me to build him an house (build him an house) at Jerusalem, which [is] in Judah.

Who [is there] among you of all his people? his God be with him, and let him go up to Jerusalem, which [is] in Judah, and build the house of the LORD God of Israel, (he [is] the God,) which [is] in Jerusalem. Ezra 1:1-3.

Remember I stated at the beginning of this publication that the book of Ezra is about the **building of the temple of the LORD**, so these verses are in the book of Ezra.

Now in the **1st** year etc, so they are in the **1st** chapter.

No. 2
Now when the adversaries of Judah and Benjamin heard that the children of the captivity builded the temple unto the LORD God of Israel;

Then they came to Zerubbabel, and to the chief of the fathers, and said unto them, Let us build with you: for we seek your God, as ye [do]; and we do sacrifice unto him since the days of Esarhaddon king of Assur, which brought us up hither.

*But Zerubbabel, and Jeshua, and the rest of the chief of the fathers of Israel, said unto them, Ye have nothing to do with us to build an house unto our God (**build an house unto our God**); but we ourselves together will build unto the LORD God of Israel, as king Cyrus the king of Persia hath commanded us.*

*Then the people of the land weakened the hands of the people of Judah, and troubled them in building (**TROUBLED THEM IN BUILDING**). Ezra 4:1-4.*

For details concerning the building of the temple see association number 1.

TROUBLED THEM IN BUILDING – 4 words, so these verses are in chapter 4.

NEHEMIAH

No. 1
*Now it came to pass, when Sanballat, and Tobiah (**TOBIAH**), and Geshem the Arabian, and the rest of our enemies, heard that I had builded the wall (**I had builded the wall**), and [that] there was no breach left therein; (though at that time I had not set up the doors*

upon the gates;)

That Sanballat and Geshem sent unto me, saying, Come, let us meet together in [some one of] the villages in the plain of Ono. But they thought to do me mischief.

And I sent messengers unto them, saying, I [am] doing a great work **(I AM DOING A GREAT WORK)**, *so that I cannot come down: why should the work cease, whilst I leave it, and come down to you?* Nehemiah 6:1-3.

Remember I stated at the beginning of this publication that the book of Nehemiah is about the **building of the wall of Jerusalem**, so these verses are in the book of Nehemiah.

I AM DOING A GREAT WORK – 6 words, so they are in chapter **6**.

Or - **TOBIAH – 6** letters.

No. 2

And all the people gathered themselves together as one man into the street that [was] before the water gate; and they spake unto Ezra the scribe to bring the book of the law of Moses, which the LORD had commanded to Israel.

And Ezra the priest brought the law before the congregation both of men and women, and all that could hear with understanding, upon the first day of the seventh month.

And he read therein before the street that [was] before the water gate from the morning until midday, before the men and the women, and those that could understand; and the ears of all the people [were attentive] unto the book of the law.

And Ezra the scribe stood upon a pulpit of wood, which they had made for the purpose; and beside him stood Mattithiah, and Shema, and Anaiah, and Urijah, and Hilkiah, and Maaseiah, on his right hand; and on his left hand, Pedaiah, and Mishael, and Malchiah, and Hashum, and Hashbadana, Zechariah, [and] Meshullam.

And Ezra opened the book in the sight of all the people; (for he was above all the people;) and when he opened it, all the people stood up:

And Ezra blessed the LORD, the great God. And all the people answered, Amen, Amen, **(AMEN AMEN)** *with lifting up their hands: and they bowed their heads, and worshipped the LORD with [their]* *faces to the ground.* Nehemiah 8:1-6.

Remember I stated at the beginning of this book that the book of Nehemiah is about the building of the wall of Jerusalem. These verses describe what happened after the wall of Jerusalem was built, so they are in the book of Nehemiah.

AMEN AMEN - 8 letters so these verses are in chapter **8**.

The only other place in Scripture where the words Amen, Amen are recorded is in Numbers 5:22. *And this water that causeth the curse shall go into thy bowels, to make [thy] belly to swell, and [thy] thigh to rot: And the woman shall say, Amen, amen.*

ESTHER

No. 1
*And the king loved Esther (**Esther**) above all the women, and she obtained grace and favour in his sight more than all the virgins; so that he set the royal crown upon her head, and made her queen instead of Vashti (**Vashti**).* Esther 2:17.

This verse is obviously in the book of **Esther**.

(1) Esther
(2) Vashti

For the purpose of association, think that there are **2** women mentioned, so it is in chapter **2**.

No. 2
*And it was so, when the king saw Esther (**Esther**) the queen standing in the court, [that] she obtained favour in his sight: and the king held out to Esther the golden sceptre that [was] in his hand. So Esther*

drew near, and touched the top of the sceptre (**So Esther drew near, and touched the top of the scepter**).

Then said the king unto her, What wilt thou, queen Esther? and what [is] thy request? it shall be even given thee to the half of the kingdom.

And Esther answered, If [it seem] good unto the king, let the king and Haman come this day unto the banquet that I have prepared for him.

Then the king said, Cause Haman to make haste, that he may do as Esther hath said. So the king and Haman came to the banquet that Esther had prepared. Esther 5:2-5.

These verses are obviously in the book of **Esther**.

ESTHER TOUCHED THE KING'S SCEPTRE – **5** words, so they are in chapter **5**.

No. 3

Then the king returned out of the palace garden into the place of the banquet of wine; and Haman was fallen upon the bed whereon Esther (**Esther**) *[was]. Then said the king, Will he force the queen also before me in the house? As the word went out of the king's mouth, they covered Haman's face.*

And Harbonah, one of the chamberlains, said before the king, Behold also, the gallows fifty cubits high, which Haman had made for Mordecai, who had spoken good for the king, standeth in the house of Haman. Then the king said, Hang him thereon.

So they hanged Haman on the gallows (**GALLOWS**) *that he had prepared for Mordecai. Then was the king's wrath pacified.*
Esther 7:8-10.

These verses are obviously in the book of **Esther**.

GALLOWS – **7** letters, so they are in chapter **7**.

JOB

No. 1

*Then Job (**Job**) arose, and rent his mantle, and shaved his head, and fell down upon the ground, and worshipped,*

*And said, Naked came I (**I**) out of my mother's womb, and naked shall I (**I**) return thither: the LORD gave, and the LORD hath taken away; blessed (**blessed**) be the name of the LORD.*

In all this Job sinned not, nor charged God foolishly. Job 1:20-22.

These verses are obviously in the book of **Job**.

If you read the whole of the first chapter of Job you will find that verses 20-22 tell us what Job did when he heard of all the tragedies that had befallen him, including the death of his seven sons and three daughters. Truly Job was a spiritual man.

For the purpose of association, think that Psalm **1** starts with *Blessed (**Blessed**) [is] the man that walketh not in the counsel of the ungodly,* so these verses are in chapter **1**.

Or - **I** looks similar to **1**, so they are in chapter **1**.

No. 2

*And the LORD said unto Satan, Hast thou considered my servant Job (**Job**), that [there is] none like him in the earth, a perfect (**perfect**) and an upright (**upright**) man, one that feareth God, and escheweth evil? and still he holdeth fast his integrity, although thou movedst me against him, to destroy him without cause.* Job 2:3.

This verse is obviously in the book of **Job**.

(1) perfect
(2) upright
2 descriptions of Job, so it is in chapter **2**.

No. 3
So went Satan forth from the presence of the LORD, and smote Job **(Job)** *with sore boils from the sole of his foot unto his crown.*
And he took him a potsherd to scrape himself withal **(And he took him a potsherd to scrape himself withal)**; *and he sat down among the ashes* **(and he sat down among the ashes)**. Job 2:7-8.

These verses are obviously in the book of **Job**.

Job did **2** things:

(1) He took a potsherd to scrape himself.
(2) He sat down among the ashes, so they are in chapter **2**.

No. 4
Then said his wife unto him **(Job)**, *Dost thou still retain thine integrity? curse God* **(CURSE GOD)**, *and die.* Job 2:9.

This verse is obviously in the book of **Job**.

CURSE GOD – **2** words, so it is in chapter **2**.

No. 5
Now when Job's **(Job's)** *three friends heard of all this evil that was come upon him, they came every one from his own place; Eliphaz the Temanite, and Bildad the Shuhite, and Zophar the Naamathite: for they had made an appointment together to come to mourn with him and to comfort him.*
And when they lifted up their eyes afar off, and knew him not, they lifted up their voice, and wept; and they rent every one his mantle, and sprinkled dust upon their heads toward heaven.
So they sat down with him upon the ground seven days and seven nights, and none spake **(NONE SPAKE)** *a word unto him: for they saw that [his] grief was very great.* Job 2:11-13.

These verses are obviously in the book of **Job**.

NONE SPAKE – **2** words, so they are is in chapter **2**.

No. 6
Yet man is born unto trouble (MAN IS BORN UNTO TROUBLE),
as the sparks fly upward. Job 5:7.

For the purpose of association, think that Job was the man who endured much trouble, so this verse is in the book of Job.

MAN IS BORN UNTO TROUBLE – **5** words, so it is in chapter **5**.

No. 7
For I know [that] my redeemer liveth, and [that] he shall stand
*at the latter [day] upon the earth (**FOR I KNOW [THAT] MY***
REDEEMER LIVETH, AND [THAT] HE SHALL STAND AT THE
***LATTER [DAY] UPON THE EARTH**):*
*And [though] after my skin [worms] destroy this [body] (**destroy***
***this [body]**), yet in my flesh shall I see God:*
*Whom I shall see for myself, and mine eyes shall behold (**MINE***
***EYES SHALL BEHOLD**), and not another; [though] my reins be*
consumed within me. Job 19:25-27.

For the purpose of association, think of Job's body as already being **destroyed**, so these verses are in the book of Job.

FOR I KNOW [THAT] MY REDEEMER LIVETH, AND [THAT] HE SHALL STAND AT THE LATTER [DAY] UPON THE EARTH – **19** words, so they are in chapter **19**.

Or - **MINE EYES SHALL BEHOLD** – **19** letters.

No. 8
*And the LORD turned the captivity of Job (**Job**), when he prayed for*
his friends: also the LORD gave Job twice as much as he had before
*(**ALSO THE LORD GAVE JOB TWICE AS MUCH AS HE HAD***
***BEFORE**).* Job 42:10.

This verse is obviously in the book of **Job**.

ALSO THE LORD GAVE JOB TWICE AS MUCH AS HE HAD BEFORE – **42** letters, so it is in chapter **42**.

No. 9
*So the LORD blessed the latter end (**latter end**) of Job (**Job**) more than his beginning: for he had fourteen thousand sheep (**SHEEP**), and six thousand camels (**CAMELS**), and a thousand yoke of oxen (**OXEN**), and a thousand she asses (**SHE ASSES**).*
*He had also seven sons (**ALSO 7 SONS**) and three daughters (**3 DAUGHTERS**).* Job 42:12-13.

These verses are obviously in the book of **Job**.

SHEEP CAMELS OXEN SHE ASSES ALSO 7 SONS 3 DAUGHTERS – **42** letters and figures, so they are in chapter **42**.

If you have memorized the number of chapters in the book of Job then you could remember that this verse about Job's **latter end** is in the **last** chapter, i.e. chapter **42**.

PSALMS

No. 1
*If the foundations (**foundations**) be destroyed (**BE DESTROYED**), what can the righteous do?* Psalm 11:3.

A Psalm is a poem, and a poem is **constructed** using words. For the purpose of association, think of **constructions** requiring **foundations**, so this verse is in the book of Psalms.

BE DESTROYED – **11** letters, so it is in Psalm **11**.

No. 2

*In my distress I called upon the LORD (**I CALLED UPON THE LORD**), and cried unto my God: he heard my voice out of his temple (**temple**), and my cry came before him, [even] into his ears.* Psalm 18:6.

A Psalm is a poem, and poems are **constructed** using words. For the purpose of association, think that a **temple** is a building, which requires to be **constructed**, so this verse is in the book of Psalms.

I CALLED UPON THE LORD – **18** letters, so it is in Psalm **18**.

The parallel verse is in 2nd Samuel 22:7.

In my distress I called upon the LORD, and cried to my God: and he did hear my voice out of his temple, and my cry [did enter] into his ears.

The above two verses contain the words of David. Remember I stated at the beginning of this publication that the book of 2nd Samuel is about David when he was king, so the above verse is in 2nd Samuel.

KING DAVID CALLS ON HIS GOD – **22** letters, so this verse is in chapter **22**.

These are the only two verses in the Old Testament where the words **'into his ears'** are recorded.

To enable you to remember which book is chapter 18 and which is chapter 22, just think that Psalm is a smaller word than Samuel, so it has the smaller number for its chapter, i.e. Psalm **18** and 2nd Samuel chapter **22**.

No. 3

*Let the words of my mouth, and the meditation of my heart (**MEDITATION OF MY HEART**), be acceptable in thy sight, O LORD, my strength and my redeemer.* Psalm 19:14.

A Psalm is a poem and a poem is **constructed** using words. For the purpose of association, think of a **construction** requiring a **foundation**. **Foundation** rhymes with **meditation**, so this verse is in the book of Psalms.

MEDITATION OF MY HEART – **19** letters, so it is in Psalm **19**.

No. 4
We will rejoice in thy salvation (SALVATION), and in the name (NAME) of our God we will set up [our] banners (BANNERS): the LORD fulfil all thy petitions. Psalm 20:5.

A Psalm is a poem, and poems are **constructed** using words. For the purpose of association, think of **erecting constructions** to display **banners**, so this verse is in the book of Psalms.

The following association is somewhat different.

SALVATION NAME BANNERS – **20** letters, so this verse is in Psalm **20**.

No. 5
My times [are] in thy hand (MY TIMES [ARE] IN THY HAND): deliver me from the hand of mine enemies, and from them that per-secute me. Psalm 31:15.

My times are in Thy hand,
My God, I wish them there;
My life, my friends, my soul I leave,
Entirely to Thy care.

You have just read the words of a well-known hymn. For the pur-pose of association, think that we **sing** hymns and we **sing** Psalms, so this verse is in the book of Psalms.

MY TIMES ARE IN THY HAND – I NEED NOT FEAR – 31 letters, so it is in Psalm **31**.

No. 6

Have mercy upon me, O God, according to thy lovingkindness: according unto the multitude of thy tender mercies blot out my transgressions.

Wash me throughly from mine iniquity, and cleanse me from my sin. For I acknowledge my transgressions: and my sin [is] ever before me.

Against thee, thee only, have I sinned, and done [this] evil in thy sight: that thou mightest be justified when thou speakest, [and] be clear when thou judgest.

Behold, I was shapen in iniquity; and in sin did my mother conceive me.

Behold, thou desirest truth in the inward parts: and in the hidden [part] thou shalt make me to know wisdom.

Purge me with hyssop, and I shall be clean: wash me, and I shall be whiter than snow.

Make me to hear joy and gladness; [that] the bones [which] thou hast broken may rejoice.

Hide thy face from my sins, and blot out all mine iniquities.

Create in me a clean heart, O God; and renew a right spirit within me.

Cast me not away from thy presence; and take not thy holy spirit from me.

Restore unto me the joy of thy salvation; and uphold me [with thy] free spirit.

[Then] will I teach transgressors thy ways; and sinners shall be converted unto thee. Psalm 51:1-13

I presume that most people would know that these verses are part of the book of Psalms.

I am using a different type of association for these verses because it is a large number.

God's grace accomplishes all that David mentions in these verses. The number of grace is **5**.

As you read through these verses you will observe that **I**, **me** and **my** are used throughout. **I**, **me** and **my** all refer to **1** person.

5 and **1** is **51**, so they are in Psalm **51**.

I am aware that **5** and **1** is also **6**. To help you remember it is **51** and not **6**, just think that the Psalmist was a **grown man** when he wrote these words. A grown man could be **51**, but if the number was 6 then that would be a child.

No. 7
O worship (worship) the LORD in the beauty of holiness (O WOR-SHIP THE LORD IN THE BEAUTY OF HOLINESS): fear before him, all the earth. Psalm 96:9.

For the purpose of association, think that when we gather together to **worship** God we sometimes sing **Psalms**, so this verse is in the book of **Psalms**.

I am taking a different approach for the following association.

O WORSHIP THE LORD IN THE BEAUTY OF HOLINESS – 9 words.

This verse is in Psalm **96**. Think of the **9** as sitting up straight with its head at the top just as we would sit in church. Then think of **6** as the head bowed down for prayer, so this verse is in Psalm **96**.

The actual verse can be memorized this time. Just think of sitting up straight again, i.e. **9** when the prayer is finished, so it is verse **9**.

No. 8
Thy word have I hid (hid) in mine heart, that I might not sin against thee. Psalm 119:11.

Psalm 119 is the longest Psalm in the Bible, or to describe it another way, it is the **big**gest Psalm. For the purpose of association, think that if you wanted to **hid**e something you would choose the **big**gest space, so this verse is in Psalm 119.

As the Psalm is very long I think you should memorize the number of the verse in this case. Just think that the first two figures in **119** are the same as **11**, so it is verse **11**.

No. 9
Thy word [is] a lamp (lamp) unto my feet, and a light (light) unto my path (path). Psalm 119:105

We **sing carols**, and we also **sing Psalms**. For the purpose of association, think that carol singers need a **light for their path**, so this verse is in the book of Psalms.

It is difficult to form an association for such a large number as 119, so I am taking a different approach.

In the previous verse the Word was **hid** in the heart. In this verse the Word is a **lamp** and a **light**. For the purpose of association, think of using a **lamp** or **light** to search for what is **hid**. So this verse is in the same Psalm i.e. Psalm 119.

This is the long Psalm, so I think you should memorize the number of the verse as was suggested in association number 8. For the purpose of association, think that when you find what is **hid** you lift it and take it **away** with you. There are **14** words in this verse, so take **14 away** from **119** and the result is **105**, so this is verse **105**.

No. 10
If thou, LORD, shouldest mark iniquities (mark iniquities), O Lord, who shall stand (stand)? Psalm 130:3.

Psalms are poems, and poems are **constructed** of words. Buildings are also **constructed**. For the purpose of association, think that it is essential that a building will remain **stand**ing, so this verse is in the book of Psalms.

This is another large number again, so I need to use a different type of association.

The only place in Scripture where the term **'mark iniquities'** is mentioned is Psalm 130:3, so just memorize that this term is only recorded in Psalms.

For the purpose of association, start at the end of the verse and work towards the beginning. When you read the words 'O Lord, who shall stand?' Answer nobody, so that is **0**, and it is at the end of the number. 'Shouldest mark iniquities' is **3** words, so **3** comes before the **0**. 'LORD' There is only **1** LORD, so **1** comes before the **3** – **130**, so this verse is in Psalm **130**.

No. 11
Whither shall I go from thy spirit? or whither shall I flee from thy presence?
If I ascend up into heaven, thou [art] there: if I make my bed in hell, behold, thou [art there].
[If] I take the wings of the morning (**the wings of the morning**), *[and] dwell in the uttermost parts of the sea;*
Even there shall thy hand lead me, and thy right hand shall hold me.
If I say, Surely the darkness shall cover me; even the night shall be light about me.
Yea, the darkness hideth not from thee; but the night shineth as the day: the darkness and the light [are] both alike [to thee].
Psalm 139:7-12.

When you read these verses, think of the well-known song:

Oh for the wings, for **the wings of a dove**,
Far away, far away would I rove.

We **sing a song**, and we also **sing a Psalm**, so these verses are in the book of Psalms.

As I have already mentioned it is difficult to form an association for a large number, so I am taking a different approach.

(1) *Whither shall I go from thy spirit? or*
(2) *whither shall I flee from thy presence?*
(3) *If I ascend up into heaven, thou [art] there:*
(4) *if I make my bed in hell, behold, thou [art there].*
(5) *[If] I take the wings of the morning, [and] dwell in the uttermost parts of the sea; Even there shall thy hand lead me, and thy right hand shall hold me.*
(6) *If I say, Surely the darkness shall cover me; even the night shall be light about me.*
(7) *Yea, the darkness hideth not from thee; but the night shineth*

as the day:
 (8) **the darkness and the light [are] both alike [to thee].**

 (9) **Lord cleanse me from my sin.**

N.B. I am not adding to the Word of God when I write **Lord cleanse me from my sin**. I am forming an association. The Word of God is in *italics* to differentiate it, and there is a space so that you can see clearly the sentence I have formed.

Notice verse 6. For the purpose of association, think that sinners would like the darkness to cover them and hide them from God. As it is impossible to hide from God, then sinners need to be **cleansed from their sin.**

The above Scripture list is 8. For the purpose of association, think of the sinner saying **"Lord cleanse me from my sin."** Add that to the list of 8 and that makes **9**. As you read the verses think of them multiplying, then you can see that **1x3=3 3x3=9. 139**, so these verses are in Psalm **139**.

No. 12
For thou hast possessed my reins: thou hast covered me in my mother's womb.
I will praise thee; for I am fearfully [and] wonderfully made: marvellous [are] thy works; and [that] my soul knoweth right well.
My substance was not hid from thee, when I was made in secret, [and] curiously wrought in the lowest parts of the earth.
Thine eyes did see my substance, yet being unperfect; and in thy book all [my members] were written, [which] in continuance were fashioned, when [as yet there was] none of them. Psalm 139:13-16.

A Psalm is a poem, and a poem is **constructed** using words. These words are about the foetus in the womb. For the purpose of association, think that God has **constructed** the foetus, so these verses are in the book of Psalms.

 (1) *For thou hast possessed my reins:*
 (2) *thou hast covered me in my mother's womb.*
 (3) *I will praise thee; for I am fearfully [and] wonderfully made:*

(4) *marvellous [are] thy works; and [that] my soul knoweth right well.*

(5) *My substance was not hid from thee, when I was made in secret, [and] curiously wrought in the lowest parts of the earth.*

(6) *Thine eyes did see my substance, yet being unperfect; and in thy book all [my members] were written, [which] in continuance were fashioned, when [as yet there was] none of them.*

The Scripture list is **6** and I need **9**.

These verses are about the foetus in the womb. After the baby is born it has to eventually get on its feet, so when it stands its head is at the top.

For the purpose of association, think of the number **9** as standing up straight with its head at the top. There are only 150 Psalms, so **9** can't be the first number and it can't be the second number, so it must be the last number.

A child grows bigger day by day. When we multiply numbers they get bigger. **1x3=3 3x3=9. 139**, so these verses are in Psalm **139**.

No. 13
*Search **(Search)** me, O God **(O God)**, and know my heart: try **(try)** me, and know my thoughts:*
And see if [there be any] wicked way in me, and lead me in the way everlasting. Psalm 139:23-24.

When you read this verse of Scripture, think immediately of the well-known **hymn**:

Search me, O God, and know my heart today;
Try me, O Saviour, know my thoughts I pray,
See if there be some wicked way in me;
Cleanse me from every sin and set me free.

For the purpose of association, think that we **sing hymns**, but we also sing Psalms, so these verses are in the book of Psalms.

This is another large number that is difficult to form an association for, so I am taking a different approach.

The Psalmist writes **Search** me, O God, and know my heart: **try** me, and know my thoughts:

Search and **try** together have 9 letters. There are 150 Psalms so 9 can't be the first figure and it can't be the second figure, so it must be the last figure.

O – 1 letter. **God** – 3 letters. Psalm 139.

PROVERBS

No. 1

Trust in the LORD with all (ALL) thine heart; and lean not unto thine own understanding.

In all thy ways acknowledge him, and he shall direct thy paths.
Proverbs 3:5-6.

If we do what these two verses instruct us to do, then we will **prove** that the LORD will direct our paths. The word **'prove'** and the first five letters of **Prove**rbs are the same, so these verses are in the book of Proverbs.

ALL – **3** letters, so they are in chapter **3**.

No. 2

These six (6) [things] doth the LORD hate: yea, seven [are] an abomination unto him:

A proud look, a lying tongue, and hands that shed innocent blood,

An heart that deviseth wicked imaginations, feet that be swift in running to mischief,

A false witness [that] speaketh lies, and he that soweth (SOWETH) discord among brethren. Proverbs 6:16-19.

This time I am forming an association for the chapter first, instead of last, because it is more suitable to do so.

The start of verse sixteen reads like this: These six **(6)** [things] doth the LORD hate: so these verses are in chapter **6.**

The word **SOWETH** has **6** letters in it and it is a **verb**. The last syllable of Pro**verbs** is **verbs**, so they are in the book of Proverbs.

No. 3
*There is a way which seemeth right unto a man, but the end thereof [are] the ways of death (**THE WAYS OF DEATH**).* Proverbs 14:12.

For the purpose of association, think that if people continue in the way that seems right to them then they will **prove** eventually that this verse is true. The word **'prove'** and the first five letters of **Prove**rbs are the same, so this verse is in the book of Proverbs.

THE WAYS OF DEATH – 14 letters, so it is in chapter **14.**

No. 4
*Righteousness exalteth a nation (**Righteousness exalteth a nation**): but sin [is] a reproach (re**pro**ach) (**SIN IS A REPROACH**) to any people.* Proverbs 14:34.

Proverbs is part of the **wisdom** literature of the Old Testament.

For the purpose of association, think that a **righteous nation** would be founded on **wisdom**, so this verse is in Proverbs.

Notice also that letters three, four and five of re**pro**ach are the same as the first three letters of **Pro**verbs.

SIN IS A REPROACH – 14 letters, so this verse is in chapter **14.**

No. 5
*The name of the LORD [is] a strong tower (**strong tower**): the righteous runneth into it, and is safe.* Proverbs 18:10.

For the purpose of association, think that the righteous **prove** that the name of the LORD is a strong tower. The word **'prove'** is the same as the first five letters of **Prove**rbs, so this verse is in the book of Proverbs.

WE HAVE A STRONG TOWER – **18** letters, so it is in chapter **18**.

No. 6
A man [that hath] friends must shew himself friendly: and there is a friend [that] sticketh closer than a brother (CLOSER THAN A BROTHER). Proverbs 18:24.

Jesus is the friend that sticks closer than a brother, and if we know Him as our Friend we will **prove** this. The word '**prove**' and the first five letters of **Prove**rbs are the same, so this verse is in the book of Proverbs.

CLOSER THAN A BROTHER – **18** letters, so it is in chapter **18**.

No. 7
Train up a child (TRAIN UP A CHILD) in the way he should go: and when he is old, he will not depart (NOT DEPART) from it. Proverbs 22:6.

Train up a child in the way he should go, and **prove** in later years that he will not depart from it. The word '**prove**' and the first five letters of **Prove**rbs are the same, so this verse is in the book of Proverbs.

TRAIN UP A CHILD – **NOT DEPART** – **22** letters, so it is in chapter **22**.

Or – **A CHILD NEEDS TO BE TRAINED** – **22** letters.

No. 8
*Withhold not correction from the child (**Withhold not correction from the child**): for [if] thou beatest him with the rod, he shall not die. Thou shalt beat him with the rod (**beat him with the rod**), and shalt deliver his soul from hell (**deliver his soul from hell**).*
Proverbs 23:13-14.

Beat him with the rod and **prove** that he does not die.
The word '**prove**' and the first five letters of **Prove**rbs are the same, so these verses are in the book of Proverbs.

For the purpose of association, think that **if one is delivered from hell** then he/she will *dwell in the house of the LORD for ever,* as Psalm **23** records for us, so these verses are in chapter **23**.

Or – **CHILDREN MUST BE CORRECTED** – **23** letters.

No. 9
*Boast not thyself of to morrow (**Boast not thyself of to morrow**); for thou knowest not what a day may bring (**bring**) forth.* Proverbs 27:1.

Bring is a **verb** and the last syllable of Pro**verbs** is **verbs**, so this verse is in the book of Proverbs.

DON'T BOAST CONCERNING TOMORROW – **27** letters, so it is in chapter **27**.

No. 10
*He, that being often reproved (**reproved**) hardeneth [his] neck (**OFTEN REPROVED HARDENETH HIS NECK**), shall suddenly be destroyed, and that without remedy.* Proverbs 29:1.

Letters three, four, five, six and seven of re**prove**d are the same as the first five letters of **Prove**rbs, so this verse is in the book of Proverbs. Also think that **hardeneth** is a **verb** and the last syllable of Pro**verbs** is **verbs**.

OFTEN REPROVED HARDENETH HIS NECK – **29** letters, so this verse is in chapter **29**.

No. 11
*Who can find a virtuous woman (**virtuous woman**)? for her price [is] far above rubies.*
*The heart of her husband doth safely trust (**trust**) in her, so that he shall have no need of spoil.*

She will do him good and not evil all the days of her life.
Proverbs 31:10-12.

The first five letters of **Prove**rbs are the same as the word '**prove**'. For the purpose of association, think that if a man finds a virtuous woman he will **prove** that all that is recorded in these verses is true, so these verses are in the book of Proverbs.

A VIRTUOUS WOMAN CAN BE FULLY TRUSTED – 31 letters, so they are in chapter **31**.

ECCLESIASTES

No.1
*Then I looked on all the works that my hands had wrought, and on the labour that I had laboured to do: and, behold, all [was] vanity and vexation of spirit (**vanity and vexation of spirit**), and [there was] no profit (**NO PROFIT**) under the sun.* Ecclesiastes 2:11.

The word 'vanity' is mentioned in many books of the Bible, and the term 'vexation of spirit' is mentioned in Ecclesiastes and Isaiah. The term **'vanity and vexation of spirit'** is only found in Ecclesiastes; therefore this verse is in the book of Ecclesiastes.

NO PROFIT – 2 words, so it is in chapter **2**.

No.2
*For [there is] not a just man (**JUST MAN**) upon earth, that doeth good, and sinneth not.* Ecclesiastes 7: 20.

Ecclesiastes means the preacher. For the purpose of association, think that this verse applies to the preacher as well as the rest of us, so this verse is in the book of Ecclesiastes.

JUST MAN – 7 letters, so it is in chapter **7**.

No. 3
Remember now thy Creator in the days of thy youth (youth), while the evil days come not, nor the years draw nigh, when thou shalt say, I have no pleasure in them; Ecclesiastes 12:1.

Ecclesiastes means preacher, and you can think of a preacher warning young people to remember their Creator, so this verse is in the book of Ecclesiastes.

YOUTHFUL DAYS – 12 letters, so it is in chapter **12**.

No. 4
Let us hear the conclusion (conclusion) of the whole matter: Fear God, and keep his commandments: for this [is] the whole [duty] of man.
For God shall bring every work into judgment, with every secret thing, whether [it be] good (BE GOOD), or whether [it be] evil (BE EVIL). Ecclesiastes 12:13-14.

Ecclesiastes means preacher, and you can think of a preacher bringing his sermon to a **conclusion**, so these verses are in the book of Ecclesiastes.

BE GOOD – BE EVIL – 12 letters, so they are in chapter **12**.

SONG OF SOLOMON

No. 1
I [am] the rose (rose) of Sharon, [and] the lily (lily) of the valleys. Song of Solomon 2:1.

When you read this verse of Scripture think immediately of the well-known **chorus:**

He's the Lily of the Valley,
He's the Bright and Morning Star,
He's the fairest of ten thousand,
Everybody ought to know.

For the purpose of association, think of the **chorus** as a **song**, so this verse is in the book of **Song** of Solomon.

(1) rose of Sharon,
(2) lily of the valleys.

2 flowers, so it is in chapter **2**.

No. 2
*He brought me to the banqueting house (**BANQUETING HOUSE**), and his banner over me [was] love.* Song of Solomon 2:4.

For the purpose of association, think of **singing a song** in the banqueting house, so this verse is in the book of **Song** of Solomon.

BANQUETING HOUSE – **2** words, so it is in chapter **2**.

No. 3
My beloved [is] mine, and I [am] his: he feedeth among the lilies (**lilies**). Song of Solomon 2:16.

Lilies are mentioned, so you could think of the well-known **chorus**:

He's the Lily of the Valley,
He's the Bright and Morning Star,
He's the fairest of ten thousand,
Everybody ought to know.

For the purpose of association, think of the **chorus** as a **song**, so this verse is in the book of **Song** of Solomon.

There are **2** people mentioned in this verse, so it is in chapter **2**.

No. 4
His mouth (mouth) [is] most sweet: yea, he [is] altogether lovely (YEA, HE [IS] ALTOGETHER LOVELY). This [is] my beloved, and this [is] my friend, O daughters of Jerusalem. Song of Solomon 5:16.

For the purpose of association, think that we sing a **song** with our **mouth**, so this verse is in the book of **Song** of Solomon.

YEA HE [IS] ALTOGETHER LOVELY – **5** words, so it is in chapter **5**.

No. 5
I [am] my beloved's, and my beloved [is] mine: he feedeth among the lilies (lilies). Song of Solomon 6:3.

Lilies are mentioned so you could think of the well-known **chorus**:

He's the Lily of the Valley,
He's the Bright and Morning Star,
He's the fairest of ten thousand,
Everybody ought to know.

For the purpose of association, think of the **chorus** as a **song**, so this verse is in the book of **Song** of Solomon.

LILIES – **6** letters, so it is in chapter **6**.

ISAIAH

No. 1
Come now, and let us reason (reason) together, saith the LORD: though your sins be as scarlet, they shall be as white as snow; though they be red like crimson, they shall be as wool. Isaiah 1:18.

We use our brains to **reason**, and they are in our **heads**. The first syllable of **Is**aiah sounds like **eyes** (plural) and they are in our heads too, so this verse is in the book of Isaiah.

The second syllable of Is**ai**ah sounds like **eye** (singular). **1** is singular, so this verse is in chapter **1**.

No. 2
I suggest that you memorize the following verses.

*In the year that king Uzziah died I (**Isaiah**) saw also the Lord sitting upon a throne, high and lifted up, and his train filled the temple.*
*Above it stood the seraphims: each one had six (**6**) wings; with twain he covered his face, and with twain he covered his feet, and with twain he did fly.*
And one cried unto another, and said, Holy, holy, holy, [is] the LORD of hosts: the whole earth [is] full of his glory.
And the posts of the door moved at the voice of him that cried, and the house was filled with smoke.
*Then said I, Woe [is] me! for I am undone; because I [am] a man of unclean lips, and I dwell in the midst of a people of unclean lips: for mine eyes have seen the King (**MINE EYES HAVE SEEN THE KING**), the LORD of hosts.* Isaiah 6:1-5.

These verses are obviously in the book of **Isaiah**.

MINE EYES HAVE SEEN THE KING – 6 words, so they are in chapter **6**.

Or - each seraphim had **6** wings.

No. 3
*Therefore the Lord himself shall give you a sign (**a sign**); Behold, a virgin (**A VIRGIN**) shall conceive, and bear a son, and shall call his name Immanuel.* Isaiah 7:14.

We can see **a sign** with our **eyes**, and the first syllable of **Is**aiah sounds the same as **eyes**, so this verse is in the book of Isaiah.

A VIRGIN – **7** letters, so it is in chapter **7**.

No. 4
And when they shall say unto you, Seek unto them that have familiar spirits, and unto wizards that peep, and that mutter: should not a people seek unto their God? for the living to the dead?
*To the law and to the testimony: if they speak not according to this word **(THIS WORD)**, [it is] because [there is] no light **(light)** in them.* Isaiah 8:19-20.

In the book of Matthew we read the following words: *The light **(light)** of the body is the eye **(eye)**: if therefore thine eye be single, thy whole body shall be full of light.* Matthew 6:22.

The second syllable of Isaiah sounds like **eye**, so these verses are in the book of Isaiah.

THIS WORD – **8** letters, so they are in chapter **8**.

No. 5
*For unto us a child is born **(a child is born)**, unto us a son is given: and the government shall be upon his shoulder: and his name shall be called Wonderful, Counsellor, The mighty God, The everlasting Father, The Prince of Peace. **(WONDERFUL, COUNSELLOR, MIGHTY GOD, EVERLASTING FATHER, PRINCE OF PEACE)**.* Isaiah 9:6.

This verse is prophesying the birth of Jesus, and when Jesus **was born as a baby** people could **see** Him. For the purpose of association, think that we **see** with our **eyes**, and the first syllable of Isaiah sounds the same as **eyes**, so this verse is in the book of Isaiah.

WONDERFUL, COUNSELLOR, MIGHTY GOD, EVERLASTING FATHER, PRINCE OF PEACE - 9 words, so it is in chapter **9**.

No. 6
*In the year that Tartan came unto Ashdod **(TARTAN CAME UNTO ASHDOD)**, (when Sargon the king of Assyria sent him,) and*

fought against Ashdod, and took it;
  *At the same time spake the LORD by Isaiah (**Isaiah**) the son of Amoz, saying, Go and loose the sackcloth from off thy loins, and put off thy shoe from thy foot. And he did so, walking naked and barefoot.*
  Isaiah 20:1-2.

These verses are obviously in the book of **Isaiah**.

TARTAN CAME UNTO ASHDOD – 20 letters, so they are in chapter **20**.

No. 7
I suggest that you memorize the following two verses.

*T**h**ou wilt keep [him] in perfect peace (**perfect peace**), [whose] mind (**mind**) [is] stayed [on thee]: because he trusteth (**trusteth**) in thee.*
  Trust ye in the LORD for ever: for in the LORD JEHOVAH [is] everlasting strength: Isaiah 26:3-4.

Whose **mind** is stayed on thee. For the purpose of association, think that the **mind** and the **eyes** are both part of the head. The first syllable of **Is**aiah sounds like **eyes**, so these verses are in the book of Isaiah.

PERFECT PEACE FOR ALL WHO TRUST – 26 letters, so they are in chapter **26**.

No. 8
*Judgment also will I lay to the line, and righteousness to the plummet: and the hail shall sweep away the refuge of lies (**refuge of lies**), and the waters shall overflow the hiding place. Isaiah 28:17.*

For the purpose of association, think that **lies** rhymes with the first syllable of **Is**aiah, so this verse is in the book of Isaiah.

ENSURE YOU HAVEN'T A REFUGE OF LIES – 28 letters, so it is in chapter **28**.

No. 9
Behold **(Behold)**, *a king shall reign in righteousness* **(a king shall reign in righteousness)**, *and princes shall rule in judgment.*
And a man shall be as an hiding place from the wind, and a covert from the tempest; as rivers of water in a dry place, as the shadow of a great rock in a weary land. Isaiah 32:1-2.

The word 'behold' is used frequently in the Old Testament and the New Testament. These two verses are prophesying the coming of Jesus; therefore they are in the Old Testament.

'**Behold**' can mean to look, and we look with our physical **eyes**. The first syllable of **Is**aiah sounds like **eyes**, so these verses are in the book of Isaiah.

JESUS CHRIST REIGNS IN RIGHTEOUSNESS – **32** letters, so they are in chapter **32**.

No. 10
[It is] he that sitteth upon the circle of the earth **(IT IS HE THAT SITTETH UPON THE CIRCLE OF THE EARTH)**, *and the inhabitants thereof [are] as grasshoppers* **(grasshoppers)**; *that stretcheth out the heavens as a curtain, and spreadeth them out as a tent to dwell in:* Isaiah 40:22.

For the purpose of association, think of **sitting** and **looking** at **grasshoppers**. We **look** with our **eyes** and the first syllable of **Is**aiah sounds the same as **eyes**, so this verse is in the book of Isaiah.

IT IS HE THAT SITTETH UPON THE CIRCLE OF THE EARTH – **40** letters, so it is in chapter **40**.

No. 11
But they that wait upon the LORD shall renew [their] strength **(But they that wait upon the LORD shall renew [their] strength)**; *they shall mount up with wings as eagles; they shall run, and not be weary; [and] they shall walk, and not faint.* Isaiah 40:31.

For the purpose of association, imagine that when you are **wait-**

ing upon the LORD you have your **eyes** closed. The first syllable of Isaiah sounds like **eyes**, so this verse is in the book of Isaiah.

WAIT UPON THE LORD DAILY AND RENEW YOUR STRENGTH – **40** letters, so it is in chapter **40**.

No. 12
Seek (seek) ye the LORD while he may be found, call (call) ye upon him while he is near: Isaiah 55:6.

If you are **seek**ing physically you use your **eyes**. The first syllable of Isaiah sounds like **eyes**, so this verse is in the book of Isaiah.

This is a big number so the association is different.

It is God's **grace** that enables you to **seek** Him, and it is God's **grace** that enables you to **call** on Him. The number of grace is five, and we have **grace** to seek (**5**), **grace** to call (**5**): **55**, so the chapter is **55**.

No. 13
But your iniquities have separated (SEPARATED) between you and your God, and your sins have hid [his] face (hid his face) from you, that he will not hear. Isaiah 59:2.

If you cover your face with your hands then your **face is hid**, and that includes your **eyes**. For the purpose of association, think that **eyes** and the first syllable of **Isa**iah sound the same, so this verse is in Isaiah.

This is another big number, so the association is different.

For the purpose of association, think that we are in great danger if we are separated from God, and only the **grace** of God can remedy our precarious situation.

5 is the number of grace.

Our problem is that we are **separated** from God.

SEPARATED – 9 letters.

When **5** and **9** are written together the number is **59**, so this verse is in chapter **59**.

No. 14
*I (I) will greatly rejoice in the LORD (**I will greatly rejoice in the LORD**), my (my) soul shall be joyful in my (my) God (**my soul shall be joyful in my God**); for he (he) hath clothed me (me) with the garments of salvation (**he hath clothed me with the garments of salvation**), he (he) hath covered me (me) with the robe of righteousness (**he hath covered me with the robe of righteousness**), as a bridegroom decketh [himself] with ornaments (**as a bridegroom decketh himself with ornaments**), and as a bride adorneth [herself] with her (her) jewels (**as a bride adorneth herself with her jewels**).*
Isaiah 61:10.

For the purpose of association, think that the **bridegroom** and **bride** have **eyes** only for each other on their special day. The first syllable of **Is**aiah sounds like **eyes**, so this verse is in the book of Isaiah.

This is another big number, so I have to take a different approach regarding the association.

There are **6** phrases in this verse, so **6** is part of the association in this case.

(1) *I will greatly rejoice in the LORD.*
(2) *my soul shall be joyful in my God;*
(3) *for he hath clothed me with the garments of salvation,*
(4) *he hath covered me with the robe of righteousness,*
(5) *as a bridegroom decketh himself with ornaments,*
(6) *and as a bride adorneth herself with her jewels.*

Singular pronouns are used frequently in this verse, and singular means **1**. Put the two figures together and that is **61**, so this verse is in chapter **61**.

No. 15

But we are all as an unclean [thing], and all our righteousnesses [are] as filthy rags (WE ARE ALL AS AN UNCLEAN [THING], AND ALL OUR RIGHTEOUSNESSES [ARE] AS FILTHY RAGS); and we all do fade as a leaf; and our iniquities, like the wind, have taken us away. Isaiah 64:6.

For the purpose of association, think that we see by the **eyes** of faith that our own righteousnesses are not good enough. The first syllable of **Is**aiah sounds like **eyes**, so this verse is in the book of Isaiah.

WE ARE ALL AS AN UNCLEAN [THING] AND ALL OUR RIGHTEOUSNESSES [ARE] AS FILTHY RAGS – 63 letters, and we need another righteousness, (Christ's righteousness), add **1** to **63** and that is **64**, so this verse is in chapter **64**.

JEREMIAH

The following seven verses need to be read as a whole, in order to understand them.

No. 1

Then the word of the LORD came unto me, saying,

Before I (I) formed thee in the belly I (I) knew thee; and before thou camest forth out of the womb I (I) sanctified thee, [and] I (I) ordained thee a prophet unto the nations.

Then said I (I), Ah, Lord GOD! behold, I (I) cannot speak (speak) for I (I) [am] a child.

But the LORD said unto me, Say not, I (I) [am] a child: for thou shalt go to all that I (I) shall send thee, and whatsoever I (I) command thee thou shalt speak (speak).

Be not afraid of their faces (faces): for I (I) [am] with thee to deliver thee, saith the LORD.

Then the LORD put forth his hand, and touched my mouth. And the LORD said unto me, Behold, I (I) have put my words in thy mouth (mouth).

110

*See, I (I) have this day set thee over the nations and over the king-
doms, to root out, and to pull down, and to destroy, and to throw
down, to build, and to plant.* Jeremiah 1:4-10.

Jeremiah was known as the weeping prophet. We use our **eyes** to
weep, and our **eyes** are part of our **faces**. These verses have quite a
lot to say about the different parts of our **faces**.
Verse 6 **speak – mouth.**
Verse 7 **speak – mouth.**
Verse 8 **faces.**
Verse 9 **mouth – speak**, so these verses are in the book of Jer-
emiah.

I is found thirteen times in these verses, and **I** looks similar to **1**,
so they are in chapter **1**.

No. 2
*For my people have committed two (2) evils; they have forsaken me
the fountain of living waters, [and] hewed them out cisterns, broken
cisterns, that can hold no water (water).* Jeremiah 2:13.

Jeremiah was known as the **weeping** prophet. This verse is all
about **water**, so it is in the book of Jeremiah.

2 evils, so this verse is in chapter **2**.

No. 3
*A wonderful and horrible thing (A WONDERFUL AND HOR-
RIBLE THING) is committed in the land;*
*The prophets (prophets) prophesy falsely, and the priests (priests)
bear rule by their means; and my people love [to have it] so: and what
will ye do in the end thereof?* Jeremiah 5:30-31.

Jeremiah was a **prophet**, and he also grew up in the **priestly** tradition – see chapter 1:1. Verse 30 speaks of the **prophets** and the
priests, so these verses are in the book of Jeremiah.

A WONDERFUL AND HORRIBLE THING – 5 words, so they
are in chapter **5**.

No. 4
For they have healed the hurt of the daughter of my people slightly (**SLIGHTLY**), *saying, Peace, peace; when [there is] no peace* (**SAYING, PEACE, PEACE; WHEN [THERE IS] NO PEACE**). Jeremiah 8:11.

This verse mentions **peace, peace**. Jeremiah grew up in the **priestly** tradition, and the Lord Jesus Christ is our Great High **Priest** through whom we have **peace** with God, so this verse is in the book of Jeremiah.

SAYING, PEACE, PEACE; WHEN THERE IS NO PEACE - 8 words, so it is in chapter **8**.

Or – **SLIGHTLY - 8** letters.

No. 5
The harvest is past, the summer is ended (***THE HARVEST IS PAST, THE SUMMER IS ENDED***)*, and we are not saved* (**NOT SAVED**). Jeremiah 8:20.

Jeremiah was known as the **weeping** prophet. Anyone who is **not saved** would need to be **weeping**, so this verse is in the book of Jeremiah.

THE HARVEST IS PAST, THE SUMMER IS ENDED – 8 words, so it is in chapter **8**.

Or - **NOT SAVED – 8** letters.

No. 6
Oh that my head were waters, and mine eyes a fountain (**A FOUN- TAIN**) *of tears, that I might weep* (**weep**) *day and night for the slain of the daughter of my people!* Jeremiah 9:1.

Jeremiah is known as the **weep**ing prophet, so this verse is in the book of Jeremiah.

A FOUNTAIN – 9 letters, so it is in chapter **9**.

No. 7

The following two verses need to be read as a complete unit in order to understand them.

Thus saith the LORD, Let not the wise [man] glory in his wisdom **(LET NOT THE WISE [MAN] GLORY IN HIS WISDOM)**, *neither let the mighty [man] glory in his might, let not the rich [man] glory in his riches:*
But let him that glorieth glory in this, that he understandeth and knoweth **(knoweth)** *me, that I [am] the LORD which exercise lovingkindness, judgment, and righteousness, in the earth: for in these [things] I delight, saith the LORD.* Jeremiah 9:23-24.

Jeremiah was brought up in the **priestly** tradition, and the Lord Jesus Christ is our Great High **Priest**. We cannot **know** God apart from Jesus, so these verses are in the book of Jeremiah.

LET NOT THE WISE MAN GLORY IN HIS WISDOM – 9 words, so they are in chapter **9**.

No. 8

But the LORD [is] the true God, he [is] the living God, and an everlasting king: at his wrath **(AT HIS WRATH)** *the earth shall tremble, and the nations shall not be able to abide his indignation* **(THE NATIONS SHALL NOT BE ABLE TO ABIDE HIS INDIGNATION)**. Jeremiah 10:10.

Jeremiah was known as the **weeping** prophet. For the purpose of association, think of the people **weeping** when they are not able to abide the **indignation** of the living God, so this verse is in the book of Jeremiah.

THE NATIONS SHALL NOT BE ABLE TO ABIDE HIS INDIGNATION – 10 words, so it is in chapter **10**.

Or – **AT HIS WRATH – 10** letters.

No. 9
T*hus saith the LORD; Cursed [be] the man that trusteth in man* **(trusteth in man)**, *and maketh flesh his arm* **(MAKETH FLESH HIS ARM)**, *and whose heart departeth from the LORD* **(and whose heart departeth from the LORD)**. Jeremiah 17:5.

Jeremiah was known as the **weeping** prophet. For the purpose of association, think of him **weeping** when men's hearts departed from the LORD, so this verse is in the book of Jeremiah.

MAKETH FLESH HIS ARM – **17** letters, so it is in chapter **17**.

No. 10
I suggest that you memorize the following two verses.

The heart [is] deceitful above all [things], and desperately wicked **(DESPERATELY WICKED)**: *who can know it?*
I the LORD search the heart, [I] try the reins, even to give every man according to his ways, [and] according to the fruit of his doings.
Jeremiah 17:9-10.

Jeremiah was known as the **weeping** prophet.

For the purpose of association, think that people should be **weeping** because their hearts are deceitful and desperately wicked, so these verses are in the book of Jeremiah.

DESPERATELY WICKED – **17** letters, so they are in chapter **17**.

No. 11
Behold, the days come, saith the LORD, that I will raise unto David a righteous Branch, and a King shall reign and prosper, and shall execute judgment and justice in the earth.
In his days Judah shall be saved, and Israel shall dwell safely: and this [is] his name whereby he shall be called, THE LORD OUR RIGHTEOUSNESS **(THE LORD OUR RIGHTEOUSNESS)**.
Jeremiah 23:5-6.

Jeremiah was grieved by the sin of the people of his day, and was known as the weeping prophet. For the purpose of association, think that he would be pleased and encouraged to hear about the coming King who would be called '**THE LORD OUR RIGHTEOUSNESS,**' so these verses are in the book of Jeremiah.

THE LORD OUR RIGHTEOUSNESS – **23** letters, so they are in chapter **23**.

No. 12

*And it came to pass in the fourth year of Jehoiakim (**Jehoiakim**) the son of Josiah king of Judah, [that] this word came unto Jeremiah (**Jeremiah**) from the LORD, saying,*

Take thee a roll of a book, and write therein all the words that I have spoken unto thee against Israel, and against Judah, and against all the nations, from the day I spake unto thee, from the days of Josiah, even unto this day. Jeremiah 36:1-2.

So the king sent Jehudi to fetch the roll: and he took it out of Elishama the scribe's chamber. And Jehudi read it in the ears of the king, and in the ears of all the princes which stood beside the king.

Now the king sat in the winterhouse in the ninth month: and [there was a fire] on the hearth burning before him.

*And it came to pass, [that] when Jehudi had read three or four leaves, he cut it with the penknife, and cast [it] into the fire that [was] on the hearth (**And it came to pass, [that] when Jehudi had read three or four leaves, he cut it with the penknife, and cast [it] into the fire that [was] on the hearth**), until all the roll was consumed in the fire that [was] on the hearth.* Jeremiah 36:21-23.

We see from the first verse that these verses are in the book of **Jeremiah.**

THE ROLL IS CUT AND BURNED BY KING JEHOIAKIM– **36** letters, so they are in chapter **36**.

LAMENTATIONS

No. 1
I suggest that you memorize the following two verses together.

*[It is of] the LORD'S mercies (**THE LORD'S MERCIES**) that we are not consumed, because his compassions (**compassions**) fail not. [They are] new (**NEW**) every morning: great [is] thy faithfulness (**faithfulness**).* Lamentations 3:22-23.

Relations rhymes with **Lamentations**, and we would like our relations to have **compassion** on us and be **faithful** to us, so these verses are in the book of Lamentations.

THE LORD'S MERCIES – **3** words, so they are in chapter **3**.

Or – **NEW** – **3** letters.

No. 2
I suggest that you memorize the following three verses.

For the Lord will not cast off for ever:
*But though he cause grief, yet will he have compassion (**compassion**) according to the multitude of his mercies.*
*For he doth not afflict willingly nor grieve (**nor grieve**) the children of men (**CHIDREN OF MEN**).* Lamentations 3:31-33.

Relations rhymes with **Lamentations**, and we would like our relations to have **compassion** on us and not **grieve** us, so these verses are in the book of Lamentations.

CHILDREN OF MEN – **3** words, so they are in chapter **3**.

EZEKIEL

No. 1

*Moreover he said unto me, Son **(SON)** of man, eat that thou findest; eat this roll **(eat this roll)**, and go speak unto the house of Israel. So I opened my mouth, and he caused me to eat that roll.*

And he said unto me, Son of man, cause thy belly to eat, and fill thy bowels with this roll that I give thee. Then did I eat [it]; and it was in my mouth as honey for sweetness.

And he said unto me, Son of man, go, get thee unto the house of Israel, and speak with my words unto them.

For thou [art] not sent to a people of a strange speech and of an hard language, [but] to the house of Israel; Ezekiel 3:1-5.

Ezekiel means **strength** of God, or God strengthens. For the purpose of association, think of Ezekiel **eating the roll** and being **strengthened**, so these verses are in the book of Ezekiel.

The term 'Son of man' is used frequently throughout these verses.

SON – 3 letters, so they are in chapter **3**.

No. 2

And he said unto me (Ezekiel), *Son of man **(Son of man)**, can these bones live **(AND HE SAID UNTO ME, SON OF MAN, CAN THESE BONES LIVE)**? And I answered, O Lord GOD, thou knowest.* Ezekiel 37:3.

'Son of man' is mentioned in this verse. Remember I stated at the beginning of this book that Ezekiel is called the son of man 93 times, so this verse is in the book of Ezekiel. Daniel is called the son of man 1 time in the book of Daniel 8:17, but this verse is not included in this publication.

HE SAID UNTO ME, SON OF MAN, CAN THESE BONES LIVE?

37 letters - so this verse is in chapter **37**.

DANIEL

No. 1

And the king appointed them a daily provision of the king's meat, and of the wine which he drank: so nourishing them three years, that at the end thereof they might stand before the king.

*Now among these were of the children of Judah, Daniel (**Daniel**), Hananiah, Mishael, and Azariah:*

Unto whom the prince of the eunuchs gave names: for he gave unto Daniel [the name] of Belteshazzar; and to Hananiah, of Shadrach; and to Mishael, of Meshach; and to Azariah, of Abednego.

But Daniel purposed in his heart that he would not defile himself with the portion of the king's meat, nor with the wine which he drank: therefore he requested of the prince of the eunuchs that he might not defile himself. Daniel 1:5-8.

I presume that most people would be aware that these verses are in the book of Daniel. **Daniel** is mentioned throughout the chapter.

Verse **1** states that king Nebuchadnezzar besieged Jerusalem. It was his **1**st siege of Jerusalem. It was also his **1**st year as king, so these verses are in chapter **1**.

No. 2

*Then Arioch brought in Daniel (**Daniel**) before the king in haste, and said thus unto him, I have found a man of the captives of Judah, that will make known unto the king the interpretation.*

*The king (**Nebuchadnezzar**) answered and said to Daniel, whose name [was] Belteshazzar, Art thou able to make known unto me the* *dream which I have seen, and the interpretation thereof?*

Daniel answered in the presence of the king, and said, The secret which the king hath demanded cannot the wise [men], the astrologers, the magicians, the soothsayers, shew unto the king;

But there is a God in heaven that revealeth secrets, and maketh known to the king Nebuchadnezzar what shall be in the latter days.
Daniel 2:25-28.

I presume that most people would realize that these verses are in the book of Daniel. **Daniel** is mentioned throughout the chapter.

For the purpose of association, think of these verses as concerning **Daniel** and king **Nebuchadnezzar**: **2** people, so they are in chapter **2**.

No. 3

Nebuchadnezzar the king made an image of gold, whose height [was] threescore cubits, [and] the breadth thereof six cubits: he set (SET) it up in the plain of Dura, in the province of Babylon.
Daniel 3:1.

I presume that most people would know that this verse is in the book of Daniel.

He **SET** it up – **3** letters, so it is in chapter **3**.

No. 4

And this [is] the writing that was written, MENE, MENE, TEKEL, UPHARSIN.

This [is] the interpretation of the thing: MENE; God hath numbered thy kingdom (GOD HATH NUMBERED THY KINGDOM), and finished it.

TEKEL (TEKEL); Thou art weighed in the balances, and art found wanting.

PERES; Thy kingdom is divided, and given to the Medes and Persians. Daniel 5:25-28.

I presume that most people would be aware that these verses are in the book of Daniel.

GOD HATH NUMBERED THY KINGDOM – **5** words, so they are in chapter **5**.

Or – **TEKEL** – **5** letters.

No. 5
*Then the king commanded, and they brought Daniel (**DANIEL**), and cast [him] into the den of lions. [Now] the king spake and said unto Daniel, Thy God whom thou servest continually (**THY GOD WHOM THOU SERVEST CONTINUALLY**), he will deliver thee.*
Daniel 6:16.

I presume that most people would realize that this verse is in the book of Daniel.

THY GOD WHOM THOU SERVEST CONTINUALLY – **6** words, so it is in chapter **6**.

Or **DANIEL** – **6** letters.

No. 6
And many of them that sleep in the dust of the earth shall awake, some to everlasting life, and some to shame [and] everlasting contempt. Daniel 12:2.

Daniel means God is my **Judge**. These are resurrection words, and the **judgment** follows the resurrection, so this verse is in the book of Daniel.

RESURRECTION – **12** letters, so it is in chapter **12**.

HOSEA

No. 1

The word of the LORD that came unto Hosea **(Hosea)**, the son of Beeri, in the days of Uzziah, Jotham, Ahaz, [and] Hezekiah, kings of Judah, and in the days of Jeroboam the son of Joash, king of Israel.

The beginning **(The beginning)** of the word of the LORD by Hosea. And the LORD said to Hosea, Go, take unto thee a wife of whoredoms and children of whoredoms: for the land hath committed great whoredom, [departing] from the LORD.

So he went and took Gomer the daughter of Diblaim; which conceived, and bare him a son.

And the LORD said unto him, Call his name Jezreel; for yet a little [while], and I will avenge the blood of Jezreel upon the house of Jehu, and will cause to cease the kingdom of the house of Israel.

And it shall come to pass at that day, that I will break the bow of Israel in the valley of Jezreel.

And she conceived again, and bare a daughter. And [God] said unto him, Call her name Loruhamah: for I will no more have mercy upon the house of Israel; but I will utterly take them away.

But I will have mercy upon the house of Judah, and will save them by the LORD their God, and will not save them by bow, nor by sword, nor by battle, by horses, nor by horsemen.

Now when she had weaned Loruhamah, she conceived, and bare a son.

Then said [God], Call his name Loammi: for ye [are] not my people, and I will not be your [God].

Yet the number of the children of Israel shall be as the sand of the sea, which cannot be measured nor numbered; and it shall come to pass, [that] in the place where it was said unto them, Ye [are] not my people, [there] it shall be said unto them, [Ye are] the sons of the living God.

Then shall the children of Judah and the children of Israel be gathered together, and appoint themselves one head, and they shall come up out *of the land: for great [shall be] the day of Jezreel.* Hosea chapter 1.

This chapter is obviously in the book of Hosea.

Verse two states: **The beginning** *of the word of the LORD by Hosea.* Chapter **1** would be the beginning, so this is chapter **1**.

No. 2
Come, and let us return unto the LORD: for he hath torn, and he will heal us; he hath smitten, and he will bind us up.
After two days will he revive us: in the third day he will raise us up, and we shall live in his sight.
*Then shall we know, [if] we follow on to know the LORD: his going forth is prepared as the morning; and he shall come unto us as the rain **(rain)**, as the latter [and] former rain **(AS THE LATTER AND FORMER RAIN)** unto the earth.* Hosea 6:1-3.

For the purpose of association, think that **rain** is water, and the last three letters of Ho**sea** is **sea**, which is also water, so these verses are in the book of Hosea.

AS THE LATTER AND FORMER RAIN – 6 words, so they are in chapter **6**.

JOEL

No. 1
*And I will restore to you the years that the locust hath eaten (**I will restore to you the years that the locust hath eaten**), the cankerworm, and the caterpiller, and the palmerworm, my great army **(GREAT ARMY)** which I sent among you.* Joel 2:25.

The first two letters of **Jo**el are the same as the first two letters of **Jo**seph.

*But as for you, ye thought evil **(evil)** against me **(Joseph)**; [but]*

God meant it unto good (good), to bring to pass, as [it is] this day, to save much people alive. Genesis 50:20.

For the purpose of association, think that God brought **good** out of **evil** for **Jo**seph. He also brought good to the people mentioned in the above verse from the book of **Jo**el by **restoring the years that the locust had eaten**, so this verse is in the book of Joel.

GREAT ARMY – **2** words, so it is in chapter **2**.

AMOS

No. 1
Can (CAN) two walk together, except they be agreed (THEY BE AGREED)? Amos 3:3.

For the purpose of association, think I **am** not walking with you because I don't agree with you.

Am and the first two letters of **Am**os are the same, so this verse is in the book of Amos.

Emphasize the word 'CAN' when saying the sentence.

CAN – **3** letters, so this verse is in chapter **3**.

No. 2
Therefore thus will I do unto thee, O Israel (O Israel): [and] because I will do this unto thee, prepare to meet thy God (prepare to MEET thy God), O Israel. Amos 4:12.

Individuals need to **prepare to meet God**. For the purpose of association, think that this preparation is **first** in importance.

A is the **first** letter of the alphabet.

Amos and Acts are the only books in Scripture beginning with **A**.

The term **'O Israel'** is not found in the book of Acts, so this verse is in the book of Amos.

MEET – **4** letters, so it is in chapter **4**.

No. 3

*Then answered Amos (**Amos**), and said to Amaziah, I [was] no prophet, neither [was] I a prophet's son; but I [was] an herdman (**HERDMAN**), and a gatherer of sycomore fruit:* Amos 7:14.

This verse is obviously in the book of **Amos**.

HERDMAN – **7** letters, so it is in chapter **7**.

OBADIAH

No. 1

*The vision of Obadiah (**Obadiah**). Thus saith the Lord GOD concerning Edom; We have heard a rumour from the LORD, and an ambassador is sent among the heathen, Arise ye, and let us rise up against her in battle.*

Behold, I have made thee small among the heathen: thou art greatly despised.

The pride of thine heart hath deceived thee, thou that dwellest in the clefts of the rock, whose habitation [is] high; that saith in his heart, Who shall bring me down to the ground?

Though thou exalt [thyself] as the eagle, and though thou set thy nest among the stars, thence will I bring thee down, saith the LORD.
Obadiah 1:1-4.

These verses are obviously in the book of **Obadiah**, which has only one chapter.

JONAH

No. 1
*Now the word of the LORD came unto Jonah **(Jonah)** the son of Amittai, saying,*

*Arise, go to Nineveh, that great city **(great city)**, and cry against it; for their wickedness is come up before me.*

But Jonah rose up to flee unto Tarshish from the presence of the LORD, and went down to Joppa; and he found a ship going to Tarshish: so he paid the fare thereof, and went down into it, to go with them unto Tarshish from the presence of the LORD. Jonah 1:1-3.

These verses are obviously in the book of **Jonah**.

For the purpose of association, think that Jonah refused to go to the **1 great city** that God wanted him to go to, so these verses are in chapter **1**.

No. 2
*Now the LORD had prepared a great fish **(great fish)** to swallow up Jonah. And Jonah **(Jonah)** was in the belly of the fish three days and three nights.* Jonah 1:17.

This verse is obviously in the book of **Jonah**.

For the purpose of association, think that it was **1 great fish** that swallowed Jonah, so this verse is in chapter **1**.

No. 3
*So Jonah **(Jonah)** went out of the city, and sat on the east side of the city, and there made him a booth, and sat under it in the shadow, till he might see what would become of the city.*

And the LORD God prepared a gourd, and made [it] to come up

over Jonah, that it might be a shadow over his head, to deliver him from his grief. So Jonah was exceeding glad of the gourd.
But God prepared a worm **(WORM)** when the morning rose the next day, and it smote the gourd that it withered. Jonah 4:5-7.

These verses are obviously in the book of **Jonah**.

WORM – **4** letters, so they are in chapter **4**.

MICAH

No. 1
*And he shall judge among many people, and rebuke strong nations afar off **(afar off)**; and they shall beat **(BEAT)** their swords into plowshares, and their spears into pruninghooks: nation shall not lift up a sword against nation, neither shall they learn war any more.* Micah 4:3.

The first syllable of **Mic**ah sounds the same as the first syllable of **mic**rophone. For the purpose of association, think of needing a microphone if someone was **afar off**, so this verse is in the book of Micah.

BEAT – **4** letters, so it is in chapter **4**.

No. 2
*But thou, Bethlehem Ephratah **(Ephratah)**, [though] thou be little among the thousands of Judah **(Judah)**, [yet] out of thee shall he come forth unto me [that is] to be ruler **(RULER)** in Israel; whose goings forth [have been] from of old, from everlasting.* Mi**cah** 5:2.

The last syllable of Ephra**tah**, Ju**dah** and Mi**cah** all rhyme, so this verse is in the book of Micah.

RULER – **5** letters, so it is in chapter **5**.

NAHUM

No. 1
The burden of Nineveh (Nineveh) (capital of Assyria). The book of the vision of Nahum the Elkoshite. Nahum 1:1.

Nahum wrote about the end of the Assyrian Empire of which Nineveh was the capital city.

The last syllable of Nine**veh** rhymes with the first syllable of **Na**hum and both words start with **N**, so this verse is in the book of Nahum.

For the purpose of association, think of Nineveh as being number **1** city because it is the capital of Assyria, so this verse is in chapter **1**.

No. 2
Behold upon the mountains the feet of him; **(him is singular)** *that bringeth good tidings, that publisheth peace* **(that bringeth good tidings, that publisheth peace)!** *O Judah, keep thy solemn feasts, perform thy vows: for the wicked shall no more pass through thee; he is utterly cut off.* Nahum 1:15.

Nahum means **comforter** or **comforting**. The last syllable of Na**hum** is **hum**, so to help you remember that it is Nahum (and not some of the other minor prophets) that means comforting, think that a mother may **hum** to her child in order to **comfort** him/her.

For the purpose of association, think that someone who **brings good tidings and publishes peace** would be a **comforting** person, so this verse is in the book of Nahum.

Him is singular and **singular** is **1**, so it is in chapter **1**.

HABAKKUK

No. 1
*A prayer of Habakkuk **(Habakkuk)** the prophet upon Shigionoth.
O LORD, I have heard thy speech, [and] was afraid: O LORD, revive
thy work **(REVIVE THY WORK)** in the midst of the years, in the
midst of the years make known; in wrath remember mercy.*
   Habakkuk 3:1-2.

These verses are obviously in the book of **Habakkuk**.

REVIVE THY WORK – **3** words, so they are in chapter **3**.

No. 2
*Although the fig tree shall not blossom, neither [shall] fruit [be] in
the vines; the labour of the olive shall fail, and the fields shall yield
no meat; the flock shall be cut off from the fold, and [there shall be]
no herd in the stalls:*
   *Yet I will rejoice **(I WILL REJOICE)** in the LORD, I will joy in the
God of my salvation.* Habakkuk 3:17-18.

Habakkuk means to **embrace**.

For the purpose of association, think that when things go wrong
we are still held in God's **embrace** and can **rejoice**, so these verses
are in the book of Habakkuk.

I WILL REJOICE – **3** words, so they are in chapter **3**.

ZEPHANIAH

No. 1
The LORD thy God in the midst of thee [is] mighty; he will save **(HE WILL SAVE)***, he will rejoice over thee with joy; he will rest in his love, he will joy over thee with singing* **(singing)***.* Zephaniah 3:17.

The first four letters of **Zeph**aniah are the same as the first four letters of **Zeph**yr. For the purpose of association, think of **singing** being carried by the **gentle breeze**, so this verse is in the book of Zephaniah.

HE WILL SAVE – 3 words, so it is in chapter **3**.

HAGGAI

No. 1
In the second year of Darius the king, in the sixth month, in the first **(1st)** *day of the month, came the word of the LORD by Haggai* **(Haggai)** *the prophet unto Zerubbabel the son of Shealtiel, governor of Judah, and to Joshua the son of Josedech, the high priest, saying,*
Thus speaketh the LORD of hosts, saying, This people say, The time is not come, the time that the LORD'S house should be built.
Then came the word of the LORD by Haggai the prophet, saying,
[Is it] time for you, O ye, to dwell in your cieled houses, and this house [lie] waste?
Now therefore thus saith the LORD of hosts; Consider your ways.
Ye have sown much, and bring in little; ye eat, but ye have not

enough; ye drink, but ye are not filled with drink; ye clothe you, but
there is none warm; and he that earneth wages earneth wages [to
put it] into a bag with holes.
  Thus saith the LORD of hosts; Consider your ways.
  Go up to the mountain, and bring wood, and build the house; and
I will take pleasure in it, and I will be glorified, saith the LORD.
  Ye looked for much, and, lo, [it came] to little; and when ye brought
[it] home, I did blow upon it. Why? saith the LORD of hosts. Because
of mine house that [is] waste, and ye run every man unto his own
house. Haggai 1:1-9.*

These verses are obviously in the book of **Haggai**.

1st day of the month, so they are in chapter **1**.

ZECHARIAH

No. 1
*In that day there shall be a fountain opened (**In that day there shall
be a fountain opened**) to the house of David and to the inhabitants
of Jerusalem for sin and for uncleanness. Zechariah 13:1.*

Zechariah is the penultimate book of the Old Testament, i.e. **just
before the end**. For the purpose of association, think that God
opened a fountain before the end of time. When we consider
what we read in 2 Peter 3:8. *But, beloved, be not ignorant of this
one thing, that one day [is] with the Lord as a thousand years, and
a thousand years as one day.* It is approximately two thousand years
since Christ was born, and that is as two days with God. Even if
the world continues for another thousand years that would be as
three days with God. In view of this, one can think of the fountain
as being opened **just before the end of time**, so this verse is in the
book of Zechariah. Remember I am not teaching anything here,
just forming an association.

THERE IS A FOUNTAIN FILLED WITH BLOOD DRAWN FROM IMMANUEL'S VEINS – FOR SINNERS – 13 words, so it is in chapter **13**.

MALACHI

No. 1
Will a man rob (ROB) God? Yet ye have robbed me. But ye say, Wherein have we robbed (robbed) thee? In tithes and offerings.
Ye [are] cursed with a curse: for ye have robbed me, [even] this whole nation. Malachi 3:8-9.

For the purpose of association, think that Christians would imagine that **robbing** God would be the **last** thing they would do. Malachi is the **last** book of the Old Testament, so these verses are in the book of Malachi.

ROB – 3 letters, so they are in chapter **3**.

No. 2
Bring ye all the tithes (ALL THE TITHES) into the storehouse, that there may be meat in mine house, and prove me now herewith, saith the LORD of hosts, if I will not open you the windows of heaven, and pour you out a blessing (blessing), that [there shall] not [be room] enough [to receive it]. Malachi 3:10.

Malachi is the **last** book of the Old Testament. For the purpose of association, think that when the **last tithe** is brought in God will pour out a **blessing**, so this verse is in the book of Malachi. Remember I am not teaching anything here, just forming an association.

ALL THE TITHES – 3 words, so it is in chapter **3**.

MATTHEW

No. 1
*And she shall bring forth a **son**, and thou shalt call his name JESUS: for he shall save his people from their sins.* Matthew 1:21.

Matthew means **gift** of God. When you read this verse think immediately of what is recorded in Isaiah 9:6: *For unto us a child is born, unto us a son is **given**:* Jesus was **given** to us, and something that is given is a **gift**.

Jesus is God's **gift** to mankind, so this verse is in the gospel of Matthew.

This is the **1**st time that Jesus is mentioned in the New Testament, so this verse is in chapter **1**.

No. 2
Then cometh Jesus from Galilee to Jordan unto John, to be baptized of him.
But John forbad him, saying, I have need to be baptized of thee, and comest thou to me?
*And Jesus answering said unto him, Suffer [it to be so] now: for thus it becometh us to fulfil all righteousness **(to fulfil all righteousness)**. Then he suffered him.*
And Jesus, when he was baptized, went up straightway out of the water: and, lo, the heavens were opened unto him, and he saw the Spirit of God descending like a dove, and lighting upon him:
*And lo a voice from heaven, saying, This is my beloved Son **(SON)**, in whom I am well pleased.* Matthew 3:13-17.

The following words are what Matthew Henry the seventeenth century Bible commentator had to say concerning the words '**to fulfil all righteousness.**' Thus Christ **filled up the righteousness** of the **ceremonial law**, which consisted in divers washings etc;

Levi is another name for Matthew: *And after these things he went forth, and saw a publican, named Levi (**Levi**), sitting at the receipt of custom: and he said unto him, Follow me.* Luke 5:27.

For the purpose of association, think that the **Levites** were employed in various duties connected with the **ceremonial law**, so these verses are in the gospel of Matthew.

SON – 3 letters, so they are in chapter **3**.

The parallel narratives are in the gospel of **Mark** chapter **1** and the gospel of **Luke** chapter **3**. The words '**to fulfil all righteousness**' are not included in Mark and Luke's narratives.

And it came to pass in those days, that Jesus came from Nazareth of Galilee, and was baptized of John in Jordan.
And straightway coming up out of the water, he saw the heavens opened, and the Spirit like a dove descending upon him:
*And there came a voice from heaven, [saying], Thou art my beloved Son (**SON**), in whom I am well pleased.*
And immediately the Spirit driveth him into the wilderness.
Mark 1:9-12.

Mark that in **Mark's** narrative of the baptism of Jesus the temptation of Jesus in the wilderness follows immediately in the same chapter, i.e. chapter 1. However, in the gospels of Matthew and Luke, the baptism is recorded at the end of chapters 3 and the temptation at the beginning of chapters 4.

For the purpose of association, think that **1** chapter contains both narratives in the gospel of Mark, so the narrative of the baptism of Jesus is in the gospel of Mark chapter **1**.

Now when all the people were baptized, it came to pass, that Jesus also being baptized, and praying, the heaven was opened,
And the Holy Ghost descended in a bodily shape like a dove upon

*him, and a voice came from heaven, which said, Thou art my beloved Son **(SON)**; in thee I am well pleased.* Luke 3:21-22.

SON – **3** letters, so these verses are in chapter **3**.

No. 3
And seeing the multitudes, he went up into a mountain: and when he was set, his disciples came unto him:
And he opened his mouth, and taught them, saying,
Blessed [are] the poor in spirit: for theirs is the kingdom of heaven.
Matthew 5:1-3.

For the purpose of association, think of the people sitting on mats as they listened to Jesus.

The first three letters of **Mat**thew are the same as the first three letters of **mat**s, so these verses are in the gospel of Matthew.

These verses are the start of the beatitudes, which are part of **THE SERMON ON THE MOUNT** – **5** words, so they are in chapter **5**.

No. 4
*Judge not, that ye be not judged **(JUDGE NOT, THAT YE BE NOT JUDGED)**.*
For with what judgment ye judge, ye shall be judged: and with what measure ye mete, it shall be measured to you again.
And why beholdest thou the mote that is in thy brother's eye, but considerest not the beam that is in thine own eye?
Or how wilt thou say to thy brother, Let me pull out the mote out of thine eye; and, behold, a beam [is] in thine own eye?
Thou hypocrite, first cast out the beam out of thine own eye; and then shalt thou see clearly to cast out the mote out of thy brother's eye. Matthew 7:1-5.

*Judge not, and ye shall not be judged **(AND YE SHALL NOT BE JUDGED)**: condemn not, and ye shall not be condemned: forgive, and ye shall be forgiven:*
Give, and it shall be given unto you; good measure, pressed down, and shaken together, and running over, shall men give into your

bosom. For with the same measure that ye mete withal it shall be measured to you again.

And he spake a parable unto them, Can the blind lead the blind? shall they not both fall into the ditch?

The disciple is not above his master: but every one that is perfect shall be as his master.

And why beholdest thou the mote that is in thy brother's eye, but perceivest not the beam that is in thine own eye?

Either how canst thou say to thy brother, Brother, let me pull out the mote that is in thine eye, when thou thyself beholdest not the beam that is in thine own eye? Thou hypocrite, cast out first the beam out of thine own eye, and then shalt thou see clearly to pull out the mote (mote) that is in thy brother's eye. Luke 6:37-42.

This time I am using one association for both chapters.

As you can see from the two portions of Scripture above, one is in the gospel of Matthew and the other in the gospel of Luke.

The first three letters of **Mat**thew are the same as **mat**.

For the purpose of association, think of your brother sitting on a **mat** (**Mat**thew) while you look (**Luke**) in his eye and try to remove the **mote** from it. These verses are in the gospels of Matthew and Luke.

Matthew says **JUDGE NOT, THAT YE BE NOT JUDGED** - 7 words, so these verses are in Matthew chapter **7**.

Luke says Judge not **AND YE SHALL NOT BE JUDGED** - 6 words, so these verses are in Luke chapter **6**.

To enable you to remember which book is chapter **7** and which is chapter **6**, just think that Matthew is a bigger word than Luke so it has the bigger number for its chapter i.e. Matthew **7** and Luke **6**.

No. 5

And as Jesus passed forth from thence, he saw a man, named Matthew (Matthew), sitting at the receipt of custom: and he saith unto him, Follow me. And he arose, and followed him.

And it came to pass, as Jesus sat at meat in the house, behold, many publicans and sinners came and sat down with him and his disciples.
*And when the Pharisees saw [it], they said unto his disciples, Why eateth **(WHY EATETH)** your Master with publicans and sinners?*
Matthew 9:9-11.

Matthew: so these verses are in the gospel of Matthew.

WHY EATETH – **9** letters, so they are in chapter **9**.

The parallel narratives are in the gospel of **Mark** chapter **2** and the gospel of **Luke** chapter **5**.

And he went forth again by the sea side; and all the multitude resorted unto him, and he taught them.
*And as he passed by, he saw Levi **(Levi)** the [son] of Alphaeus **(Alphaeus)** sitting at the receipt of custom, and said unto him, Follow me. And he arose and followed him.*
And it came to pass, that, as Jesus sat at meat in his house, many publicans and sinners sat also together with Jesus and his disciples: for there were many, and they followed him.
And when the scribes and Pharisees saw him eat with publicans and sinners, they said unto his disciples, How is it that he eateth and drinketh with publicans and sinners?
When Jesus heard [it], he saith unto them, They that are whole have no need of the physician, but they that are sick: I came not to call the righteous, but sinners to repentance. Mark 2:13-17.

Mark that **Mark's** narrative mentions **2** names –
(1) Alphaeus – Father's name
(2) Levi – Son's name, so these verses are in chapter **2**.

*And after these things he went forth, and saw a publican, named Levi **(Levi)**, sitting at the receipt of custom: and he said unto him, Follow me.*
And he left all, rose up, and followed him.
And Levi made him a great feast in his own house: and there was a great company of publicans and of others that sat down with them.
*But their scribes and Pharisees murmured against his disciples, saying, Why do ye eat and drink **(DRINK)** with publicans and sinners?*

And Jesus answering said unto them, They that are whole need not a physician; but they that are sick.
I came not to call the righteous, but sinners to repentance.
Luke 5:27-32.

Matthew is called **Levi** in Luke's narrative. Levi and Luke both start with **L** so these verses are in the gospel of Luke.

DRINK – **5** letters, so they are in chapter **5**.

Notice that drink is not mentioned in the gospel of Matthew and in the gospel of Mark it is drinketh.

To enable you to remember which book is chapter **9** and which is chapter **5**, just think that Matthew is a bigger word than Luke, so it has the bigger number for its chapter, i.e. Matthew **9** and Luke **5**.

No. 6
I suggest that you memorize the following three verses.

Come unto me, all [ye] that labour and are heavy laden, and I will give you rest.
Take my yoke upon you, and learn of me; for I am meek and lowly in heart: and ye shall find rest unto your souls.
For my yoke [is] easy, and my burden is light. Matthew 11:28-30.

Matthew was a **tax** collector before Jesus called him to follow Him. Verse 28 speaks of being heavy laden. If one is heavy laden it is very **tax**ing, so these verses are in the gospel of Matthew.

The first letter of **l**abour and **l**aden is **l**, put the two letters together **ll** and it looks like **11**, so they are in chapter **11**.

No. 7
And he spake many things unto them in parables, saying, Behold, a sower (SOWER) went forth to sow;
And when he sowed, some [seeds] (SEEDS) fell by the way side, and the fowls came and devoured them up:
Some fell upon stony places, where they had not much earth: and

forthwith they sprung up, because they had no deepness of earth:
*And when the sun (**SUN**) was up, they were scorched; and because*
they had no root, they withered away. Matthew 13:3-6.

For the purpose of association, think of the sower spreading down
a **mat** to sit on when he was having his tea break.

The first three letters of **Mat**thew are the same as **mat**, so these
verses are in the gospel of Matthew.

SOWER SEEDS SUN – **13** letters, so they are in chapter **13**.

The parallel narratives are in the gospel of **Mark** chapter **4** and
the gospel of **Luke** chapter **8**.

And he said unto them, Know ye not this parable? and how then
*will ye know all parables (**Know ye not this parable? and how then***
***will ye know all parables**)?*
The sower soweth the word.
*And these are they by the way side, where the word is sown (**SOWN**);*
but when they have heard, Satan cometh immediately, and taketh
away the word that was sown in their hearts. Mark 4:13-15.

Mark that **Mark** includes a question in his narrative: ***Know ye not***
this parable? and how then will ye know all parables?

These verses are in the gospel of **Mark**.

Mark that the word **SOWN** is only found in **Mark's** narrative.

SOWN – **4** letters, so these verses are in chapter **4**.

But that on the good ground are they, which in an honest and good
*heart, having heard the word, keep [it], and bring forth fruit (**fruit**)*
*with patience (**PATIENCE**).* Luke 8:15.

For the purpose of association, think of the sower going out to
look (Luke) for **fruit**, so this verse is in the gospel of Luke.

PATIENCE – **8** letters, so it is in chapter **8**.

To enable you to remember which book is chapter **13** and which is chapter **8**, just think that Matthew is a bigger word than Luke so it has the bigger number for its chapter i.e. Matthew **13** and Luke **8**.

No. 8

Is not this the carpenter's son (CARPENTER'S SON)? is not his mother called Mary? and his brethren, James (James), and Joses (Joses), and Simon, and Judas (Judas)?

And his sisters, are they not all with us? Whence then hath this [man] all these things? Matthew 13:55-56.

James, Joses and Judas are all mentioned in verse fifty-five, and all these names start with **J**. Matthew and Mark both start with **M**, so these verses are in the gospels of Matthew and Mark.

CARPENTER'S SON – **13** letters, so they are in chapter **13**.

The parallel narrative is in the gospel of Mark chapter 6.

And when the sabbath day was come, he began to teach in the synagogue: and many hearing [him] were astonished, saying,

From whence hath this [man] these things? and what wisdom [is] this which is given unto him, that even such mighty works are wrought by his hands?

Is not this the carpenter, the son (THE SON) of Mary, the brother of James, and Joses, and of Juda, and Simon? and are not his sisters here with us? And they were offended at him. Mark 6:2-3.

THE SON - **6** letters, so these verses are in chapter **6**.

To enable you to remember which book is chapter **6** and which is chapter **13**, just think that Matthew is a bigger word than Mark so it has the bigger number for its chapter i.e. Matthew chapter **13** and Mark chapter **6**.

No. 9

But when Herod's birthday (HEROD'S BIRTHDAY) was kept, the daughter of Herodias (Herodias) danced before them, and pleased Herod.

Whereupon he promised with an oath to give her whatsoever she would ask.

And she, being before instructed of her mother, said, Give me here John Baptist's head in a charger. Matthew 14:6-8.

Herod and **Herod**ias are mentioned in these verses. Both names start with **Herod**. Both **Ma**tthew and **Ma**rk start with **Ma**, so these verses are in the gospels of Matthew and Mark.

HEROD'S BIRTHDAY – **14** letters, so they are in chapter **14**.

The parallel narrative is in the gospel of **Mark** chapter **6**.

*And when a convenient day was come, that Herod on his birthday made a supper **(SUPPER)** to his lords, high captains, and chief [estates] of Galilee;* Mark 6:21.

SUPPER – **6** letters, so this verse is in chapter **6**.

The word **supper** is not mentioned in Matthew's narrative.

To enable you to remember which book is chapter **14** and which is chapter **6**, just think that Matthew is a bigger word than Mark so it has the bigger number for its chapter i.e. Matthew **14** and Mark **6**.

No. 10
But he (Jesus) *turned, and said unto Peter **(Peter)**, Get thee behind me, Satan: thou art an offence unto me: for thou savourest not the things that be of God **(the things that be of God)**, but those that be of men.* Matthew 16:23.

We know that this verse is in one of the four gospels because it records the words of Jesus. For the purpose of association, think of **the things that be of God** as being of **1st** importance.

Matthew is the **1st** gospel, so this verse is in the gospel of Matthew.

PETER GETS IT WRONG – **16** letters, so it is in chapter **16**.

The parallel narrative is in the gospel of **Mark** chapter **8**.

And he began to teach them, that the Son of man must suffer many things, and be rejected (REJECTED) of the elders, and [of] the chief priests, and scribes, and be killed, and after three days rise again.
And he spake that saying openly. And Peter took him, and began to rebuke him.
But when he had turned about and looked on his disciples, he rebuked Peter, saying, Get thee behind me, Satan: for thou savourest not the things that be of God, but the things that be of men.
Mark 8:31-33.

Mark that the word **rejected** is not in the Matthew narrative, so these verses are in the gospel of **Mark**.

REJECTED – **8** letters, so they are in chapter **8**.

To enable you to remember which book is chapter **16** and which is chapter **8**, just think that Matthew is a bigger word than Mark, so it has the bigger number for its chapter i.e. Matthew **16** and Mark **8**.

No. 11
For what is a man profited (PROFITED), if he shall gain the whole world, and lose his own soul? or what shall a man give in exchange for his soul? Matthew 16:26.

Think of the soul as being number **1** in importance because it is eternal, and Matthew is number **1** of the gospels, so this verse is in the gospel of Matthew.

The most precious possession a human being has is his/her soul.

PRECIOUS – **8** letters and **PROFITED** – **8** letters. **8+8=16**, so this verse is in chapter **16**.

The parallel narrative is in the gospel of **Mark** chapter **8**.

For what shall it profit a man, if he shall gain the whole world, and lose his own soul?
Or what shall a man give in exchange (EXCHANGE) for his soul?
Mark 8:36-37.

For the purpose of association, think that if ever people needed to **mark** something, it is the fact that if a man should gain the whole world and lose his soul, he is a loser and lost for all eternity. These verses are in the gospel of **Mark**.

EXCHANGE – 8 letters, so they are in chapter **8**.

Or: The most precious possession that a human being has is his/her soul. **PRECIOUS** – 8 letters.

To enable you to remember which book is chapter **16** and which book is chapter **8** just think that Matthew is a bigger word than Mark, so it has the bigger number for its chapter i.e. Matthew **16** and Mark **8**.

No. 12

*And after six days Jesus taketh Peter, James, and John (**PETER, JAMES, AND JOHN**) his brother, and bringeth them up into an high mountain apart,*

*And was transfigured before them: and his face did shine as the sun (**and his face did shine as the sun**), and his raiment was white as the light.*

*And, behold, there appeared unto them Moses (**Moses**) and Elias talking with him. Matthew 17:1-3.*

In this account of the transfiguration of Jesus we read ***his face did shine as the sun***. In the parallel chapter in Mark His face is not mentioned.

In Exodus 34:29. We read concerning **Moses** that the **skin of his face shone**.

*And it came to pass, when Moses came down from mount Sinai with the two tables of testimony in Moses' hand, when he came down from the mount, that Moses wist not that the skin of his face shone (**the skin of his face shone**) while he talked with him. Exodus 34:29.*

The narrativies about Moses are in the Old Testament. For the purpose of association, think that another name for Matthew is **Levi**, and the **Levites** are mentioned frequently in the Old Testament, so these verses are in the gospel of Matthew.

PETER JAMES AND JOHN – **17** letters, so they are in chapter **17**.

The parallel narrative is in the gospel of **Mark** chapter **9**.

*And as they came down from the mountain, he charged them that they should tell no man (**TELL NO MAN**) what things they had seen, till the Son of man were risen from the dead.* Mark 9:9.

Mark that the Face of Jesus is not mentioned in this narrative as it is in the gospel of Matthew. **Mark** also that the words **TELL NO MAN** are in the gospel of **Mark**. In Matthew's narrative it is tell the vision to no man.

TELL NO MAN – **9** letters, so this verse is in chapter **9**.

To enable you to remember which book is chapter **17** and which is chapter **9**, just think that Matthew is a bigger word than Mark so it has the bigger number for its chapter i.e. Matthew **17** and Mark **9**.

No. 13
*For where two or three are gathered together in my name, there am I in the midst of them (**For where two or three are gathered together in my name, there am I in the midst of them**).* Matthew 18:20.

Jesus was in the midst of the congregation in the tabernacle and that included **Levites**. For the purpose of association, think that another name for Matthew is **Levi**, so this verse is in the gospel of Matthew.

JESUS GATHERS WITH US – **18** letters, so it is in chapter **18**.

No. 14
*Wherefore they are no more twain, but one flesh. What therefore God hath joined together, let not man put asunder (**LET NOT MAN PUT ASUNDER**).*
*They say unto him, Why did Moses (**Moses**) then command to give a writing of divorcement, and to put her away?*

He saith unto them, Moses because of the hardness of your hearts suffered you to put away your wives: but from the beginning it was not so. Matthew 19:6-8.

Moses is mentioned, and he was with the **Levites** during his lifetime. For the purpose of association, think that another name for Matthew is **Levi**, so these verses are in the gospel of Matthew.

LET NOT MAN PUT ASUNDER – **19** letters, so they are in chapter **19**.

No. 15
The following narrative is in the gospels of Matthew, Mark and Luke.

And when they drew nigh unto Jerusalem, and were come to Bethphage, unto the mount of Olives, then sent Jesus two disciples,
Saying unto them, Go into the village over against you, and straightway ye shall find an ass tied, and a colt with her: loose [them], and bring [them] unto me.
*And if any [man] say ought unto you, ye shall say, The Lord hath need of them (**THE LORD HATH NEED OF THEM**); and straightway he will send them.*
All this was done, that it might be fulfilled which was spoken by the prophet, saying,
Tell ye the daughter of Sion, Behold, thy King cometh unto thee, meek, and sitting upon an ass, and a colt the foal of an ass.
Matthew 21:1-5.

Zechariah prophesied concerning Jesus.

Rejoice greatly, O daughter of Zion; shout, O daughter of Jerusalem: behold, thy King cometh unto thee: he [is] just, and having salvation; lowly, and riding upon an ass, and upon a colt the foal of an ass. Zechariah 9:9.

Notice that in Matthew's narrative there is an ass and a colt mentioned. In Mark and Luke's narratives there is just a colt mentioned. An ass and a colt are 2 animals (the Lord hath need of **them**), and a colt is 1 animal (the Lord hath need of **him**). The number 2 is bigger than the number 1. Matthew is a bigger word than Mark or Luke, so it is not difficult to remember that Matthew's narrative uses the words **the Lord hath need of them**.

THE LORD HATH NEED OF THEM – 21 letters, so these verses are in chapter **21**.

*And if any man say unto you, Why do ye this (**WHY DO YE THIS**)? say ye that the Lord hath need of him; and straightway he will send him hither.* Mark 11:3.

WHY DO YE THIS – 11 letters, so this verse is in chapter **11**.

And as they were loosing the colt, the owners thereof said unto them, Why loose ye the colt?
And they said, The Lord hath need of him.
*And they brought him to Jesus: and they cast their garments upon the colt, and they set Jesus thereon (**THEY SET JESUS THEREON**).*
 Luke 19:33-35.

THEY SET JESUS THEREON – 19 letters, so these verses are in chapter **19**.

It is easy to remember which one of these is Mark and which one is Luke. The association for the number of the chapter in the gospel of Luke is '**THEY SET JESUS THEREON**,' so you just think that you hear the people saying '**look (Luke)** at Jesus sitting on the colt.'

No. 16
*But the wise took oil (**oil**) in their vessels with their lamps.*
While the bridegroom tarried, they all slumbered and slept.
*And at midnight there was a cry made, Behold, the bridegroom cometh (**BEHOLD THE BRIDEGROOM COMETH**); go ye out to meet him.* Matthew 25:4-6.

Oil is mentioned in these verses, and oil was used in the **tabernacle** in the Old Testament. For the purpose of association, think that **Levi** is another name for Matthew, and the **Levites** were in the tabernacle, so these verses are in the gospel of Matthew.

145

BEHOLD, THE BRIDEGROOM COMETH – 25 letters, so they are in chapter **25**.

No. 17
Then shall he say also unto them on the left hand, Depart from me, ye cursed, into everlasting fire (everlasting fire), prepared for the devil and his angels: Matthew 25:41.

Just remember that the gospel of Matthew is the only book in the New Testament that records the words **'everlasting fire.'**

In Isaiah 33:14 the following words are recorded: *The sinners in Zion are afraid; fearfulness hath surprised the hypocrites. Who among us shall dwell with the devouring fire? who among us shall dwell with **everlasting burnings**?*

EVERLASTING FIRE FOR SINNERS – 25 letters, so this verse is in chapter **25**.

MARK

No. 1
And he said unto them, The sabbath was made for man, and not man for the sabbath:
Therefore the Son of man is Lord also of the sabbath. Mark 2:27-28.

For the purpose of association, when you read these words, **mark** That Jesus said *"The Sabbath (**Sabbath**) was made for man (**man**), and not man (**not man**) for the Sabbath (**Sabbath**)."*

These verses are in the gospel of **Mark**.

(1) *The sabbath was made for man,*

(2) *and not man for the sabbath:*

2 clear statements, so they are in chapter **2**.

No. 2
And they brought young children to him, that he should touch them: and [his] disciples rebuked those that brought [them].

But when Jesus saw [it], he was much displeased **(DISPLEASED)**, *and said unto them, Suffer the little children to come unto me, and forbid them not: for of such is the kingdom of God.*

Verily I say unto you, Whosoever shall not receive the kingdom of God as a little child, he shall not enter therein.

And he took them up in his arms, put [his] hands upon them, and blessed them. Mark 10:13-16.

Mark that **Mark's** narrative states that Jesus was **displeased**, but the narrative in the gospel of Matthew doesn't mention this, so these verses are in the gospel of **Mark**.

DISPLEASED – 10 letters, so they are in chapter **10**.

The parallel narrative is in the gospel of **Matthew** chapter **19**.

Then were there brought unto him little children, that he should put [his] hands on them, and pray **(pray)**: *and the disciples rebuked them.*

But Jesus said, Suffer little children, and forbid them not, to come unto me: for of such is the kingdom of heaven.

And he laid [his] hands on them, and departed thence.
Matthew 19:13-15.

For the purpose of association, think that there have been children in the world since Cain was born at the **beginning** of time. Matthew is the **beginning** of the gospels, so these verses are in the gospel of Matthew.

MATTHEW MENTIONS PRAY – 19 letters, so they are in chapter **19**.

The narrative in the gospel of Mark doesn't mention pray.

No. 3

*And Jesus sat over against the treasury, and beheld how the people (**people**) cast money into the treasury and many that were rich cast in much.*

And there came a certain poor widow, and she threw in two mites, which make a farthing.

And he called [unto him] his disciples, and saith unto them, Verily I say unto you, That this poor widow hath cast more in, than all they which have cast into the treasury:

*For all [they] did cast in of their abundance; but she of her want did cast in all that she had, [even] all her living. (**ALL HER LIVING**).*

Mark 12:41-44.

Mark that this narrative tells us: Jesus beheld how the **people** cast money into the treasury. In Luke's narrative it is just the rich men and the widow who are mentioned, so these verses are in the gospel of **Mark**.

ALL HER LIVING – 12 letters, so they are in chapter **12**.

*And he looked up (and he **look**ed up), and saw the rich men casting their gifts into the treasury.*

*And he saw also a certain poor widow (**And he saw also a certain poor widow**) casting in thither two mites.*

And he said, Of a truth I say unto you, that this poor widow hath cast in more than they all:

For all these have of their abundance cast in unto the offerings of God: but she of her penury hath cast in all the living that she had.

Luke 21:1-4.

And he **look**ed up (**Luke**), so these verses are in the gospel of Luke.

JESUS SEES THE POOR WIDOW – 21 letters, so they are in chapter **21**.

In order to avoid confusion between these two chapters, just think of the association '**JESUS SEES THE POOR WIDOW.**' In order to **see** something we must **look** (**Luke**) at it, so this association belongs to the gospel of Luke.

No. 4

*And Jesus **(Jesus)** answered him, The first **(first)** of*
all the commandments [is], Hear, O Israel; The Lord our God is
one Lord:
And thou shalt love the Lord thy God with all thy heart, and with
all thy soul, and with all thy mind, and with all thy strength: this [is]
the first commandment.
*And the second **(second)** [is] like, [namely] this, Thou shalt love*
thy neighbour as thyself. There is none other commandment greater
than these. Mark 12:29-31.

The parallel passage is in the book of Deuteronomy chapter 6.

Hear, O Israel: The LORD our God [is] one LORD:
And thou shalt love the LORD thy God with all thine heart, and
with all thy soul, and with all thy might. Deuteronomy 6:4-5.

Moses spoke these words to the Israelites, but a greater than Moses
spoke these words too. **Mark** that **Jesus** spoke them, so these verses
are in the gospel of **Mark**.

This association is a little different, but I trust that you can remember it.

There are **two** commandments recorded in these verses.

COMMANDMENTS – 12 letters, so they are in chapter **12**.

No. 5

But in those days, after that tribulation, the sun shall be darkened,
and the moon shall not give her light,
And the stars of heaven shall fall, and the powers that are in heaven
shall be shaken.
*And then shall they see the Son of man coming in the clouds **(then***
***shall they see the Son of man coming in the clouds)** with great*
power and glory. Mark 13:24-26.

The parallel narrative is in the gospel of **Matthew** chapter **24**.

These narratives are about the second coming of Jesus. When you read them, think immediately of what is recorded in Acts 1:11: *Ye men of Galilee, why stand ye gazing up into heaven? this same* ***(same)*** *Jesus, which is taken up from you into heaven, shall so come in like manner as ye have seen him go into heaven.*

For the purpose of association, think that **Ma**tthew and **Ma**rk both start with the **same** letters, so these verses are in the gospels of Matthew and Mark.

JESUS IS COMING – **13** letters, so they are in chapter **13**.

Immediately after the tribulation of those days shall the sun be darkened, and the moon shall not give her light, and the stars shall fall from heaven, and the powers of the heavens shall be shaken:
And then shall appear the sign of the Son of man in heaven: and then shall all the tribes of the earth mourn, and they shall see the Son of man coming in the clouds of heaven ***(they shall see the Son of man coming in the clouds of heaven)*** *with power and great glory.*
Matthew 24:29-30.

JESUS CHRIST IS COMING AGAIN – **24** letters, so these verses are in chapter **24**.

To enable you to remember which book is chapter **24** and which is chapter **13**, just think that Matthew is a bigger word than Mark so it has the bigger number for its chapter i.e. Matthew **24** and Mark **13**.

LUKE

No. 1
And, behold ***(behold)****, thou shalt conceive in thy womb, and bring forth a son, and shalt call his name JESUS.*
He shall be great, and shall be called the Son of the Highest: and the Lord God shall give unto him the throne of his father David:

And he shall reign over the house of Jacob for ever; and of his kingdom there shall be no end.

Then said Mary unto the angel, How shall this be, seeing I (I) know not a man?

And the angel answered and said unto her, The Holy Ghost shall come upon thee, and the power of the Highest shall overshadow thee: therefore also that holy thing which shall be born of thee shall be called the Son of God. Luke 1:31-35.

'**Behold**' can be defined as to gaze upon. If one is gazing then he/she is **look**ing (**Luke**), so these verses are in the gospel of Luke.

I know not a man. **I** is similar to **1**, so they are in chapter **1**.

No. 2

*And the angel said unto them, Fear not: for, behold (**behold**), I bring you good tidings of great joy, which shall be to all people.*

For unto you is born this day in the city of David a Saviour, which is Christ the Lord.

*And this [shall be] a sign unto you; Ye shall find the babe wrapped in swaddling clothes (**wrapped in swaddling clothes**), lying in a manger (**lying in a manger**).* Luke 2:10-12.

To '**behold**' can be defined as to gaze upon. If one is gazing then he/she is **look**ing (**Luke**), so these verses are in the gospel of Luke.

The sign was **2**-fold.

(**1**) **wrapped in swaddling clothes,**
(**2**) **lying in a manger.**

These verses are in chapter **2**.

No. 3

*And he said unto them, How is it that ye sought me (**How is it that ye sought me**)? wist ye not that I must be about my Father's business (**wist ye not that I must be about my Father's business**)?* Luke 2:49.

Mary and Joseph were **look**ing (**Luke**) for Jesus, so this verse is in the gospel of Luke.

Jesus said:

(1) *How is it that ye sought me?*

(2) *wist ye not that I must be about my Father's business?*

2 questions, so this verse is in chapter **2**.

No. 4

And Jesus himself began to be about thirty years of age, being (as was supposed) ***(AS WAS SUPPOSED)*** *the son* ***(SON)*** *of Joseph, which was [the son] of Heli, Luke 3:23.*

For the purpose of association, think that Jesus would **look (Luke)** like the son of Joseph, but he actually was the Son of God, so this verse is in the gospel of **Luke**.

AS WAS SUPPOSED – **3** words, so it is in chapter **3**.

Or: **SON** - **3** letters. The word 'son' appears the whole way through Luke chapter 3.

No. 5

And he closed the book, and he gave [it] again to the minister ***(And he closed the book, and he gave [it] again to the minister)****, and sat down. And the eyes of all them that were in the synagogue were fastened on him* ***(And the eyes of all them that were in the synagogue were fastened on him)****.*

And he began to say unto them, This ***(THIS)*** *day is this* ***(THIS)*** *scripture fulfilled in your ears. Luke 4:20-21.*

And the eyes of all them that were in the synagogue were fastened on him. If their eyes were fastened on him then they were **look**ing **(Luke)** at Him, so these verses are in the gospel of Luke.

THIS day.

THIS scripture.

THIS - **4** letters, so they are in chapter **4**.

No. 6

And it came to pass in those days, that he went out into a mountain to pray, and continued all night in prayer to God ***(continued all night in prayer to God).***

And when it was day, he called [unto him] his disciples: and of them he chose twelve ***(TWELVE)****, whom also he named apostles;*

Simon, (whom he also named Peter,) and Andrew his brother, James and John, Philip and Bartholomew,

Matthew and Thomas, James the [son] of Alphaeus, and Simon called Zelotes,

And Judas [the brother] of James, and Judas Iscariot, which also was the traitor. Luke 6:12-16.

We should **look (Luke)** at verses twelve and thirteen carefully. Here we read that **Jesus spent the whole night in prayer before he chose His twelve apostles,** so these verses are in the gospel of Luke.

TWELVE – 6 letters, so they are in chapter **6**.

No. 7

And Jesus answering said, A certain [man] went down from Jerusalem to Jericho, and fell among thieves, which stripped him of his raiment, and wounded [him], and departed, leaving [him] half dead.

And by chance there came down a certain priest that way: and when he saw him, he passed by on the other side.

And likewise a Levite, when he was at the place, came and looked ***(look****ed) [on him], and passed by on the other side.*

But a certain Samaritan, as he journeyed, came where he was: and when he saw him, he had compassion [on him],

And went to [him], and bound up his wounds, pouring in oil and wine ***(OIL AND WINE)****, and set him on his own beast, and brought him to an inn, and took care of him. Luke 10:30-34.*

Verse thirty-two tells us that a Levite **look**ed **(Luke)** on this man, so these verses are in the gospel of Luke.

OIL AND WINE– 10 letters, so they are in chapter **10**.

If you have difficulty remembering who was the first person to encounter this man who fell among the thieves, and who was the second person to encounter him, then the following associations should be helpful.

The priest passed by. **P** for priest and **p** for passed.
The Levite looked on him. **L** for Levite and **l** for looked.
The Samaritan stopped. **S** for Samaritan and **s** for stopped.

Notice also that each person who encountered this man came a little closer to him.
The priest passed by on the other side. He kept his distance.
The Levite came and looked on him. He came closer.
The Samaritan bound up his wounds, and set him on his own beast. He touched him.

No. 8
*Now it came to pass, as they went, that he entered into a certain village: and a certain woman named Martha (**MARTHA**) received him into her house.*

*And she had a sister called Mary (**MARY**), which also sat at Jesus' feet, and heard his word.*

But Martha was cumbered about much serving, and came to him, and said, Lord, dost thou not care that my sister hath left me to serve alone? bid her therefore that she help me.

And Jesus answered and said unto her, Martha, Martha, thou art careful and troubled about many things:

But one thing is needful: and Mary hath chosen that good part, which shall not be taken away from her. Luke 10:38-42.

For the purpose of association think of Martha saying "**look (Luke)** at Mary sitting at the feet of Jesus instead of helping me to serve," so these verses are in the gospel of Luke.

Remember this is only an association. I am not saying that Martha said these words.

MARTHA MARY – **10** letters, so these verses are in chapter **10**.

No. 9
And he said, This will I do: I will pull down my barns, and build greater (BUILD GREATER); and there will I bestow all my fruits and my goods. Luke 12:18.

For the purpose of association, visualize this rich man saying "**look (Luke)** at my plentiful harvest," so this verse is in the gospel of Luke.

BUILD GREATER – **12** letters, so it is in chapter **12**.

No. 10
What man of you, having an hundred sheep, if he lose one of them, doth not leave the ninety and nine in the wilderness, and go after that which is lost (THAT WHICH IS LOST), until he find it? Luke 15:4.

This verse is about a lost sheep. If a sheep is lost, the shepherd has to **look (Luke)** for it, so this verse is in the gospel of Luke.

THAT WHICH IS LOST – **15** letters, so it is in chapter **15**.

No. 11
There was a certain rich man, which was clothed in purple and fine linen, and fared sumptuously (FARED SUMPTUOUSLY) every day:
And there was a certain beggar named Lazarus, which was laid at his gate, full of sores,
And desiring to be fed with the crumbs which fell from the rich man's table: moreover the dogs came and licked his sores.
And it came to pass, that the beggar died, and was carried by the angels into Abraham's bosom: the rich man also died, and was buried;
And in hell he lift up his eyes, being in torments, and seeth (seeth) Abraham afar off, and Lazarus in his bosom. Luke 16:19-23.

And seeth Abraham afar off. If he saw Abraham then he was **looking (Luke)** at Abraham, so these verses are in the gospel of Luke.

FARED SUMPTUOUSLY – **16** letters, so they are in chapter **16**.

No. 12

Two men went up into the temple to pray; the one a Pharisee (A PHARISEE), and the other a publican (A PUBLICAN).
The Pharisee stood and prayed thus with himself, God, I thank thee, that I am not as other men [are], extortioners, unjust, adulterers, or even as this publican.
I fast twice in the week, I give tithes of all that I possess.
Luke 18:10-12.

For the purpose of association think of saying, "**Look (Luke)** at that self-righteous Pharisee boasting about what he does," so these verses are in the gospel of Luke.

A PHARISEE A PUBLICAN – 18 letters, so they are in chapter **18**.

No. 13

*And when Jesus came to the place, he looked (**looked**) up, and saw him (**HE LOOKED UP AND SAW HIM**), and said unto him, Zacchaeus, make haste, and come down; for to day I must abide at thy house.* Luke 19:5.

Looked – **Luke**. This verse is in the gospel of Luke.

HE LOOKED UP AND SAW HIM – 19 letters, so it is in chapter **19**.

No. 14

And the Lord said, Simon, Simon, behold, Satan hath desired [to have] you, that he may sift [you] as wheat:
But I have prayed for thee, that thy faith fail not: and when thou art converted, strengthen thy brethren. Luke 22:31-32.

I would imagine that the Lord would be **look**ing (**Luke**) at Peter while he was talking to him, so this verse is in the gospel of **Luke**.

For the purpose of association, just think that Simon's name was spoken **2** times, and the Lord always goes the 2nd mile. Think of this as two 2's i.e. **22**, so this verse is in chapter **22**.

If you would like to know the location of other repeated names in the Bible, read the following list:

Abraham, Abraham – when Abraham was about to slay Isaac. Genesis 22:11.
Jacob, Jacob – before going to Egypt to see Joseph. Genesis 46:2.

Moses, Moses – at the burning bush. Exodus 3:4.

Samuel, Samuel – when Samuel was in bed. 1 Samuel 3:10.

Lord, Lord – Jesus said many would say unto Him Lord, Lord, but they would not enter into the kingdom of Heaven. Matthew 7:21.

Jerusalem, Jerusalem – when Jesus was speaking to the scribes and Pharisees and told them their house was left desolate. Matthew 23:37.

Eli, Eli – one of the sayings of Jesus when He was on the cross. Matthew 27:46.

Eloi, Eloi – one of the sayings of Jesus when He was on the cross. Mark 15:34.

Martha, Martha – when Martha was cumbered about much serving. Luke 10:41.

Saul, Saul – when he was travelling to Damascus on an evil mission. Acts 9:4.

No. 15
And Jesus said unto him, Verily I say unto thee, To day shalt thou be with me in paradise. Luke 23:43.

For the purpose of association, think of **look**ing at someone when you speak to him/her, so this verse is in the gospel of **Luke**.

JESUS LOVED THE DYING THIEF – **23** letters, so it is in chapter **23**.

No. 16

*And the sun was darkened (**And the sun was darkened**), and the veil of the temple was rent in the midst (**the veil of the temple was rent in the midst**).* Luke 23:45.

Imagine someone saying, "**Look (Luke)** the veil is rent," so this verse is in the gospel of **Luke**.

NO SUNSHINE AS GOD'S SON DIES – **23** letters, so it is in chapter **23**.

The rending of the veil is also mentioned in the gospels of Matthew and Mark.

*And, behold, the veil (**veil**) (**RENT VEIL**) of the temple was rent in twain from the top to the bottom; and the earth did quake (**earth did quake**), and the rocks rent (**rocks rent**);* Matthew 27:51.

Another name for **Matthew** is **Levi** and the **priests** were from the **tribe of Levi.** The high priest entered within the **vail** with blood (once every year) for the atonement of his own sins and the sins of the people, so this verse is in the gospel of Matthew.

In some King James editions of the Bible it is **vail** in the Old Testament and **veil** in the New Testament.

RENT VEIL – EARTHQUAKE – RENT ROCKS – **27** letters, so this verse is in chapter **27**.

*And the veil of the temple (**veil of the temple**) was rent in twain from the top to the bottom.* Mark 15:38.

VEIL OF THE TEMPLE – **15** letters, so this verse is in chapter **15**.

Mark that the association for the number of the chapter in the gospel of **Mark** actually states that it was the **VEIL OF THE TEMPLE**, so it is chapter **15**.

To enable you to remember which book is chapter **27** and which is chapter **23**, just think that Matthew is a bigger word than Luke so it has the bigger number for its chapter, i.e. Matthew **27** and Luke **23**.

No. 17
*Behold **(Behold)** my hands and my feet **(Behold my hands and my feet)**, that it is I myself **(it is I myself)**: handle me, and see **(handle me and see)**; for a spirit hath not flesh and bones **(a spirit hath not flesh and bones, as ye see me have)**, as ye see me have. Luke 24:39.*

One of the definitions for '**behold**' is to gaze upon, so that is the same as **look (Luke)** at my hands and my feet. This verse is in the gospel of **Luke**.

Hands and feet have **10** fingers and **10** toes, so that is **20**.

(1) Behold my hands and my feet,
(2) it is I myself:
(3) handle me, and see;
(4) a spirit hath not flesh and bones, as ye see me have,

20+4=24, so this verse is in chapter **24**.

JOHN

No. 1
*In the beginning **(beginning)** was the Word (**Word**), and the Word was with God, and the Word was God. John 1:1.*

*But as many as received **(received)** him, to them gave he power to become the sons of God, [even] to them that believe on his name: John 1:12.*

It is widely believed that **John** was the apostle who leaned on the bosom of Jesus. For the purpose of association think of this as proof that **John received** Him, so these verses are in the gospel of **John**.

For the purpose of association, think of the beginning as being at the start and therefore number **1**, so these verses are in chapter **1**.

'Thy word have I hid in mine heart.'

Notice the capital **W** for **W**ord.

No. 2
And the third day there was a marriage in Cana of Galilee; and the mother of Jesus was there:
And both (both) Jesus was called, and his disciples, to the marriage.
John 2:2.

Jesus saith unto them, Fill the waterpots with water (water). And they filled them up to the brim. John 2:7.

In this chapter, **water** is mentioned. For the purpose of association, think of **John** the Baptist baptizing with **water**, so these verses are in the gospel of **John**.

Both means **2**, so they are in chapter **2**.

No. 3
The following three verses need to be read as a whole in order to understand them.
There was a man of the Pharisees, named Nicodemus, a ruler of the Jews:
The same came to Jesus by night, and said unto him, Rabbi, we know that thou art a teacher come from God: for no man can do these miracles that thou doest, except God be with him.
Jesus answered and said unto him, Verily, verily, I say unto thee, Except a man be born again (born of God), he cannot see (SEE) the kingdom of God. John 3:1-3.

When you read these verses, think immediately of what is recorded in **John** 1:12-13. *But as many as received him, to them gave he power to become the sons of God, [even] to them that believe on his name:*
Which were born (born), not of blood, nor of the will of the flesh, nor of the will of man, but of God (of God).

These verses are in the gospel of **John**.

SEE – **3** letters, so they are in chapter **3**.

No. 4

I suggest that you memorize the following three verses.

For God so loved the world, that he gave his only begotten Son ***(SON)****, that whosoever believeth in him should not perish, but have everlasting life.*

For God sent not his Son into the world to condemn the world; but that the world through him might be saved.

He that believeth on him is not condemned: but he that believeth not is condemned already, because he hath not believed in the name of the only begotten Son ***(only begotten Son)*** *of God.* John 3:16-18.

The words 'only begotten Son' are used five times in Scripture. In the above verse it is actually 'only begotten Son of God.' **John** is the only person who uses the words 'only begotten Son' and 'only begotten Son of God' **in referring to Jesus**. He uses these words three times in the gospel of John: John 1:18, 3:16, 3:18, and once in 1st John 4:9.

It is easy to remember that these verses are in the gospel of John because John 3:16 is probably one of the best-known verses in Scripture.

SON – 3 letters, so these verses are in the gospel of John chapter **3**.

The words 'only begotten son' are mentioned in Hebrews 11:17, but **they refer to Isaac** in this instance.

By faith Abraham, when he was tried, offered up Isaac: and he that had received the promises offered up his only begotten [son] ***(only begotten Son)****,* Hebrews 11:17.

No. 5

God [is] a Spirit ***(GOD [IS] A SPIRIT)****: and they that worship him must worship [him] in spirit and in truth* ***(truth)****.* John 4:24.

It is in **John's** gospel that we read: *Jesus saith unto him, I am the way, the truth* ***(truth)****, and the life: no man cometh unto the Father, but by me.* John 14:6.

It is also in John's gospel that we read about Jesus sending the **Spirit**.

And I will pray the Father, and he shall give you another Comforter, that he may abide with you for ever;
*[Even] the Spirit of truth (**Spirit of truth**); whom the world cannot receive, because it seeth him not, neither knoweth him: but ye know him; for he dwelleth with you, and shall be in you.* John 14:16-17.

*But when the Comforter is come, whom I will send unto you from the Father, [even] the Spirit of truth (**Spirit of truth**), which proceedeth from the Father, he shall testify of me:* John 15:26.

*Howbeit when he, the Spirit of truth (**Spirit of truth**), is come, he will guide you into all truth: for he shall not speak of himself; but whatsoever he shall hear, [that] shall he speak: and he will shew you things to come.* John 16:13.

For the purpose of association, think **Spirit** and **truth**, so this verse is in the gospel of John.

GOD IS A SPIRIT – **4** words, so it is in chapter **4**.

No. 6
*Search the scriptures; for in them ye think ye have eternal life: and they are they which testify (**testify**) of me.*
And ye will not come to me, that ye might have life. John 5:39-40.

For the purpose of association, think of the book of Revelation as **testifying** of Jesus. It is The Revelation of Jesus Christ. **John** wrote the book of Revelation, so these verses are in the gospel of **John**.

THE SCRIPTURES TESTIFY OF JESUS – **5** words, so they are in chapter **5**.

No. 7
*For had ye believed Moses (**MOSES**), ye would have believed me: for he wrote (**wrote**) of me.*
But if ye believe not his writings, how shall ye believe my words? John 5:46-47.

These verses state that **Moses wrote** of Jesus. For the purpose of association, think that **John wrote** of Jesus in the book of Revelation, so these verses are in the gospel of **John**.

MOSES – 5 letters, so they are in chapter **5**.

No. 8
And Jesus said unto them, I am (I am) the bread of life (I AM THE BREAD OF LIFE): he that cometh to me shall never hunger (HUNGER); and he that believeth on me shall never thirst. John 6:35.

Remember I stated at the beginning of this book that the **'I am's'** of Jesus are in the gospel of John, so you don't need an association this time.

I AM THE BREAD OF LIFE – **6** words, so this verse is in chapter **6**.

Or – **HUNGER** – **6** letters.

No. 9
Then spake Jesus again unto them, saying, I am (I am) the light of the world: he that followeth me shall not walk in darkness (DARKNESS), but shall have the light of life. John 8:12.

See association number 8 for details concerning the 'I am's' of Jesus.

DARKNESS – **8** letters, so this verse is in chapter **8**.

No. 10
Your father (father) Abraham (Abraham) rejoiced to see my day and he saw [it] and was glad. John 8:56.

We know that these words were spoken by Jesus, so this verse is in some one of the gospels.

Remember I stated at the beginning of this book that the gospel of **John** portrays Jesus as the **Son of God**.

For the purpose of association, think that these people to whom Jesus was speaking were sons of **Abraham**, but **Jesus is the Son of** God, so this verse is in the gospel of **John**.

Fathers have bonds with their families, and bonds start with **B**, which is similar in appearance to **8**, so this verse is in the gospel of John chapter **8**.

No. 11
*And when he putteth forth his own sheep, he goeth before them, and the sheep follow him: for they know his voice (**for they know his voice**). John 10:4.*

*And other sheep (**OTHER SHEEP**) I have, which are not of this fold: them also I must bring, and they shall hear my voice; and there shall be one fold, [and] one shepherd. John 10:16.*

It is widely believed that **John** was the apostle who leaned on the bosom of Jesus. For the purpose of association, think that if **John** leaned on the bosom of Jesus he would be the one who would **know his voice**, so these verses are in the gospel of **John**.

OTHER SHEEP – **10** letters, so they are in chapter **10**.

No. 12
*I am (**I am**) the door (**I AM THE DOOR**): by me if any man enter in, he shall be saved, and shall go in and out, and find pasture. John 10:9.*

See association number 8 for details concerning the 'I am's.' of Jesus.

I AM THE DOOR –**10** letters, so this verse is in chapter **10**.

No. 13
*I am (**I am**) the good shepherd (**good shepherd**): the good shepherd giveth his life for the sheep. John 10:11.*

See association number 8 for details concerning the 'I am's.' of Jesus.

The Good Shepherd will bring in the **OTHER SHEEP - 10** letters, so this verse is in chapter **10**.

No. 14
Therefore his sisters sent unto him, saying, Lord, behold, he (**Lazarus**) *whom thou lovest (lovest) is sick.* John 11:3.

It is widely believed that **John** was the apostle whom Jesus **loved**. For the purpose of association, notice the word '**lovest**,' so this verse is in the gospel of **John**.

LAZARUS DIES – 11 letters, so it is in chapter **11**.

No. 15
Jesus said unto her, I am (I am) the resurrection, and the life: he that believeth in me, though he were dead, yet shall he live: John chapter 11:25.

See association number 8 for details concerning the 'I am's.' of Jesus.

Remember also, I stated that this verse is in the narrative of the death of Lazarus.

LAZARUS DIES – 11 letters, so it is in chapter **11**.

No. 16
I suggest that you memorize the following six verses.

*Let not your heart be troubled: ye believe in God (**YE BELIEVE IN GOD**), believe also in me.*
*In my Father's house are many mansions: if [it were] not [so], I would have told you. I go to prepare a place for you (**I go to prepare a place for you**).*
And if I go and prepare a place for you, I will come again, and receive

you unto myself; that where I am, [there] ye may be also.
And whither I go ye know, and the way ye know.
Thomas saith unto him, Lord, we know not whither thou goest; and how can we know the way?
Jesus saith unto him, I am the way, the truth, and the life: no man cometh unto the Father, but by me **(Jesus saith unto him, I am the way, the truth, and the life: no man cometh unto the Father, but by me.)** John 14:1-6.

It is widely believed that **John** was the apostle whom Jesus loved. For the purpose of association, think that if Jesus loved **John** He would **go to prepare a place** for him, so these verses are in the gospel of **John**.

YE BELIEVE IN GOD – **14** letters, so they are in chapter **14**.

Jesus saith unto him, I am **(I am)** *the way, the truth, and the life: no man cometh unto the Father, but by me.* John 14:6.

See association number 8 for details concerning the 'I am's' of Jesus.

If you memorize John 14:1-6 you will realize that this verse is in chapter 14.

No. 17
If ye love **(love)** *me* **(IF YE LOVE ME)**, *keep my commandments* **(MY COMMANDMENTS)**. John 14:15.

The above words were spoken by Jesus, so they are in some one of the four gospels. It is widely believed that **John** was the disciple whom Jesus **loved**, so this verse is in the gospel of **John**.

This association is slightly different.

IF YE LOVE ME - **4** words. There are **10** commandments. **4+10=14**, so this verse is in chapter **14**.

Or - **MY COMMANDMENTS** – **14** letters.

No. 18

*And I will pray the Father, and he shall give you another Comforter,
that he may abide with you for ever;*

*[Even] the Spirit of truth **(Spirit of truth)**; whom the world cannot
receive, because it seeth him not, neither knoweth him: but ye know
him; for he dwelleth with you, and shall be in you.* John **14**:16-17.

*But when the Comforter is come, whom I will send unto you from
the Father, [even] the Spirit of truth **(Spirit of truth)**, which proceedeth from the Father, he shall testify of me:* John **15**:26.

*Howbeit when he, the Spirit of truth **(Spirit of truth)**, is come, he
will guide you into all truth: for he shall not speak of himself; but
whatsoever he shall hear, [that] shall he speak: and he will shew you
things to come.* John **16**:13.

These verses are taken from different chapters, but they are all
relating to Jesus telling His disciples that He will **send the Spirit.**

It is widely believed that **John** was the apostle who leaned on Jesus'
bosom. *Now there was leaning on Jesus' bosom one of his disciples,
whom Jesus loved.* John 13:23.

For the purpose of association, think that if **John** was the apostle
who leaned on the bosom of Jesus, then he would be the one who
was closest to Him, and would know about the **Spirit** coming, so
these verses are in the gospel of John. I am not suggesting that is
how it happened, as Jesus told all of the apostles about the coming
of the Holy Spirit. I am merely forming an association.

If you can remember that the high priestly prayer of Jesus is in the
gospel of John chapter **17**, then it is relatively simple to find these
verses about Jesus sending the Spirit, because when you look at
them you will see that they are in chapters **14, 15** and **16**.

No. 19

*I am **(I am)** the true vine, and my Father is the husbandman.*

*Every branch in me that beareth not fruit **(BEARETH NOT FRUIT)**
he taketh away: and every [branch] that beareth fruit, he purgeth it,
that it may bring forth more fruit.*

Now ye are clean through the word which I have spoken unto you.
John 15:1-3.

See association number 8 for details concerning the 'I am's.' of Jesus.

BEARETH NOT FRUIT - **15** letters, so these verses are in chapter **15**.

No. 20
These words spake Jesus **(These words spake Jesus)**, *and lifted up his eyes to heaven, and said, Father, the hour is come; glorify thy Son, that thy Son also may glorify thee:*
As thou hast given him power over all flesh, that he should give eternal life to as many as thou hast given him.
And this is life eternal, that they might know thee the only true God, and Jesus Christ, whom thou hast sent.
I have glorified thee on the earth: I have finished the work which thou gavest me to do.
And now, O Father, glorify thou me with thine own self with the glory which I had with thee before the world was. John 17:1 -5.

These verses are part of **our Saviour's High Priestly prayer**. The prayer lasts for the whole chapter.

It is widely believed that **John** was the apostle whom Jesus loved.
For the purpose of association, think that if **John** was the apostle whom Jesus loved, then he would be the one who was closest to Him, and would be the one most likely to hear His prayer, so these verses are in the gospel of **John**. I am not suggesting that is how it happened; I am merely forming an association.

THE SAVIOUR'S PRAYER – **17** letters, so these verses are in chapter **17**.

No. 21
Sanctify them through thy truth: thy word is truth. John 17:17.

I am using a different type of association for this verse. Just remember that this verse is part of our Saviour's High Priestly prayer. This verse is number **17** of chapter **17**, so that is a good association.

No. 22
*As soon then as he had said unto them, I am (**I am**) [he], they went backward, and fell to the ground (**AND FELL TO THE GROUND**).* John 18:6.

Remember I said at the beginning of this book that the seven 'I am's' of Jesus are in the gospel of John. This is not one of the seven, but for the purpose of association, think that the words are *'I am he,'* so this verse is in the gospel of John.

AND FELL TO THE GROUND – 18 letters, so it is in chapter **18**.

It is interesting to note that the words *'I am he,'* are recorded seven times in the gospel of John. None of the other gospels contain these words.

No. 23
*When Jesus therefore had received the vinegar, he said, It is finished (**finished**) and he bowed his head, and gave up the ghost.* John 19:30.

For the purpose of association, think of the gospels being **finished** with the gospel of John because it is the final gospel, so this verse is in the gospel of John.

When Jesus said *"It is finished"* - **HIS WORK WAS COMPLETED – 19** letters, so this verse is in chapter **19**.

ACTS

No. 1
*The former treatise have I made, O Theophilus, of all that Jesus began (**began**) both to do and teach,*
Until the day in which he was taken up, after that he through the Holy Ghost had given commandments unto the apostles whom he had chosen:

To whom also he shewed himself alive **(he showed himself alive)** after his passion by many infallible proofs, being seen of them forty days, and speaking of the things pertaining to the kingdom of God:

And, being assembled together with [them], commanded them that they should not depart from Jerusalem, but wait for the promise of the Father, which, [saith he], ye have heard of me.

For John truly baptized with water **(baptized with water)**; but ye shall be baptized with the Holy Ghost not many days hence.

When they therefore were come together, they asked of him, saying, Lord, wilt thou at this time restore again the kingdom to Israel?

And he said unto them, It is not for you to know the times or the seasons, which the Father hath put in his own power.

But ye shall receive power, after that the Holy Ghost is come upon you: and ye shall be witnesses unto me both in Jerusalem, and in all Judaea, and in Samaria, and unto the uttermost part of the earth.

And when he had spoken these things, while they beheld, he was taken up; and a cloud received him out of their sight **(while they beheld, he was taken up; and a cloud received him out of their sight)**. Acts 1:1-9.

In these verses we have:

The **act** of Jesus showing himself alive to His disciples.

The **act** of John baptizing with water.

The **act** of Jesus ascending to Heaven, so they are in the book of **Acts**.

Began is the beginning and the 1st chapter is the beginning, so these verses are in chapter **1**.

No. 2

And they appointed two, Joseph called Barsabas, who was surnamed Justus, and Matthias.

And they prayed, and said, Thou, Lord, which knowest the hearts of all [men], shew whether of these two thou hast chosen,

That he may take part of this ministry and apostleship, from which Judas by transgression fell, that he might go to his own place.

And they gave forth their lots; and the lot fell upon Matthias; and he was numbered with the eleven apostles. Acts 1:23-26.

Remember I stated at the beginning of this book that the choosing of an apostle to replace Judas Iscariot is recorded in the book of Acts, so these verses are in the book of Acts.

1 man was chosen, so they are in chapter **1**.

No. 3

And when the day of Pentecost **(the day of Pentecost)** *was fully come, they were all with one accord in one place.*

And suddenly there came a sound from heaven as of a rushing mighty wind, and it filled all the house where they were sitting. And there appeared unto them cloven tongues like as of fire, and it sat upon each of them.

And they were all filled with the Holy Ghost, and began to speak with other tongues, as the Spirit gave them utterance. Acts 2:1-4.

Remember I stated at the beginning of this book that the coming of the Holy Spirit on the **day of Pentecost** is recorded in the book of Acts chapter 2; therefore these verses are in chapter 2.

Ye men of Israel, hear these words; Jesus of Nazareth, a man approved of God among you by miracles and wonders and signs, which God did by him in the midst of you, as ye yourselves also know:

Him, being delivered by the determinate counsel and foreknowledge of God, ye have taken, and by wicked hands have crucified and slain:

Whom God hath raised up, having loosed the pains of death: because it was not possible that he should be holden of it.

For David speaketh concerning him, I foresaw the Lord always before my face, for he is on my right hand, that I should not be moved:

Therefore did my heart rejoice, and my tongue was glad; moreover also my flesh shall rest in hope:

Because thou wilt not leave my soul in hell, neither wilt thou suffer thine Holy One to see corruption.

(Because thou wilt not leave my soul in hell, neither wilt thou suffer thine Holy One to see corruption.)

Thou hast made known to me the ways of life; thou shalt make me full of joy with thy countenance.

Men [and] brethren, let me freely speak unto you of the patriarch David, that he is both dead and buried, and his sepulchre is with us unto this day.

Therefore being a prophet, and knowing that God had sworn with an oath to him, that of the fruit of his loins, according to the flesh, he would raise up Christ to sit on his throne;

He seeing this before spake of the resurrection of Christ, that his soul was not left in hell, neither his flesh did see corruption.

This Jesus hath God raised up, whereof we all are witnesses.

Therefore being by the right hand of God exalted, and having received of the Father the promise of the Holy Ghost, he hath shed forth this, which ye now see and hear.

For David is not ascended into the heavens: but he saith himself, The LORD said unto my Lord, Sit thou on my right hand,

Until I make thy foes thy footstool.

Therefore let all the house of Israel know assuredly,

that God hath made that same Jesus, whom ye have crucified, both Lord and Christ.

Now when they heard [this], they were pricked in their heart, and said unto Peter and to the rest of the apostles, Men [and] brethren, what shall we do?

Then Peter said unto them, Repent, and be baptized **(repent, and be baptized)** every one of you in the name of Jesus Christ for the remission of sins, and ye shall receive the gift of the Holy Ghost.

Acts 2:22-38.

These verses are part of Peter's sermon on the day of Pentecost, so they are in the book of Acts chapter 2.

Or – Peter told the people to **repent** and be **baptized**. **2** things they were to do, so these verses are in chapter **2**.

I would draw your attention to verse 27 of the above narrative, as everyone may not be aware that this verse is part of Peter's sermon on the day of Pentecost.

Because thou wilt not leave my soul in hell, neither wilt thou suffer thine Holy One to see corruption.

The parallel passage is in Psalm 16:10. *For thou wilt not leave my soul in hell; neither wilt thou suffer thine Holy One to see corruption.*

No. 4

Now Peter and John **(Peter and John)** *went up together into the* *temple at the hour of prayer, [being] the ninth [hour].*

And a certain man lame from his mother's womb was carried, whom they laid daily at the gate of the temple which is called Beautiful, to ask alms of them that entered into the temple;

Who seeing Peter and John about to go into the temple asked an alms.

And Peter, fastening his eyes upon him with John, said, Look on us (LOOK ON US).

And he gave heed unto them, expecting to receive something of them.

Then Peter said, Silver and gold have I none; but such as I have give I thee: In the name of Jesus Christ of Nazareth rise up and walk.

And he took him by the right hand, and lifted [him] up: and immediately his feet and ancle bones received strength.

And he leaping up stood, and walked, and entered with them into the temple, walking, and leaping, and praising God. Acts 3:1-8.

These verses describe a miracle performed by God through Peter, so they are in the book of Acts.

LOOK ON US - **3** words, so these verses are in chapter **3**.

No. 5

Repent ye therefore (REPENT YE THEREFORE), and be converted, that your sins may be blotted out, when the times of refreshing shall come from the presence of the Lord;

And he shall send Jesus Christ, which before was preached unto you:

Whom the heaven must receive until the times of restitution of all things, which God hath spoken by the mouth of all his holy prophets since the world began. Acts 3:19-21.

Peter is preaching in these verses, so they are in the book of Acts.

REPENT YE THEREFORE – **3** words, so these verses are in chapter **3**.

No. 6

This is the stone (the stone) which was set at nought (the stone which was set at nought) of you builders, which is become the head of the corner (HEAD OF THE CORNER).

Neither is there salvation in any other: for there is none other name under heaven given among men, whereby we must be saved (WE MUST BE SAVED). Acts 4:11-12.

The Lord Jesus is referred to as a tried Stone, a precious corner Stone, that Stone, this Stone, the chief corner Stone, a living Stone and a Stone of stumbling. The words 'set at nought' are used five times in Scripture, and the words 'set him at nought' is used once. However, the book of Acts chapter 4:11 is the only place in Scripture where the words **'the stone which was set at nought'** are used.

For the purpose of association, think that a **stone** is used for building, and the book of Acts is about the building of the church. Also for the purpose of association, think that there was an **act** of despising **(set at nought)** in verse 11, so these verses are in the book of **Acts**.

HEAD OF THE CORNER – **4** words, so they are in chapter **4**.
Or – Jesus is the **HEAD** of the corner – **4** letters in **HEAD**.
Or – **WE MUST BE SAVED** – **4** words.

No. 7
But a certain man named Ananias, with Sapphira his wife, sold a possession,
And kept back [part] of the price (PRICE), his wife also being privy [to it], and brought a certain part, and laid [it] at the apostles' feet. Acts 5:1-2.

This was a sinful **act** committed by Ananias and Sapphira, so these verses are in the book of **Acts**.

PRICE - **5** letters, so they are in chapter **5**.

No. 8
And in those days, when the number of the disciples was multiplied, there arose a murmuring of the Grecians against the Hebrews, because their widows (WIDOWS) were neglected in the daily ministration.
Then the twelve called the multitude of the disciples [unto them], and said, It is not reason that we should leave the word of God, and

serve tables.

Wherefore, brethren, look ye out among you seven men **(seven men)** *of honest report, full of the Holy Ghost and wisdom, whom we may appoint over this business.*

But we will give ourselves continually to prayer, and to the ministry of the word.

And the saying pleased the whole multitude: and they chose Stephen, a man full of faith and of the Holy Ghost, and Philip, and Prochorus, and Nicanor, and Timon, and Parmenas, and Nicolas a proselyte of Antioch:

Whom they set before the apostles: and when they had prayed, they laid [their] hands on them. Acts 6:1-6.

Remember I stated at the beginning of this book that the choosing of the **seven deacons** in the early church is recorded in the book of Acts, so these verses are obviously in the book of Acts.

WIDOWS – 6 letters, so they are in chapter **6**.

No. 9
And they stoned Stephen **(STEPHEN)**, *calling upon [God], and saying, Lord Jesus, receive my spirit.*

And he kneeled down, and cried with a loud voice, Lord, lay not this sin to their charge. And when he had said this, he fell asleep. Acts 7:59-60.

Verses 2-56 of this chapter record Stephen's oration; therefore they are in the book of Acts.

The above two verses record his murder.

STEPHEN – 7 letters, so these verses are in chapter **7**.

No. 10
And when Simon saw that through laying on of the apostles' hands the Holy Ghost was given, he offered them money.

Saying, Give me also this power, that on whomsoever I lay hands, he may receive the Holy Ghost.

But Peter said unto him, Thy money **(THY MONEY)** *perish with* *thee, because thou hast thought that the gift of God may be purchased with money.* Acts 8:18-20.

These verses are about a manifestation of the Holy Spirit through the apostle Peter; therefore they are in the book of Acts.

Simon thought he could **buy** the power that Peter was demonstrating, so you could think of **money** as being the problem on this occasion.

THY MONEY - **8** letters, so these verses are in chapter **8**.

No. 11
And the angel of the Lord spake unto Philip, saying, Arise, and go toward the south unto the way that goeth down from Jerusalem unto Gaza, which is desert.
*And he arose and went: and, behold, a man of Ethiopia (**ETHIO-PIA**), an eunuch of great authority under Candace queen of the Ethiopians, who had the charge of all her treasure, and had come to Jerusalem for to worship,* Acts 8:26-27.

*Then Philip opened his mouth, and began at the same scripture, and preached (**preached**) unto him Jesus.* Acts 8:35.

This was a sermon by Philip the evangelist. He was one of the seven deacons chosen in the early church, so these verses are in the book of Acts.

ETHIOPIA – **8** letters, so they are in chapter **8**.

No. 12
*And he (Saul) said, Who art thou, Lord? And the Lord said, I am Jesus whom thou persecutest: [it is] hard for thee to kick against the pricks (**THE PRICKS**).* Acts 9:5.

I imagine most people would be aware that this verse is in the book of Acts.

THE PRICKS – **9** letters, so it is in chapter **9**.

Pricks are only mentioned in one other verse of Scripture and that is Numbers 33:55. *But if ye will not drive out the inhabitants of the land from before you; then it shall come to pass, that those which ye let remain of them [shall be] pricks (pricks) in your eyes, and thorns in your sides, and shall vex you in the land wherein ye dwell.*

No. 13
Now there was at Joppa a certain disciple named Tabitha, which by interpretation is called Dorcas: this woman was full of good works and almsdeeds (ALMSDEEDS) which she did.

And it came to pass in those days, that she was sick, and died: whom when they had washed, they laid [her] in an upper chamber.

And forasmuch as Lydda was nigh to Joppa, and the disciples had heard that Peter was there, they sent unto him two men, desiring [him] that he would not delay to come to them.

Then Peter arose and went with them. When he was come, they brought him into the upper chamber: and all the widows stood by him weeping, and shewing the coats and garments which Dorcas made, while she was with them.

But Peter put them all forth, and kneeled down, and prayed; and turning [him] to the body said, Tabitha, arise. And she opened her eyes: and when she saw Peter, she sat up.

And he gave her [his] hand, and lifted her up, and when he had called the saints and widows, presented her alive. Acts 9:36-41.

A mighty miracle performed by God through Peter is recorded in these verses, so they are in the book of Acts.

ALMSDEEDS – **9** letters, so these verses are in chapter **9**.

This is the only place in Scripture where the word 'almsdeeds' is used.

No. 14
There was a certain man in Caesarea called Cornelius (Cornelius), a centurion of the band called the Italian [band],

[A] devout [man], and one that feared God with all his house, which gave much alms to the people, and prayed to God alway.

He saw in a vision evidently about the ninth hour of the day an angel

of God coming in to him, and saying unto him, Cornelius.
And when he looked on him, he was afraid, and said, What is it,
Lord? And he said unto him, Thy prayers and thine alms are come
up for a memorial before God.
And now send men to Joppa, and call for [one] Simon, whose sur-
name is Peter: Acts 10:1-5.

And as Peter was coming in, Cornelius met him, and fell down at
*his feet, and worshipped **(WORSHIPPED)** [him].*
But Peter took him up, saying, Stand up; I myself also am a man.
Acts 10:25-26.

These verses record a manifestation from Heaven to **Cornelius**
in which the Lord requires him to summon Simon Peter, so they
are in the book of Acts.

WORSHIPPED – 10 letters, so these verses are in chapter **10**.

No. 15
On the morrow, as they went on their journey, and drew nigh unto
the city, Peter went up upon the housetop to pray about the sixth hour:
And he became very hungry, and would have eaten: but while they
made ready, he fell into a trance,
And saw heaven opened, and a certain vessel descending unto him,
*as it had been a great sheet **(GREAT SHEET)** knit at the four corners,*
and let down to the earth:
Wherein were all manner of fourfooted beasts of the earth, and wild
beasts, and creeping things, and fowls of the air.
And there came a voice to him, Rise, Peter; kill, and eat.
But Peter said, Not so, Lord; for I have never eaten any thing that
is common or unclean. Acts 10:9-14.

Remember I stated at the beginning of this book that any manifestations from Heaven to the disciples when Jesus is not present
are recorded in the book of Acts; therefore these verses are in the
book of Acts.

GREAT SHEET – 10 letters, so they are in chapter **10**.

No. 16

Peter therefore was kept in prison: but prayer was made without ceasing of the church unto God for him.

And when Herod would have brought him forth, the same night Peter was sleeping between two soldiers, bound with two chains: and the keepers before the door kept the prison.

And, behold, the angel of the Lord came upon [him], and a light shined in the prison: and he smote Peter on the side, and raised him up, saying, Arise up quickly. And his chains fell off from [his] hands.

And the angel said unto him, Gird thyself, and bind on thy sandals. And so he did. And he saith unto him, Cast thy garment about thee, and follow me. Acts 12:5-8.

And when he had considered [the thing], he came to the house of Mary the mother of John, whose surname was Mark; where many were gathered together praying.

And as Peter knocked at the door of the gate, a damsel came to hearken, named Rhoda.

And when she knew Peter's voice, she opened not the gate for gladness, but ran in, and told how Peter stood before the gate.

*And they said unto her, Thou art mad. But she constantly affirmed that it was even so. Then said they, It is his angel (**IT IS HIS ANGEL**).* Acts 12:12-15.

Remember I stated at the beginning of this book that any manifestations from Heaven to the disciples when Jesus is not present are recorded in the book of Acts; therefore these verses are in the book of Acts.

IT IS HIS ANGEL – **12** letters, so they are in chapter **12**.

This is the only place in Scripture where the words '*It is his angel*' are recorded.

No. 17

Now as soon as it was day, there was no small stir among the soldiers, what was become of Peter.

And when Herod had sought for him, and found him not, he examined the keepers, and commanded that [they] should be put to death. And he went down from Judaea to Caesarea, and [there] abode.

And Herod was highly displeased with them of Tyre and Sidon: but they came with one accord to him, and, having made Blastus the king's chamberlain their friend, desired peace; because their country was nourished by the king's [country].

And upon a set day Herod, arrayed in royal apparel, sat upon his throne, and made an oration unto them.

And the people gave a shout, [saying, It is] the voice of a god, and not of a man.

And immediately the angel of the Lord smote him, because he gave not God the glory: and he was eaten of worms, **(EATEN OF WORMS)***, and gave up the ghost.* Acts 12:18-23.

These verses are about Peter, so they are in the book of Acts.

EATEN OF WORMS – **12** letters, so these verses are in chapter **12**.

No. 18

Now there were in the church that was at Antioch certain prophets and teachers; as Barnabas, and Simeon **(SIMEON)** *that was called Niger* **(NIGER)***, and Lucius* **(LUCIUS)** *of Cyrene* **(CYRENE)***, and Manaen, which had been brought up with Herod the tetrarch, and Saul.*

As they ministered to the Lord, and fasted, the Holy Ghost said, Separate me Barnabas and Saul for the work whereunto I have called them.

And when they had fasted and prayed, and laid [their] hands on them, they sent [them] away.

So they, being sent forth by the Holy Ghost, departed unto Seleucia; and from thence they sailed to Cyprus. Acts 13:1-4.

These verses are about Barnabas and Saul, so they are in the book of Acts.

SIMEON NIGER - **11** letters
LUCIUS CYRENE - **12** letters
Chapter   - **13**

This association is different. I think it is self- explanatory.

No. 19

And when they had gone through the isle unto Paphos, they found a certain sorcerer, a false prophet, a Jew, whose name [was] Barjesus:

Which was with the deputy of the country, Sergius Paulus (SERGIUS PAULUS), a prudent man; who called for Barnabas and Saul, and desired to hear the word of God.

But Elymas the sorcerer (for so is his name by interpretation) withstood them, seeking to turn away the deputy from the faith.

Then Saul (Saul), (who also [is called] Paul (Paul),) filled with the Holy Ghost, set his eyes on him,

And said, O full of all subtilty and all mischief, [thou] child of the devil, [thou] enemy of all righteousness, wilt thou not cease to pervert the right ways of the Lord?

And now, behold, the hand of the Lord [is] upon thee, and thou shalt be blind, not seeing the sun for a season. And immediately there fell on him a mist and a darkness; and he went about seeking some to lead him by the hand.

Then the deputy, when he saw what was done, believed, being astonished at the doctrine of the Lord. Acts 13:6-12.

Remember I stated at the beginning of this book that any miracles performed by God through the disciples are recorded in the book of Acts; therefore these verses are in the book of Acts.

SERGIUS PAULUS – 13 letters, so they are in chapter **13**.

If you wish to remember where **Saul** was first called **Paul** that is quite simple, because it is in the narrative about Sergius **Paul**us.

No. 20

Then Paul and Barnabas (Paul and Barnabas) waxed bold, and said, It was necessary that the word of God should first have been spoken to you: but seeing ye put it from you, and judge yourselves unworthy of everlasting life, lo, we turn to the Gentiles (TO THE GENTILES). Acts 13:46.

Remember I stated at the beginning of this book that the phrase '**Paul and Barnabas**' is only found in the book of Acts; therefore this verse is in the book of Acts.

TO THE GENTILES – **13** letters, so it is in chapter **13**.

No. 21
And there sat a certain man at Lystra, impotent in his feet, being a cripple from his mother's womb, who never had walked:
The same heard Paul speak: who stedfastly beholding him, and perceiving that he had faith to be healed,
Said with a loud voice, Stand upright on thy feet. And he leaped and walked.
And when the people saw what Paul had done, they lifted up their voices, saying in the speech of Lycaonia, The gods are come down to us in the likeness of men.
*And they called Barnabas, Jupiter (**BARNABAS, JUPITER**); and Paul, Mercurius (**PAUL MERCURIUS**), because he was the chief speaker.* Acts 14:8-12.

These verses are about Paul and Barnabas, so they are in the book of Acts.

BARNABAS JUPITER	- **15** letters
Chapter	- **14**
PAUL MERCURIUS	- **13** letters

This is a different type of association. I think it is self-explanatory.

No. 22
And some days after Paul said unto Barnabas, Let us go again and visit our brethren in every city where we have preached the word of the Lord, [and see] how they do.
And Barnabas determined to take with them John, whose surname was Mark.
But Paul thought not good to take him with them, who departed from them from Pamphylia, and went not with them to the work.
*And the contention was so sharp between them, that they departed asunder (**DEPARTED ASUNDER**) one from the other: and so Barnabas took Mark, and sailed unto Cyprus;*
And Paul chose Silas, and departed, being recommended by the brethren unto the grace of God.
And he went through Syria and Cilicia, confirming the churches. Acts 15:36-41.

These verses are about one of Paul's journeys, so they are in the book of Acts.

DEPARTED ASUNDER – **15** letters, so these verses are in chapter **15**.

No. 23
Then came he to Derbe and Lystra: and, behold, a certain disciple was there, named Timotheus, the son of a certain woman, which was a Jewess, and believed; but his father [was] a Greek:
Which was well reported of by the brethren that were at Lystra and Iconium.
Him would Paul have to go forth with him; and took and circumcised him because of the Jews **(BECAUSE OF THE JEWS)** *which were in those quarters: for they knew all that his father was a Greek.*
And as they went through the cities, they delivered them the decrees for to keep, that were ordained of the apostles and elders which were at Jerusalem.
And so were the churches established in the faith, and increased in number daily. Acts 16:1-5.

These verses are about Paul travelling around, so they are in the book of Acts.

BECAUSE OF THE JEWS – **16** letters, so these verses are in chapter **16**.

No. 24
And a vision appeared to Paul in the night; There stood a man of Macedonia, and prayed him, saying, Come over into Macedonia **(Come over into Macedonia)**, *and help us.*
And after he had seen the vision, immediately we endeavoured to go into Macedonia, assuredly gathering that the Lord had called us for to preach the gospel unto them. Acts 16:9-10.

These verses are about Paul journeying around, so they are in the book of Acts.

VISIT TO MACEDONIA – **16** letters, so these verses are in chapter **16**.

No. 25

And on the sabbath we went out of the city by a river side, where prayer was wont to be made; and we sat down, and spake unto the women which resorted [thither].

*And a certain woman named Lydia (**And a certain woman named Lydia**), a seller of purple, of the city of Thyatira, which worshipped God, heard [us]: whose heart the Lord opened, that she attended unto the things which were spoken of Paul.*

And when she was baptized, and her household, she besought [us], saying, If ye have judged me to be faithful to the Lord, come into my house, and abide [there]. And she constrained us. Acts 16:13-15.

These verses inform us that the apostle Paul had spoken to a woman named Lydia, so they are in the book of Acts.

A WOMAN NAMED LYDIA – **16** letters, so these verses are in chapter **16**.

No. 26

*And it came to pass, as we went to prayer (**AS WE WENT TO PRAYER**), a certain damsel possessed with a spirit of divination met us, which brought her masters much gain by soothsaying:*

The same followed Paul and us, and cried, saying, These men are the servants of the most high God, which shew unto us the way of salvation.

And this did she many days. But Paul, being grieved, turned and said to the spirit, I command thee in the name of Jesus Christ to come out of her. And he came out the same hour.

And when her masters saw that the hope of their gains was gone, they caught Paul and Silas, and drew [them] into the marketplace unto the rulers,

And brought them to the magistrates, saying, These men, being Jews, do exceedingly trouble our city,

And teach customs, which are not lawful for us to receive, neither to observe, being Romans. Acts 16:16-21.

These verses are about Paul, so they are in the book of Acts.

AS WE WENT TO PRAYER – **16** letters, so these verses are in chapter **16**.

No. 27

*And at midnight Paul and Silas prayed, and sang praises unto God:
and the prisoners heard them.*

*And suddenly there was a great earthquake (A GREAT EARTH-
QUAKE), so that the foundations of the prison were shaken: and
immediately all the doors were opened, and every one's bands were
loosed. Acts 16:25-26.*

These verses are about Paul, so they are in the book of Acts.

A GREAT EARTHQUAKE – 16 letters, so these verses are in
chapter **16**.

No. 28

*Now when they had passed through Amphipolis and Apollonia, they
came to Thessalonica, where was a synagogue of the Jews:*

*And Paul, as his manner was, went in unto them, and three sabbath
days reasoned with them out of the scriptures,*

*Opening and alleging, that Christ must needs have suffered, and
risen again from the dead; and that this Jesus, whom I preach unto
you, is Christ.*

*And some of them believed, and consorted with Paul and Silas;
and of the devout Greeks a great multitude, and of the chief women
not a few.*

*But the Jews which believed not, moved with envy, took unto them
certain lewd fellows of the baser sort, and gathered a company, and
set all the city on an uproar, and assaulted the house of Jason, and
sought to bring them out to the people.*

*And when they found them not, they drew Jason and certain breth-
ren unto the rulers of the city, crying, These that have turned the world
upside down are come hither also;*

*Whom Jason hath received (JASON HATH RECEIVED): and these
all do contrary to the decrees of Caesar, saying that there is another
king, [one] Jesus.*

*And they troubled the people and the rulers of the city, when they
heard these things.*

*And when they had taken security of Jason, and of the other, they
let them go. Acts 17:1-9.*

These verses are about Paul journey around, so they are in the
book of Acts.

185

JASON HATH RECEIVED – **17** letters, so these verses are in chapter **17**.

No. 29
*And the brethren immediately sent away Paul and Silas by night unto Berea **(Berea)**: who coming [thither] went into the synagogue of the Jews.*

*These were more noble **(noble)** than those in Thessalonica, in that they received the word with all readiness of mind, and searched the scriptures daily, whether those things were so.*

Therefore many of them believed; also of honourable women which were Greeks, and of men, not a few.

But when the Jews of Thessalonica had knowledge that the word of God was preached of Paul at Berea, they came thither also, and stirred up the people. Acts 17:10-13.

These verses are about Paul journeying around, so they are in the book of Acts.

BEREA FOLK ARE NOBLE – **17** letters, so these verses are in chapter **17**.

The above sentence should be '**Berean folk are noble,**' but that would render 18 letters.

No. 30
And they took him (Paul), *and brought him unto Areopagus **(ARE-OPAGUS)**, saying, May we know what this new doctrine, whereof thou speakest, [is]?*

For thou bringest certain strange things to our ears: we would know therefore what these things mean.

(For all the Athenians and strangers which were there spent their time in nothing else, but either to tell, or to hear some new thing.)

*Then Paul stood in the midst of Mars' hill **(MARS' HILL)**, and said, [Ye] men of Athens, I perceive that in all things ye are too superstitious.*

For as I passed by, and beheld your devotions, I found an altar with this inscription, TO THE UNKNOWN GOD. Whom therefore ye ignorantly worship, him declare I unto you.

God that made the world and all things therein, seeing that he is Lord of heaven and earth, dwelleth not in temples made with hands;

Neither is worshipped with men's hands, as though he needed any thing, seeing he giveth to all life, and breath, and all things;

And hath made of one blood all nations of men for to dwell on all the face of the earth, and hath determined the times before appointed, and the bounds of their habitation;

That they should seek the Lord, if haply they might feel after him, and find him, though he be not far from every one of us:

For in him we live, and move, and have our being; as certain also of your own poets have said, For we are also his offspring.

Forasmuch then as we are the offspring of God, we ought not to think that the Godhead is like unto gold, or silver, or stone, graven by art and man's device.

And the times of this ignorance God winked at; but now commandeth all men every where to repent:

Because he hath appointed a day, in the which he will judge the world in righteousness by [that] man whom he hath ordained; [whereof] he hath given assurance unto all [men], in that he hath raised him from the dead. Acts 17:19-31.

This is a sermon by Paul, so these verses are in the book of Acts.

AREOPAGUS MARS' HILL – 17 letters, so they are in chapter **17**.

No. 31

Then spake the Lord to Paul in the night by a vision, Be not afraid, but speak, and hold not thy peace:

For I am with thee, and no man shall set on thee to hurt thee: for I have much people **(FOR I HAVE MUCH PEOPLE)** *in this city.* (Corinth). Acts 18:9-10.

This is a manifestation from Heaven to Paul, so these verses are in the book of Acts.

FOR I HAVE MUCH PEOPLE – 18 letters, so they are in chapter **18**.

No. 32

And it came to pass, that, while Apollos was at Corinth, Paul having passed through the upper coasts came to Ephesus: and finding certain disciples,

He said unto them, Have ye received the Holy Ghost since ye believed? And they said unto him, We have not so much as heard whether there be any Holy Ghost.

And he said unto them, Unto what then were ye baptized? And they said, Unto John's baptism.

Then said Paul, John verily baptized with the baptism of repentance **(BAPTISM OF REPENTANCE)**, *saying unto the people, that they should believe on him which should come after him, that is, on Christ Jesus.*

When they heard [this], they were baptized in the name of the Lord Jesus.

And when Paul had laid [his] hands upon them, the Holy Ghost came on them; and they spake with tongues, and prophesied.

And all the men were about twelve. Acts 19:1-7.

These verses are about Paul journeying around, so they are in the book of Acts.

BAPTISM OF REPENTANCE – 19 letters, so these verses are in chapter **19**.

No. 33

Then certain of the vagabond Jews, exorcists, took upon them to call over them which had evil spirits the name of the Lord Jesus, saying, We adjure you by Jesus whom Paul preacheth. **(We adjure you by Jesus whom Paul preacheth).**

And there were seven sons of [one] Sceva **(SEVEN SONS OF [ONE] SCEVA)**, *a Jew, [and] chief of the priests, which did so.*

And the evil spirit answered and said, Jesus I know, and Paul I know; but who are ye?

And the man in whom the evil spirit was leaped on them, and overcame them, and prevailed against them, so that they fled out of that house naked and wounded. Acts 19:13-16.

Paul had been preaching: '**We adjure you by Jesus whom Paul preacheth**,' so these verses are in the book of Acts.

SEVEN SONS OF [ONE] SCEVA – 19 letters, so they are in chapter **19**.

No. 34
*And many that believed **(many that believed)** came, and confessed, and shewed their deeds.*
Many of them also which used curious arts brought their books together, and burned them before all [men]: and they counted the price of them, and found [it] fifty thousand [pieces] of silver.
So mightily grew the word of God and prevailed. Acts 19:18-20.

This happening was in **Ephesus**.

The people believed the message of the apostle Paul - '*many that believed,*' so these verses are in the book of Acts.

BOOKS BURNT AT EPHESUS – 19 letters, so they are in chapter **19**.

No. 35
*And there sat in a window **(SAT IN A WINDOW)** a certain young man named Eutychus **(EUTYCHUS)**, being fallen into a deep sleep: and as Paul was long preaching, he sunk down with sleep, and fell down from the third loft, and was taken up dead.*
And Paul went down, and fell on him, and embracing [him] said, Trouble not yourselves; for his life is in him.
When he therefore was come up again, and had broken bread, and eaten, and talked a long while, even till break of day, so he departed.
And they brought the young man alive, and were not a little comforted. Acts 20:9-12.

These verses record a miracle performed by God through Paul, so they are in the book of Acts.

EUTYCHUS SAT IN A WINDOW – 20 letters, so these verses are in chapter 20.

No. 36

I suggest that you commit the following two verses to memory.

For I (Paul) *have not shunned to declare unto you all the counsel of* **God (For I have not shunned to declare unto you all the counsel of God).**

Take heed therefore unto yourselves, and to all the flock, over the which the Holy Ghost hath made you overseers, to feed the church of God **(TO FEED THE CHURCH OF GOD)**, *which he hath purchased with his own blood.* Acts 20:27-28.

***For I* (Paul)** *have not shunned to declare unto you all the counsel of God.* Paul preached the whole counsel of God, so these verses are in the book of Acts.

This is the only place in Scripture where the words 'all the counsel of God' are recorded.

TO FEED THE CHURCH OF GOD – **20** letters, so these verses are in chapter **20**.

No. 37

And as we tarried [there] (Caesarea) *many days, there came down from Judaea a certain prophet, named Agabus* **(Agabus).**

And when he was come unto us, he took Paul's girdle **(he took Paul's girdle)**, *and bound his own hands and feet, and said, Thus saith the Holy Ghost, So shall the Jews at Jerusalem bind the man that owneth this girdle, and shall deliver [him] into the hands of the Gentiles.*

And when we heard these things, both we, and they of that place, besought him not to go up to Jerusalem.

Then Paul answered, What mean ye to weep and to break mine heart? for I am ready not to be bound only, but also to die at Jerusalem for the name of the Lord Jesus. Acts 21:10-13.

These verses are about Paul being bound by the Jews for preaching about Jesus, so they are in the book of Acts.

AGABUS TOOK PAUL'S GIRDLE – **21** letters, so these verses are in chapter **21**.

No. 38

*And when Paul's sister's son heard of their lying in wait (**HEARD OF THEIR LYING IN WAIT**), he went and entered into the castle, and told Paul.*

Then Paul called one of the centurions unto [him], and said, Bring this young man unto the chief captain: for he hath a certain thing to tell him.

So he took him, and brought [him] to the chief captain, and said, Paul the prisoner called me unto [him], and prayed me to bring this young man unto thee, who hath something to say unto thee.

Then the chief captain took him by the hand, and went [with him] aside privately, and asked [him], What is that thou hast to tell me?

And he said, The Jews have agreed to desire thee that thou wouldest bring down Paul to morrow into the council, as though they would inquire somewhat of him more perfectly. Acts 23:16-20.

These verses are about Paul, so they are in the book of Acts.

HEARD OF THEIR LYING IN WAIT – **23** letters, so these verses are in chapter **23**.

Or - **PAUL'S NEPHEW SAVES HIS LIFE** – **23** letters.

No. 39

And after certain days, when Felix came with his wife Drusilla, which was a Jewess, he sent for Paul, and heard him concerning the faith in Christ.

*And as he reasoned of righteousness, temperance, and judgment to come, Felix trembled, and answered (**FELIX TREMBLED AND ANSWERED**), Go thy way for this time; when I have a convenient season, I will call for thee. Acts 24:24-25.*

Paul speaks to Felix concerning the gospel, so these verses are in the book of Acts.

FELIX TREMBLED AND ANSWERED – **24** letters, so they are in chapter 24.

Or - **FELIX THE GOVERNOR TREMBLED** – **24** letters.

No. 40
*Then Agrippa said unto Paul, Almost thou persuadest me (**Then Agrippa said unto Paul, Almost thou persuadest me**) to be a Christian.* Acts 26:28.

This verse is about Paul, so it is in the book of Acts.

KING AGRIPPA ALMOST PERSUADED – **26** letters, so this verse is in chapter **26**.

ROMANS

No. 1
*For I am not ashamed of the gospel of Christ: for it is the power of God unto salvation to every one that believeth; to the Jew first (**first**), and also to the Greek.* Romans 1:16.

For the purpose of association, think about not being ashamed of the gospel of Christ no matter where you are, and that includes being under Roman domination, so this verse is in the book of Romans.

First means number **1**, so it is in chapter **1**.

No. 2
*For he is not a Jew (**Jew**), which is one outwardly (**outwardly**); neither [is that] circumcision, which is outward in the flesh:*
*But he [is] a Jew, which is one inwardly (**inwardly**); and circumcision [is that] of the heart, in the spirit, [and] not in the letter; whose praise [is] not of men, but of God.* **Romans** 2:28-29.

The **Jews** demanded that Jesus be crucified and the **Romans** crucified Him. Two groups of people, so when you read these verses, think of the Jews and the Romans, and then you will remember that they are in the book of Romans.

(1) outwardly
(2) inwardly

2 states, so these verses are in chapter **2**.

No. 3
*For all (ALL) have sinned (ALL HAVE SINNED), and come short
of the glory of God;* Ro**man**s 3:23.

This association is somewhat different.
Letters three, four and five of Ro**man**s spell **man** and this verse
is referring to **man**kind, (**ALL** of **man**kind have sinned), so this
verse is in the book of Romans.

ALL HAVE SINNED - 3 words, so it is in chapter **3**.

Or: **ALL – 3** letters.

No. 4
*For what saith the scripture (WHAT SAITH THE SCRIPTURE)?
Abraham believed God, and it was counted unto him for righteous-
ness.* **R**omans 4:3.

This verse is about the imputed righteousness of Christ to Abraham. The imputed righteousness (**R** for righteousness and **R** for
Romans) of Abraham is mentioned in both the Old Testament
and the New Testament, and is a cardinal doctrine of the Christian
faith. The books of Romans and Revelation are the only books of
the New Testament starting with **R**. If you have some knowledge
of Scripture you would know that this verse is not in the book of
Revelation, therefore it is in the book of Romans.

WHAT SAITH THE SCRIPTURE? This is the question that
believers must always ask - **4** words, so this verse is in chapter **4**.

Or - **WHAT saith the scripture? 4** letters.

No. 5
*Blessed [is] the man (**BLESSED IS THE MAN**) to whom the Lord will not impute sin (**WILL NOT IMPUTE SIN**).* Romans 4:8.

The parallel passage is Psalm 32:2.
Blessed [is] the man unto whom the LORD imputeth not iniquity, and in whose spirit [there is] no guile. Psalm 32:2.

Blessed can be defined as enjoying great happiness. Even under Roman rule, a man to whom the Lord will not impute sin can be happy, so this verse is in the book of Romans.

The man to whom the Lord will not impute sin is **FREE**. There are **4** letters in free, so this verse is in chapter **4**.

Or - **BLESSED IS THE MAN** – **4** words.

Or - **WILL NOT IMPUTE SIN** – **4** words.

No. 6
*Therefore being justified by faith, we have peace with God (**WE HAVE PEACE WITH GOD**) through our Lord Jesus Christ:* Romans 5:1.

For the purpose of association, think that even under **Roman** rule if one was justified by faith then thy had **peace with God**, so this verse is in the book of Romans.

WE HAVE PEACE WITH GOD – **5** words, so it is in chapter **5**.

No. 7
*For as by one man's (**ADAM'S**) disobedience (**disobedience**) many were made sinners, so by the obedience of one* (Jesus) *shall many be made righteous.* Romans 5:19.

One would probably feel like being **disobedient** under Roman rule, so this verse is in the book of Romans.

ADAM'S - **5** letters, so it is in chapter **5**.

No. 8
*For the wages of sin [is] death (**THE WAGES OF SIN IS DEATH**); but the gift of God [is] eternal life through Jesus Christ our Lord.* Romans 6:23.

For the purpose of association, think that **sin** and **death** were rampant when the Romans were in power, so this verse is in the book of Romans.

Just remember that **THE WAGES OF SIN IS DEATH – 6** words, so this verse is in chapter **6**.

No. 9
*[There is] therefore now no condemnation to them which are in Christ Jesus (**no condemnation to them which are in Christ Jesus**), who walk not after the flesh, but after the Spirit.* Romans 8:1.

For the purpose of association, think that even though the **Romans** condemned people, there is **no condemnation** to those who are in Christ Jesus, so this verse is in the book of Romans.

NO CONDEMNATION FOR THE FOLLOWERS OF JESUS CHRIST – 8 words, so it is in chapter **8**.

I would suggest that you memorize at least the first seventeen verses of Romans chapter 8.

No. 10
*But ye are not in the flesh, but in the Spirit, if so be that the Spirit of God dwell in you. Now if any man have not the Spirit of Christ (**Now if any man have not the Spirit of Christ**), he is none of his.* Romans 8:9.

For the purpose of association, think that the **Romans** definitely did not have the **Spirit of Christ** when they were persecuting the Christians, so this verse is in the book of Romans.

NOBODY BELONGS TO CHRIST WITHOUT HAVING HIS SPIRIT – 8 words, so it is in chapter **8**

No. 11
I suggest that you memorize the following five verses.

*Who shall separate us from the love of Christ? [shall] tribulation, or distress, or persecution (**persecution**), or famine, or nakedness, or peril, or sword?*
As it is written, For thy sake we are killed all the day long; we are accounted as sheep for the slaughter.
*Nay, in all these things we are more than conquerors through him that loved us (**MORE THAN CONQUERORS THROUGH HIM THAT LOVED US**).*
For I am persuaded, that neither death, nor life, nor angels, nor principalities, nor powers, nor things present, nor things to come,
*Nor height, nor depth, nor any other creature, shall be able to separate (**SEPARATE**) us from the love of God, which is in Christ Jesus our Lord.* Romans 8:35-39.

It's not difficult to get an association for these verses. The Romans used persecution, and the word **persecution** is actually recorded in verse 35, so they are in the book of Romans.

MORE THAN CONQUERORS THROUGH HIM THAT LOVED US - **8** words, so these verses are in chapter **8**.

Or: **SEPARATE** – **8** letters.

No. 12
*For with the heart man believeth (**believeth**) unto righteousness; and with the mouth confession (**confession**) is made unto salvation.* Romans 10:10.

For the purpose of association, think that **confession** of salvation would be necessary even under **Roman** rule, so this verse is in the book of Romans.

This is the only place in Scripture where the word **confession** is used concerning salvation.
The only other place in the New Testament where the word confession is used is in 1st Timothy 6:13. *I give thee charge in the sight of God, who quickeneth all things, and [before] Christ Jesus, who*

before Pontius Pilate witnessed a good **confession;**

The number **10** signifies the perfection of Divine order; surely this verse clearly shows Divine order, **believing first** and **then confessing**, so it is in chapter **10**.

No. 13
For whosoever shall call upon the name of the Lord (call upon the name of the Lord) shall be saved. Romans 10:13.

Even under Roman domination it was possible to **call upon the name of the Lord,** so this verse is in the book of Romans.

For the purpose of association, think of lifting up your hands in prayer as you call upon God. Paul speaks of this in his epistle to Timothy: 1 Timothy 2:8. *I will therefore that men pray every where, lifting up holy hands, without wrath and doubting.*

Also for the purpose of association, think that each hand has 5 fingers making a total of **10** fingers, so this verse is in chapter **10**.

No. 14
I suggest that you memorize the following 4 verses.

How then shall they call on him in whom they have not believed? and how shall they believe in him of whom they have not heard? and how shall they hear without a preacher?
*And how shall they preach, except they be sent? as it is written, How beautiful are the feet of them that preach the gospel of peace, and bring glad tidings of good things (**GOOD THINGS**)!*
But they have not all obeyed the gospel. For Esaias saith, Lord, who hath believed our report?
*So then faith [cometh] by hearing, and hearing by the word of God **(faith [cometh] by hearing, and hearing by the word of God).***
Romans 10:14-17.

As the **Roman** Empire expanded, and began to include people from a variety of cultures, the worship of an ever-increasing number of gods was tolerated and accepted.

In the midst of a multi-god culture it was still true that *'faith [cometh] by hearing, and hearing by the word of God.'* Romans 10:17, so these verses are in the book of **Romans**.

GOOD THINGS – **10** letters, so they are in chapter **10**.

No. 15
For it is written, [As] I live, saith the Lord, every knee shall bow to me, and every tongue shall confess to God.
*So then every one of us shall give account (**account**) of himself to God. Romans 14:11-12.*

For the purpose of association, think that the Romans will have to give an **account** for all of their wickedness if they did not repent, so these verses are in the book of Romans.

AN ACCOUNT TO GOD – **14** letters, so they are in chapter **14**.

No. 16
*For whatsoever things were written aforetime were written for our learning, that we through patience (**THROUGH PATIENCE**) and comfort of the scriptures (**patience and comfort of the scriptures**) might have hope. Romans 15:4.*

For the purpose of association, think that you would certainly need **patience and the comfort of the Scriptures** under Roman rule, so this verse is in the book of Romans.

THROUGH PATIENCE – **15** letters, so it is in chapter **15**

No. 17
*Now I beseech you, brethren, mark them which cause divisions and offences (**offences**) contrary to the doctrine which ye have learned; and avoid them.*
*For they that are such serve not our Lord Jesus Christ, but their own belly; and by good words and fair speeches deceive the hearts (**DECEIVE THE HEARTS**) of the simple. Romans 16:17-18.*

For the purpose of association, think that the Romans were **offensive**, so these verses are in the book of Romans.

DECEIVE THE HEARTS – 16 letters, so they are in chapter **16**.

No. 18
*And the God of peace shall bruise Satan **(SHALL BRUISE SATAN)** under your feet **(under your feet)** shortly. The grace of our Lord Jesus Christ [be] with you. Amen.* Romans 16:20.

For the purpose of association, think that the Romans would have trampled the people **under their feet** in times of persecution, so this verse is in the book of Romans.

SHALL BRUISE SATAN – 16 letters, so it is in chapter **16**.

1ST CORINTHIANS

No. 1
*For the preaching of the cross **(preaching of the cross)** is to them that perish foolishness; but unto us which are saved it is the power **(power)** of God.* 1st Corinthians 1:18.

This verse mentions 'them that perish:' that is a corporate group. The first syllable of **cor**porate is the same as the first syllable of **Cor**inthians, so this verse is in some book of Corinthians.

The preaching of the cross is the **1st** priority, so it is in the book of **1st** Corinthians.

For the purpose of association, think that the **1st power**ful work that the preaching of the cross effects is conviction of sin by the **power** of God, so this verse is in chapter **1**.

No. 2
I suggest that you commit the following three verses to memory.

For after that in the wisdom of God the world by wisdom knew not God, it pleased God by the foolishness of preaching to save them that believe.
For the Jews require a sign, and the Greeks seek after wisdom:
*But we preach Christ crucified (**But we preach Christ crucified**), unto the Jews a stumblingblock, and unto the Greeks foolishness;*
1st Corinthians 1:21-23.

For the purpose of association, think of the Jews as a **cor**porate group. The first three letters of corporate are the same as the first three letters of **Cor**inthians, so these verses are in some book of Corinthians.

Think that to '**preach Christ crucified**' is of **1st** importance, so they are in the book of **1st** Corinthians.

Also for the purpose of association, think that Christ was crucified **1** time, so these verses are in chapter **1**.

No. 3
*For who maketh thee to differ (**differ**) [from another]? and what hast thou that thou didst not receive? now if thou didst receive [it], why dost thou glory (**WHY DOST THOU GLORY**), as if thou hadst not received [it]?* 1st Corinthians 4:7.

This verse mentions that we **differ** one from another, so for the purpose of association, think of the human race as being a non-corporate group.

The first syllable of **cor**porate is the same as the first syllable of **Cor**inthians, so this verse is in some book of Corinthians.

When you read the question '*who maketh thee to differ [from another].*' answer '**God.**' For the purpose of association, think that God is **1st** because He is before all things, so this verse is in the book of **1st** Corinthians.

200

WHY DOST THOU GLORY - **4** words, so it is in chapter **4**.

No. 4
*For though I preach (**preach**) the gospel (**THE GOSPEL**), I have nothing to glory of: for necessity is laid upon me; yea, woe is unto me, if I preach not the gospel!* 1st Corinthians 9:16.

Ministers **preach** when people are gathered corporately. The first syllable of **cor**porately is the same as the first syllable of **Cor**inthians, so this verse is in some book of Corinthians.

When you read these words say to yourself there is only **1** gospel, so this verse is in the book of **1**st Corinthians.

THE GOSPEL - **9** letters so it is in chapter **9**.

No. 5
*Ye cannot drink the cup of the Lord, and the cup of devils: ye cannot be partakers of the Lord's table (**LORD'S TABLE**), and of the table of devils (**ye cannot be partakers of the Lord's table, and of the table of devils**).* 1st Corinthians 10:21.

For the purpose of association, think that a group of believers at the Lord's Table are a corporate group. The first syllable of **cor**porate is the same as the first syllable of **Cor**inthians, so this verse is in some book of Corinthians.

You cannot be partakers of 2 tables, just 1, so this verse is in the book of **1**st Corinthians.

LORD'S TABLE – **10** letters, so it is in chapter **10**.

This is the only place in Scripture where the term the '**Lord's table**' is used.

No. 6
*But I would have you know, that the head (**head**) of every man is Christ; and the head of the woman [is] the man; and the head of*

Christ [is] God.

Every man praying or prophesying, having [his] head covered **(HEAD COVERED)**, *dishonoureth his head.*

But every woman that prayeth or prophesieth with [her] head **(head)** *uncovered dishonoureth her head: for that is even all one as if she were shaven.*

For if the woman be not covered, let her also be shorn: but if it be a shame for a woman to be shorn or shaven, let her be covered.

For a man indeed ought not to cover [his] head **(head)**, *forasmuch as he is the image and glory of God: but the woman is the glory of the man.*

For the man is not of the woman; but the woman of the man.

Neither was the man created for the woman; but the woman for the man. 1st Corinthians 11:3-9.

These verses are about people gathering corporately for worship.

The first syllable of **cor**porate is the same as the first syllable of **Cor**inthians, so they are in some book of Corinthians.

These verses concern the head covering for women in the place of worship, so the word **'head'** is used frequently in these verses. Head is singular i.e. **1**, so these verses are in the book of **1**st Corinthians.

HEAD COVERED - **11** letters, so they are in chapter **11**.

No. 7

Wherefore tongues **(TONGUES)** *are for a sign* **(a sign)**, *not to them that believe, but to them that believe not: but prophesying [serveth] not for them that believe not, but for them which believe.* 1st Corinthians 14:22.

This verse mentions 'them that believe:' that is a corporate group.

The first syllable of **cor**porate is the same as the first syllable of **Cor**inthians, so this verse is in some book of Corinthians.

For the purpose of association, think that **a** sign means **1** sign, so it is in the book of **1**st Corinthians.

Tongues is a plural word, so for the purpose of association think not 1 tongue (singular) but 2 tongues (plural) i.e. **TONGUES, TONGUES - 14** letters, so this verse is in chapter **14**.

No. 8
*For God is not [the author] (**[the author]**) of confusion (**CONFU-SION**), but of peace (**PEACE**), as in all churches of the saints.*
1st Corinthians 14:33.

For the purpose of association, think of the churches of the saints as a corporate group. The first syllable of **cor**porate is the same as the first syllable of Corinthians, so this verse is in some book of **Cor**inthians.

Also for the purpose of association, think of an **author** as someone who **begins** something. 1st Corinthians is the **beginning** of the books of Corinthians, so this verse is in the book of 1st Corinthians.

CONFUSION PEACE – 14 letters, so it is in chapter **14**.

No. 9
Now this I say, brethren, that flesh and blood cannot inherit the kingdom of God; neither doth corruption inherit incorruption.
*Behold, I shew you a mystery (**SHEW YOU A MYSTERY**); We shall not all sleep, but we (**we**) shall all be changed,*
*In a moment, in the twinkling of an eye, at the last trump (**the last trump**): for the trumpet shall sound, and the dead shall be raised incorruptible, and we shall be changed.*
For this corruptible must put on incorruption, and this mortal [must] put on immortality.
So when this corruptible shall have put on incorruption, and this mortal shall have put on immortality, then shall be brought to pass the saying that is written, Death is swallowed up in victory. 1st Corinthians 15:50-54.

We shall all be changed: For the purpose of association, think of 'we' as a corporate group. The first syllable of **cor**porate is the same as the first syllable of **Cor**inthians, so these verses are in some book of Corinthians.

For the purpose of association think of **the last trump** as being **1** trump, so they are in the book of **1**st Corinthians.

SHEW YOU A MYSTERY – **15** letters, so these verses are in chapter **15**.

2ND CORINTHIANS

No. 1
*Who also hath made us able ministers **(ministers)** of the new **(NEW)** testament; not of the letter, but of the spirit: for the letter killeth **(the letter killeth)**, but the spirit giveth life **(the spirit giveth life)**.* 2nd Corinthians 3:6.

Think of ministers as a corporate group of people. The first 3 letters of **cor**porate are the same as the first three letters of **Cor**inthians, so this verse is in some book of Corinthians.

(1) *the letter killeth*
(2) *the spirit giveth life.*

2 statements, so it is in the book of **2**nd Corinthians.

NEW – **3** letters, so this verse is in chapter **3**.

No. 2
*For we must all appear **(FOR WE MUST ALL APPEAR)** before the judgment seat of Christ; that every one may receive the things [done] in [his] body, according to that he hath done, whether [it be] good or bad **(good or bad)**.* 2 Corinthians 5:10.

We must all appear – For the purpose of association, think of 'we' as a corporate body. The first syllable of **cor**porate is the same as the first syllable of **Cor**inthians, so this verse is in some book of Corinthians.

The verse mentions **good and bad** – **2** kinds of doing, so it is in the book of 2nd Corinthians.

At the judgment there will be a judge: **JUDGE has 5** letters, so this verse is in chapter **5**.

Or - **FOR WE MUST ALL APPEAR** – **5** words

No. 3
Therefore if any man [be] in Christ (in Christ), [he is] a new creature ([HE IS] A NEW CREATURE): old (old) things are passed away; behold, all things are become new (new).
2nd Corinthians 5:17.

This verse is obviously in the New Testament, and it speaks of being **in** Christ. The only books in the New Testament that contain the word **in** are 1st and 2nd Cor**in**thians, so this verse is in some book of Corinthians.

(1) old
(2) new

2 different types of things are mentioned, so it is in the book of 2nd Corinthians.

HE IS A NEW CREATURE – **5** words, so this verse is in chapter **5**.

No. 4
I suggest that you memorize the following two verses.

Now then we are ambassadors (ambassadors) for Christ, as though God did beseech [you] by us: we pray [you] in Christ's stead, be ye reconciled to God (BE YE RECONCILED TO GOD).
For he hath made him [to be] sin for us, who knew no sin; that we might be made the righteousness of God in him.
2nd Corinthians 5:20-21.

For the purpose of association, think of **ambassadors** as being a corporate group. The first syllable of **cor**porate is the same as the first syllable of **Cor**inthians, so these verses are in some book of Corinthians.

(**1**) Jesus was made sin.
(**2**) We are made righteous.

2 happenings, so they are in the book of **2**nd Corinthians.

BE YE RECONCILED TO GOD – **5** words, so these verses are in chapter **5**.

No. 5

Be ye not unequally yoked together **(BE YE NOT UNEQUALLY YOKED TOGETHER)** *with unbelievers: for what fellowship hath righteousness with unrighteousness? and what communion hath light* **(light)** *with darkness* **(darkness)**? 2nd Corinthians 6:14.

For the purpose of association, think of unbelievers as a corporate group. The first syllable of **cor**porate is the same as the first syllable of **Cor**inthians, so this verse is in some book of Corinthians.

Light and **darkness** are mentioned – **2** states, so it is in the book of **2**nd Corinthians.

BE YE NOT UNEQUALLY YOKED TOGETHER – **6** words, so this verse is in chapter **6**.

No. 6

For ye know the grace of our Lord Jesus Christ, that, though he was rich **(RICH)**, *yet for your* **(your)** *sakes he became poor* **(POOR)**, *that ye through his poverty might be rich.* 2 Corinthians 8:9.

For the purpose of association, think of '**your**' as being a corporate group. The first syllable of **cor**porate is the same as the first syllable of **Cor**inthians, so this verse is in some book of Corinthians.

Riches and poverty are mentioned – **2** things, so it is in the book of **2**nd Corinthians.

RICH POOR – **8** letters, so this verse is in chapter **8**.

No. 7
*And lest I should be exalted above measure through the abundance of the revelations (**revelations**), there was given to me a thorn in (**in**) the flesh, the messenger of Satan to buffet me, lest I should be exalted above measure.*
For this thing I besought the Lord thrice, that it might depart from me.
*And he said unto me, My grace is sufficient (**IS SUFFICIENT**) for thee: for my strength is made perfect in weakness. Most gladly therefore will I rather glory in my infirmities (**infirmities**), that the power of Christ may rest upon me.* 2nd Corinthians 12:7-9.

The thorn was **in** Paul's flesh. 1st and 2nd Cor**in**thians are the only books in the New Testament that contain the word '**in**' so these verses are in some book of Corinthians.

Revelations and **infirmities** are **plural** words. For the purpose of association, think of **1**st Corinthians as being **1** and singular, and **2**nd Corinthians as being **2** and plural, so these verses are in the book of 2nd Corinthians.

IS SUFFICIENT – **12** letters, so they are in chapter **12**.

No. 8
*Examine yourselves (**Examine yourselves**), whether ye be in the faith; prove your own selves (**prove your own selves**). Know ye not your own selves, how that Jesus Christ is in you, except ye be reprobates (**reprobates**)?* 2nd Corinthians 13:5.

Examine yourselves: For the purpose of association, think of yourselves as a corporate group. The first syllable of **cor**porate is the same as the first syllable of **Cor**inthians, so this verse is in some book of Corinthians.

We are told to do **2** things:

(1) *Examine yourselves.*

(2) *Prove your own selves.*

2 things we are to do, so this verse is the book of 2nd Corinthians.

Reprobates are mentioned in this chapter. Also for the purpose of association, think that reprobates are rebellious and the number of rebellion is **13**, so this verse is in chapter **13**.

No. 9
The grace of the Lord Jesus Christ, and the love of God, and the communion of the Holy Ghost, **(PARACLETE)** *[be] with you all. Amen.*
2nd Corinthians 13:14.

I am taking a different approach to form an association for this verse.

I have used the word Paraclete instead of Holy Ghost because there would not be the correct number of words for the chapter if I used Holy Ghost.

N.B. I am not adding to the word of God when I use the word Paraclete, I am merely forming an association. The word of God is in *italics* to differentiate it.

The words of the above verse are spoken at the **end** of a worship service, i.e. they are the **final** words, so we can understand them being at the **end** of the **final** chapter.

GRACE OF THE LORD JESUS CHRIST LOVE OF GOD COMMUNION OF THE PARACLETE – **13** words, so this verse is in chapter **13**.

Or – **HOLY PARACLETE** – **13** letters.

2nd Corinthians and Hebrews are the only two books of the New Testament that have **13** chapters.

Hebrews 13:25 ends with the following words. *Grace [be] with you all. Amen.*

208

To enable you to remember that it is the book of 2nd Corinthians chapter 13 and not the book of Hebrews chapter 13, just think that there is 1st and 2nd Corinthians, which together have a total of 29 chapters. Hebrews has 13 chapters. 29 is a bigger number than 13, so the book of 2nd Corinthians ends with a bigger verse than the book of Hebrews.

GALATIANS

No. 1
I suggest that you memorize the following four verses.

I marvel that ye are so soon removed from him that called you into the grace of Christ unto another gospel:
Which is not another; but there be some that trouble you, and would pervert the gospel of Christ.
But though we, or an angel from heaven, preach any other gospel unto you than that which we have preached unto you, let him be accursed.
As we said before, so say I now again, If any [man] preach any other gospel unto you than that ye have received, let him be accursed.
Galatians 1:6-9.

If any man preach any other gospel unto you than that ye have received, let him be accursed. Even if he is a close **relation** we must not listen to him. For the purpose of association, think that **relation** rhymes with **Galatian**, so these verses are in the book of Galatians.

As you read these verses say to yourself there is only **1** gospel, so they are in chapter **1**.

No. 2
But contrariwise, when they saw that the gospel of the uncircumcision was committed unto me (**Paul**)*, as [the gospel] of the circumcision [was] unto Peter* (**Peter**)*;* Galatians 2:7.

For the purpose of association, think of Paul and Peter being brothers in Christ, and having a relationship with Christ and with each other. The second and third syllables of re**lation**ship rhyme with the last two syllables of Ga**latian**, so this verse is in the book of Galatians.

(1) Paul
(2) Peter

2 people – so it is in chapter **2**.

No. 3
I (I) **(Paul)** *am crucified with Christ* **(Christ)**: *nevertheless I live; yet not I, but Christ liveth in me: and the life which I now live in the flesh I live by the faith of the Son of God, who loved me, and gave himself for me.* Galatians 2:20.

This verse is about Paul being crucified with Christ. When you read this verse of Scripture always think **'I Paul.'** When Jesus was crucified they offered Him vinegar mingled with gall. For the purpose of association, think that Paul rhymes with gall, and the first three letters of **Gal**atians is the same as the first three letters of **gal**l, so this verse is in the book of Galatians.

This verse mentions **2** people: **Paul** and **Christ**, so it is in chapter **2**.

No. 4
O foolish Galatians **(O FOOLISH GALATIANS)**, *who hath bewitched you, that ye should not obey the truth, before whose eyes Jesus Christ hath been evidently set forth, crucified among you?*
This only would I learn of you, Received ye the Spirit by the works of the law, or by the hearing of faith?
Are ye so foolish? having begun in the Spirit, are ye now made perfect by the flesh? Galatians 3:1-3.

These verses are obviously in the book of Galatians.

O FOOLISH GALATIANS – **3** words, so they are in chapter **3**.

No. 5
But that no man is justified by the law (BY THE LAW) in the sight of God, [it is] evident: for, The just shall live by faith. Galatians 3:11.

When you read this verse of Scripture always think no man is justified by the law, or by being privileged to have a Christian father and mother. Each individual must have his or her own saving faith in order to be justified. His **relation**ship to his parents does not justify him.

For the purpose of association, think that the second and third syllables of re**lation**ship sound the same as the second and third syllables of Ga**latian**, so this verse is in the book of Galatians.

BY THE LAW – 3 words, so it is in chapter 3.

Or - **LAW** – 3 letters.

No. 6
Christ hath redeemed (redeemed) us from the curse of the law, being made a curse for us: for it is written, Cursed [is] every one that hangeth on a tree (ON A TREE): Galatians 3:13.

When you read this verse of scripture think of the following verse of a well-known hymn.

Redeemed how I love to proclaim it,
Redeemed by the Blood of the Lamb,
Redeemed by His infinite mercy,
His **child** and forever I am.

A **child** has a family re**lation**ship with his/her father.
The second and third syllables of re**lation**ship sound the same as the second and third syllables of Ga**latian**, so this verse is in the book of Galatians.

ON A TREE – 3 words, so it is in chapter 3.

The parallel verses are in the book of Deuteronomy 21:22-23.

*And if a man have committed a sin worthy of death, and he be to be put to death, and thou hang him on a tree **(on a tree)**:*

*His body shall not remain all night upon the tree, but thou shalt in any wise bury him that day; (for he that is hanged [is] **accursed** (accursed) of God;) that thy land be not defiled, which the LORD thy God giveth thee [for] an inheritance.*

No. 7

*Now to Abraham and his seed **(seed)** were the promises made. He saith not, And to seeds, as of many; but as of one **(ONE)**, And to thy seed, which is Christ.* Galatians 3:16.

The word 'seed' in this verse refers to people who are **related** to Abraham. **Relations** rhymes with Galatians, so this verse is in the book of Galatians.

Jesus is always the special **One** and when you read this verse think of accentuating **One**.

ONE - **3** letters, so this verse is in chapter **3**.

No. 8

*And this I say, [that] the covenant, that was confirmed before of God in Christ, the law, which was four hundred and thirty **(430)** years after, cannot disannul, that it should make the promise of none effect.* Galatians 3:17.

If you look at the previous association you will see that Christ was the seed of Abraham. In this verse we read that the covenant was confirmed in Christ, so there is still the thought of a re**lation**ship, therefore this verse is in the book of Ga**latian**s.

430 – **3** figures, so it is in chapter **3**

No. 9

*Stand **(STAND)** fast therefore in the liberty **(liberty)** wherewith Christ hath made us free, and be not entangled again with the yoke of bondage.* Galatians 5:1.

For the purpose of association, think that we have **liberty** when we are with our **relations**. Relations rhymes with Galatians, so this verse is in the book of Galatians.

STAND - **5** letters, so it is in chapter **5**.

No. 10
But the fruit (FRUIT) of the Spirit is love, joy, peace, longsuffering, gentleness, goodness, faith,
Meekness, temperance: against such there is no law.
Galatians 5:22-23.

When you read these verses of Scripture always ask yourself are these qualities of character evident in my life?

As the fruit of the Spirit is love, joy, peace, longsuffering, gentleness, goodness, faith, meekness and temperance, then all Christians should be amicable. If this is the case then they will have good relationships. The second and third syllables of re**lation**ships sound the same as the second and third syllables of Ga**latian** so these verses are in the book of Galatians.

FRUIT - **5** letters, so they are in chapter **5**.

No. 11
And they that are Christ's (they that are Christ's) have crucified the flesh (FLESH) with the affections and lusts. Galatians 5:24.

In this verse we read that the people belong to Christ *(they that are Christ's)*. If they belong to Him then they have a relationship with Him. We think of our children as belonging to us, and we have a relationship with them.

For the purpose of association, think that the second and third syllables of re**lation**ship sound the same as the second and third syllables of Ga**latian**, so this verse is in Galatians.

FLESH – **5** letters, so it is in chapter **5**.

No. 12
*If we live in the (IN THE) Spirit (If we live in the Spirit), let us
also walk in the (IN THE) Spirit.* Galatians 5:25.

When we are born into this world (physical birth) we live in it
and have a relationship with our family. When we are born again
(spiritual birth) **we live in the Spirit** and have a relationship with
God. The second and third syllables of re**lation**ship sound the same
as the second and third syllables of Ga**latian**, so this verse is in the
book of Galatians.

Live **IN THE** Spirit,
Walk **IN THE** Spirit.

IN THE – **5** letters, so it is in chapter **5**.

No. 13
*Be not deceived; God is not mocked: for whatsoever a man soweth,
that shall he also reap.*
*For he that soweth to his flesh shall of the flesh reap corruption; but
he that soweth to the Spirit shall of the Spirit reap life everlasting.*
Galatians 6:7-8.

A farmer sows and reaps and he may get some help from his
relations. **Relations** rhymes with **Galatians**, so these verses are in
the book of Galatians.

A **sickle** is a curved, hand-held agricultural tool typically used
for harvesting grain crops before the advent of modern harvesting machinery. The first syllable of sickle and six sound almost the
same, so these verses are in chapter **6**.

No. 14
*But God forbid (FORBID) that I should glory, save in the cross of
our Lord Jesus Christ, by whom the world (world) is crucified unto
me, and I unto the world.* Galatians 6:14.

For the purpose of association, think that the **world** consists of
nations, and **nations** rhymes with **Galatians**, so this verse is in the

book of Galatians.

FORBID – **6** letters, so it is in chapter **6**.

EPHESIANS

No. 1
I would suggest that you memorize the following five verses together.

Blessed [be] the God and Father of our Lord Jesus Christ, who hath blessed us with all spiritual blessings in heavenly [places] in Christ:
*According as he hath chosen us in him before the foundation of the world **(before the foundation of the world)**, that we should be holy and without blame before him in love:*
*Having predestinated us unto the adoption of children **(adoption of children)** by Jesus Christ to himself, according to the good pleasure of his will,*
To the praise of the glory of his grace, wherein he hath made us accepted in the beloved.
In whom we have redemption through his blood, the forgiveness of sins, according to the riches of his grace; Ephesians 1:3-7.

Union is one definition of fusion, and fusion sounds similar to the 2nd and 3rd syllables of Ephesian.

For the purpose of association think that **adopted children** are part of their new family and thus in **union** with them, so these verses are in the book of Ephesians.

Also for the purpose of association, think that '**before the foundation of the world**' is as far back as we can think. So these verses are as far back in the book of Ephesians as they can be, so they are in chapter 1.

No. 2
*For by grace **(grace)** are ye saved through faith **(faith)**; and that not of yourselves **(not of yourselves)**: [it is] the gift of God.* Ephesians 2:8.

Notice that this verse states that when we are saved by grace through faith it is not of ourselves.

For the purpose of association, think that if it is not of ourselves then we are in union with someone else. When we are saved by God's grace we are in union with Christ. Union is one definition of fusion and **fusion** sounds similar to the last two syllables of E**phesian**, so this verse is in the book of Ephesians.

We are saved by **grace** through **faith**. **2** important words, so this verse is in chapter **2**.

No. 3
*But now in Christ Jesus **(in Christ Jesus)** ye who sometimes were far off **(far off)** are made nigh by the blood of Christ.* Ephesians 2:13.

When we are *'in Christ Jesus'* we are in union with Him. As I have already mentioned, union is one definition of fusion. **Fusion** sounds similar to the last two syllables of E**phesian**, so this verse is in the book of Ephesians.

We are told **2** things in this verse:

(1) These people are **in Christ Jesus**.
(2) They were at one time **far off**.

2 different states of being, so this verse is in chapter **2**.

No. 4
*Unto me, who am less than the least of all saints **(less than the least of all saints)**, is this grace given **(grace given)**, that I should preach among the Gentiles **(AMONG THE GENTILES)** the unsearchable riches of Christ **(the unsearchable riches of Christ)**.* Ephesians 3:8.

Diffusion almost rhymes with **Ephesian**. **Diffusion** means to

216

spread and Paul is **spreading** the unsearchable riches of Christ among the Gentiles, so this verse is in the book of Ephesians.

(1) Paul says he is **less than the least of all saints**.
(2) He says **grace** has been **given** to him.
(3) He says he is preaching **the unsearchable riches of Christ**.

3 things Paul said, so this verse is in chapter **3**.

Or: **AMONG THE GENTILES – 3** words.

No. 5
*And **grieve not the Holy Spirit** of God, whereby ye are sealed* **(SEAL)** *unto the day of redemption.* Ephesians 4:30.

Remember that the book of Revelation tells us that the church at **Ephes**us had left its first love. *Nevertheless I have [somewhat] against thee, because thou hast left thy first love.* Revelation 2:4.

For the purpose of association, think that if we leave our first love then **we grieve the Holy Spirit,** so this verse is in the book of Ephesians.

All born again believers have the **SEAL** of the Holy Spirit.
SEAL – 4 letters, so this verse is in chapter **4**.

No. 6
*Be ye therefore followers of God, as dear children **(children)**;*
*And walk in love **(love)**, as Christ also hath loved us, and hath given himself for us an offering and a sacrifice **(AN OFFERING AND A SACRIFICE)** to God for a sweetsmelling savour.* Ephesians 5:1-2.

Fusion can be defined as **union**. **Fusion** sounds similar to the last two syllables of E**phesian**.

For the purpose of association, think that two people **united** in marriage have **children** and **love** each other, so these verses are in the book of Ephesians.

AN OFFERING AND A SACRIFICE – **5** words, so they are in chapter **5**.

No. 7
I suggest that you memorize the following verses.

Wives, submit yourselves unto your own husbands, as unto the Lord.
For the husband is the head of the wife, even as Christ is the head of the church: and he is the saviour of the body.
Therefore as the church is subject unto Christ, so [let] the wives [be] to their own husbands in every thing.
Husbands, love your wives, even as Christ also loved the church, and gave himself for it;
That he might sanctify and cleanse it with the washing of water by the word,
That he might present it to himself a glorious church, not having spot, or wrinkle, or any such thing; but that it should be holy and without blemish.
So ought men to love their wives as their own bodies. He that loveth his wife loveth himself.
For no man ever yet hated his own flesh (FLESH); but nourisheth and cherisheth it, even as the Lord the church:
For we are members of his body, of his flesh (FLESH), and of his bones.
For this cause shall a man leave his father and mother, and shall be joined unto his wife, and they two shall be one flesh (FLESH).
This is a great mystery: but I speak concerning Christ and the church.
Nevertheless let every one of you in particular so love his wife even as himself; and the wife [see] that she reverence [her] husband.
Ephesians 5:22-33.

Marriage is a union, and fusion can be defined as a union.
Fusion and the last two syllables of E**phesian** sound similar, so these verses are in the book of Ephesians.

FLESH - **5** letters, so they are in chapter **5**.

No. 8

Wherefore take unto you the whole armour of God, that ye may be able to withstand in the evil day, and having done all, to stand.

*Stand therefore, having your loins girt about with truth (**loins girt about with truth**), and having on the breastplate of righteousness (**having on the breastplate of righteousness**);*

*And your feet shod with the preparation of the gospel of peace (**feet shod with the preparation of the gospel of peace**);*

*Above all, taking the shield of faith **taking the shield of faith**, wherewith ye shall be able to quench all the fiery darts of the wicked.*

*And take the helmet of salvation (**take the helmet of salvation**), and the sword of the Spirit (**and the sword of the Spirit**), which is the word of God:*

Praying always with all prayer and supplication in the Spirit, and watching thereunto with all perseverance and supplication for all saints; Ephesians 6:13-18.

These are words concerning spiritual warfare, so they must be addressed to believers. Believers are in **union** with Christ. One definition of **union** is **fusion**.

For the purpose of association, think that **fusion** sounds similar to the last two syllables of E**phesian**, so these verses are in the book of Ephesians.

(1) *loins girt about with truth,*
(2) *having on the breastplate of righteousness;*
(3) *feet shod with the preparation of the gospel of peace;*
(4) *taking the shield of faith,*
(5) *take the helmet of salvation,*
(6) *and the sword of the Spirit,*

6 pieces of armour, so the above verses are in chapter **6**.

PHILIPPIANS

No. 1
For to me to live [is] Christ, and to die [is] gain.
But if I (I) live in the flesh, this [is] the fruit of my labour: yet what I (I) shall choose I (I) wot not.
For I (I) am in a strait betwixt two, having a desire to depart, and to be with Christ; which is far better:
*Nevertheless to abide in the flesh [is] more needful for you (**Nevertheless to abide in the flesh [is] more needful for you**).*
Philippians 1:21-24.

Remember I stated at the beginning of this book that the church at Philippi was the first church in Europe.

For the purpose of association, think that **it was needful for Paul to abide in the flesh** so that he could form more churches. So these verses are in the book of Philippians.

'I' is used frequently in these verses and it is similar to **1**, so they are in chapter **1**.

No. 2
I suggest that you memorize all of the following verses.

[Let] nothing [be done] through strife or vainglory; but in lowliness of mind let each esteem other better than themselves.
Look not every man on his own things, but every man also on the things of others.
Let this mind be in you, which was also in Christ Jesus:
Who, being in the form of God, thought it not robbery to be equal with God:

But made himself of no reputation, and took upon him the form of a servant, and was made in the likeness of men:
And being found in fashion as a man, he humbled himself, and became obedient unto death, even the death of the cross.
Wherefore God also hath highly exalted him, and given him a name which is above every name:
That at the name of Jesus every knee (EVERY KNEE) should bow, of [things] in heaven, and [things] in earth, and [things] under the earth;
And [that] every tongue (tongue) should confess that Jesus Christ [is] Lord, to the glory of God the Father. Philippians 2:3-11.

We use our **lip**s along with our **tongues** to confess that Jesus Christ is Lord. For the purpose of association, think that the second syllable of Phi**lip**pians is **lip**, so these verses are in the book of Philippians.

Or if you prefer to think of the well known hymn:

At the name of Jesus,
Every knee shall bow;
Every tongue confess Him,
King of Glory now.

We use our lips when singing hymns. The second syllable of Phi**lip**pians is **lip**, so these verses are in the book of Philippians.

EVERY KNEE - **2** words. So they are in chapter **2**.

No. 3
But what things were gain to me, those I counted loss for Christ.
Yea doubtless, and I count all things [but] loss for the excellency of the knowledge of Christ Jesus my Lord: for whom I have suffered the loss of all things, and do count them [but] dung, that I may win Christ,
And be found in him, not having mine own righteousness, which is of the law, but that which is through the faith of Christ, the righteousness which is of God by faith: Phillipians 3:7-9.

The apostle Paul knew what it was to be **fill**ed with all the fullness of God. *And to know the love of Christ, which passeth knowledge, that ye might be **fill**ed with all the fulness of God.* Ephesians 3:19.

As a result of this he was willing to suffer the loss of all things. The first syllable of **fill**ed and **Phil**ippians sound the same, so these verses are in the book of Philippians.

The apostle Paul was **complete** in Christ. *And ye are **complete** in him, which is the head of all principality and power:* Colossians 2:10.

3 is the number of completion, so these verses are in chapter **3**.

No. 4
*Finally, brethren, whatsoever things are true (**TRUE**), whatsoever things [are] honest, whatsoever things [are] just, whatsoever things [are] pure, whatsoever things [are] lovely, whatsoever things [are] of good report; if [there be] any virtue, and if [there be] any praise (**praise**), think on these things (**THINK ON THESE THINGS**).* Philippians 4:8.

For the purpose of association, think that we **praise** with our **lip**s, so this verse is in the book of Phi**lip**pians.

TRUE - **4** letters, so it is in chapter **4**.

Or: **THINK ON THESE THINGS** – **4** words.

No. 5
*I can (**I CAN**) do all things through Christ which strengtheneth me (**CHRIST WHICH STRENGTHENETH ME**).* Philippians 4:13.

Remember that Philip the evangelist (not Philip the apostle) preached at Samaria and he preached Jesus to the Ethiopian eunuch. See Acts 8:5-6. Acts 8:12-13. Acts 8:35.

For the purpose of association only, think that Philip the evangelist wouldn't have spent as much time with Christ as the twelve apostles did. Then think that the apostles would be **strengthened** as a result of spending so much time with Christ. When you read this verse, think of Christ **strengthening Philip** for his mighty work, so this verse is in the book of **Philip**pians.

I CAN – **4** letters, so it is in chapter **4**.

Or - **CHRIST WHICH STRENGTHENETH ME** – **4** words.

COLOSSIANS

No. 1
I suggest that you memorize the following verses.

Giving thanks unto the Father, which hath made us meet to be partakers of the inheritance of the saints in light:
Who hath delivered us from the power of darkness **(the power of darkness)**, *and hath translated [us] into the kingdom of his dear Son:*
In whom we have redemption through his blood, [even] the forgiveness of sins:
Who is the image of the invisible God, the firstborn of every creature:
For by him were all things created, that are in heaven, and that are in earth, visible and invisible, whether [they be] thrones, or dominions, or principalities, or powers: all things were created by him, and for him:
And he is before all things, and by him all things consist.
And he is the head of the body, the church: who is the beginning, the firstborn from the dead; that in all [things] he might have the preeminence **(preeminence)**.
For it pleased [the Father] that in him should all fulness dwell;
And, having made peace through the blood of his cross, by him to reconcile all things unto himself; by him, [I say], whether [they be] things in earth, or things in heaven.
And you, that were sometime alienated and enemies in [your] mind by wicked works, yet now hath he reconciled
In the body of his flesh through death, to present you holy and unblameable and unreproveable in his sight: Colossians 1:12-22.

I presume most people would know that these verses are in one of the epistles.

If we have been delivered from '**the power of darkness**' then we have heard the Saviour's **call**.

The word '**call**' and the first syllable of **Col**ossians sound the same, so these verses are in the book of Colossians.

Colossians is the only **epistle** where the words '**the power of darkness**' are recorded.

There is only one other place in Scripture where the words **the power of darkness** are recorded and that is Luke 22:53.

When I (Jesus) *was daily with you in the temple, ye stretched forth no hands against me: but this is your hour, and the power of darkness (power of darkness).*

This is the only place in Scripture where the word preeminence is recorded concerning Jesus. Preeminence can be defined as being exalted above others.

For the purpose of association think that if someone is exalted above others then they are 1st in importance, so these verses are in the 1st chapter.

No. 2
I suggest that you memorize the following verses.

As ye have therefore received Christ (received Christ) Jesus the Lord, [so] walk (walk) ye in him:
Rooted and built up in him, and stablished in the faith, as ye have been taught, abounding therein with thanksgiving.
Beware lest any man spoil you through philosophy and vain deceit, after the tradition of men, after the rudiments of the world, and not after Christ.
For in him dwelleth all the fulness of the Godhead bodily.
And ye are complete in him, which is the head of all principality and power: Colossians 2:6-10.

If you have **received Christ** then you must have heard His **call**. The word '**call**' and the first syllable of **Col**ossians sound the same, so these verses are in the book of Colossians.

In verse 6 we are encouraged to **walk** with Christ.
In verse 8 we are warned about other things that take us away from Christ.

2 opposite lifestyles – so these verses are in chapter **2**.

No. 3

*If ye then be risen with Christ **(RISEN WITH CHRIST)**, seek those things which are above, where Christ sitteth on the right hand of God.*
*Set **(SET)** your affection on things above, not on things on the earth.*
For ye are dead, and your life is hid with Christ in God.
When Christ, [who is] our life, shall appear, then shall ye also appear with him in glory. Colossians 3:1-4.

If you are **risen with Christ** then you must have heard His **call**. The word 'call' and the first syllable of **Col**ossians sound the same, so these verses are in the book of Colossians.

RISEN WITH CHRIST – **3** words, so they are in chapter **3**.

Or – **SET** – **3** letters.

No. 4

I suggest that you memorize the following verses.

*Put on therefore, as the elect of God **(the elect of God)**, holy and beloved, bowels of mercies, kindness, humbleness of mind, meekness, longsuffering;*
Forbearing one another, and forgiving one another, if any man have a quarrel against any: even as Christ forgave you, so also [do] ye.
*And above all these things [put on] charity **([PUT ON] CHARITY)**, which is the bond of perfectness.*
And let the peace of God rule in your hearts, to the which also ye are called in one body; and be ye thankful. Colossians 3:12-15.

Anyone who is **the elect of God** must have heard His **call**. The word 'call' and the first syllable of **Col**ossians sound the same, so these verses are in the book of Colossians.

PUT ON CHARITY - **3** words, so they are in chapter **3**.

No. 5
I suggest that you memorize the following two verses.

Let the word of Christ dwell in you richly **(let the word of Christ dwell in you richly)** *in all wisdom; teaching and admonishing one another in psalms and hymns and spiritual songs, singing with grace in your hearts to the Lord.*
And whatsoever ye do in word or deed **(WORD OR DEED)**, *[do] all in the name of the Lord Jesus, giving thanks to God and the Father by him.* Colossians 3:16-17.

The word of Christ will only dwell richly in those who have heard His **call**. The word **'call'** and the first syllable of **Col**ossians sound the same, so these verses are in the book of Colossians.

Whatever we do for Jesus can only be done **in word or deed**.

WORD OR DEED - **3** words, so these verses are in chapter **3**.

No. 6
Wives, submit yourselves unto your own husbands, as it is fit in the Lord.
Husbands, love [your] wives **(LOVE [YOUR] WIVES)**, *and be not bitter against them.*
Children, obey [your] parents in all things: for this is well pleasing unto the Lord.
Fathers, provoke not your children [to anger], lest they be discouraged. Colossians 3:18-21.

Think of the apostle Paul **call**ing wives, husbands and children to listen to what he has to say to each one of them. The word **'call'** and the first syllable of **Col**ossians sound the same, so these verses are in the book of Colossians.

LOVE YOUR WIVES – **3** words, so they are in chapter **3**.

No. 7
Servants, obey in all things [your] masters according to the flesh; not with eyeservice, as menpleasers; but in singleness of heart, fearing God:
And whatsoever ye do, do [it] heartily **(DO [IT] HEARTILY)***, as to the Lord, and not unto men;* Colossians 3:22-23.

Think of the apostle Paul **call**ing servants to listen to what he has to say to each one of them. The word **'call'** and the first syllable of **Col**ossians sound the same, so these verses are in the book of Colossians.

Everything we do for the Lord should be done **heartily**.

DO IT HEARTILY – **3** words, so these verses are in chapter **3**.

No. 8
Masters, give unto [your] servants that which is just and equal; knowing that ye also have a Master in heaven **(A MASTER IN HEAVEN)***.* Colossians 4:1.

Think of the apostle Paul **call**ing all masters to listen to what he has to say to them. The word **'call'** and the first syllable of **Col**ossians sound the same, so this verse is in the book of Colossians.

A MASTER IN HEAVEN – **4** words, so it is in chapter **4**.

1ST THESSALONIANS

No. 1
I suggest that you memorize the following five verses.

For this we say unto you by the word of the Lord, that we which are alive [and] remain unto the coming of the Lord shall not prevent them which are asleep.

For the Lord himself shall descend from heaven with a shout, with the voice of the archangel, and with the trump of God: and the dead in Christ shall rise first (the dead in Christ shall rise first (1st):
Then we which are alive [and] remain shall be caught up together with them in the clouds, to meet the Lord in the air: and so shall we ever be with the Lord. 1st Thessalonians 4:15-17.

In these verses we read about the dead being resurrected. Now each person who is dead is **alone** in the grave. By this I mean that they are all put into the grave in separate coffins, they are **alone**: no one goes with them. Syllables two and three of Thess**alon**ians sound the same as **alone**, so these verses are in some book of Thessalonians.

The dead in Christ shall rise first (**1st**), so these verses are in the book of **1st** Thessalonians.

In verses 16-17 we read about:
(1) **The Lord**
(2) **The Archangel,**
(3) **The dead in Christ**
(4) **We which are alive**

These verses are in chapter **4**.

No. 2
I suggest that you memorize the following verses.

But of the times and the seasons, brethren, ye have no need that I write unto you.
*For yourselves know perfectly that the day of the Lord (**THE DAY OF THE LORD**) so cometh as a thief in the night.*
For when they shall say, Peace and safety; then sudden destruction cometh upon them, as travail upon a woman with child; and they shall not escape.
*But ye, brethren, are not in darkness (**darkness**), that that day should overtake you as a thief.* 1st Thessalonians 5:1-4.

These verses are about the second coming of the Lord Jesus Christ. In 1st Thessalonians 4:16 we read the following words: *For the Lord himself shall descend from heaven with a shout, with the voice of the archangel, and with the trump of God: and the dead in Christ shall rise first:*

For the purpose of association, think that the dead are **alone** in their graves and there is **darkness** in the graves. Syllables two and three of Thess**alon**ians sound the same as **alone**, so these verses are in some book of Thessalonians.

Also for the purpose of association, think that 'the day of the Lord' is 1 special day, so they are in the book of 1st Thessalonians.

THE DAY OF THE LORD – 5 words, so these verses are in chapter 5.

No. 3
*Pray without ceasing (**Pray without ceasing**).*
1st Thessalonians 5:17.

For the purpose of association, think that you are not **alone** when you pray without ceasing. The Lord is listening to your prayers. Syllables two and three of Thess**alon**ians sound the same as **alone**, so this verse is in Thessalonians.

Also for the purpose of association, think that the **1st** requirement from a repentant sinner with regard to salvation is **pray**er. *For whosoever shall call upon the name of the Lord shall be saved.* Romans 10:13. Therefore this verse is in **1st** Thessalonians

WE MUST PRAY WITHOUT CEASING – 5 words, so this verse is in chapter 5.

2ND THESSALONIANS

No. 1

And to you who are troubled rest with us, when the Lord Jesus shall be revealed from heaven with his mighty angels,

*In flaming fire taking vengeance on them that know not God (**them that know not God**), and that obey not the gospel of our Lord Jesus Christ:*

Who shall be punished with everlasting destruction from the presence of the Lord, and from the glory of his power;

*When he shall come to be glorified in his saints (**saints**), and to be admired in all them that believe (because our testimony among you was believed) in that day (**that day**).* 2nd Thessalonians 1:7-10.

These verses are about the second coming of the Lord Jesus Christ. In 1st Thessalonians 4:16 we read the following words: *For the Lord himself shall descend from heaven with a shout, with the voice of the archangel, and with the trump of God: and the dead in Christ shall rise first:*

For the purpose of association think that the dead are **alone** in their graves. Syllables two and three of Thess**alon**ians sound the same as **alone**, so these verses are in some book of Thessalonians.

There are **2** groups of people mentioned in these verses:
(1) them that know not God
(2) saints, so they are in the book of **2**nd Thessalonians.

Also for the purpose of association think of '**that day**' as **1** day, so these verses are in chapter **1**.

No. 2
I suggest that you memorize the following verses.

*Now we beseech you, brethren, by the coming of our Lord Jesus Christ (**our Lord Jesus Christ**), and [by] our gathering together unto him,*

That ye be not soon shaken in mind, or be troubled, neither by spirit, nor by word, nor by letter as from us, as that the day of Christ is at hand.

*Let no man deceive you by any means: for [that day shall not come], except there come a falling away (**a falling away**) first, and that man of sin (**that man of sin**) be revealed, the son of perdition;*

*Who opposeth and exalteth himself above all that is called God, or that is worshipped; so that he as God sitteth in the temple of God, shewing himself that he is God (**shewing himself that he is God**).*

Remember ye not, that, when I was yet with you, I told you these things?

And now ye know what withholdeth that he might be revealed in his time.

For the mystery of iniquity doth already work: only he who now letteth [will let], until he be taken out of the way.

*And then shall that Wicked (**that Wicked**) be revealed, whom the Lord shall consume with the spirit of his mouth, and shall destroy with the brightness of his coming:*

*[Even him], whose coming is after the working of Satan (**Satan**) with all power and signs and lying wonders,*

And with all deceivableness of unrighteousness in them that perish; because they received not the love of the truth, that they might be saved.

*And for this cause God shall send them strong delusion (**strong delusion**), that they should believe a lie:*

*That they all might be damned (**be damned**) who believed not the truth, but had pleasure in unrighteousness.*

2nd Thessalonians 2:1-12.

These verses mention the second coming of the Lord Jesus Christ. In 1st Thessalonians 4:16 we read the following words: *For the Lord himself shall descend from heaven with a shout, with the voice of the archangel, and with the trump of God: and the dead in Christ shall rise first:*

For the purpose of association think that the dead are **alone** in their graves and there is **darkness** in the graves even as there is **darkness** recorded in these verses.

> **a falling away** is darkness.
> **that man of sin** is darkness.
> **shewing himself that he is God** is darkness.
> **that Wicked** is darkness.
> **Satan** is darkness.
> **strong delusion** is darkness.
> **Be damned** is darkness.

Syllables two and three of Thess**alon**ians sound the same as **alone**, so these verses are in some book of Thessalonians.

The narrative mentions the **2nd** coming of Jesus Christ, so they are in the book of **2nd** Thessalonians.
This narrative is about **2** men:

(1) the sinless Man i.e. **our Lord Jesus Christ**,
(2) **that man of sin**, so these verses are in chapter **2**.

1ST TIMOTHY

No. 1
For [there is] one (1) God, and one (1) mediator between God and men, the man Christ Jesus; 1st Timothy 2:5.

While we are living here on earth we are living in **time**, and we need a mediator to gain access to God. When we finish with **time** and enter eternity a mediator will no longer be necessary. We will be with our great Mediator. The first three letters of **time** and **Tim**othy are the same, so this verse is in some book of Timothy.

The **1st** thing that this verse says is there is one **(1)** God, so it is in the book of **1st** Timothy.

It then says and one **(1)** mediator **1+1=2**, so it is in chapter **2**.

No. 2
Let the woman learn in silence with all subjection.
But I suffer not a woman to teach, nor to usurp authority over the man, but to be in silence.
*For Adam **(Adam)** was first **(1st)** formed, then Eve **(Eve)**.*
And Adam was not deceived, but the woman being deceived was in the transgression. 1st Timothy 2:11-14.

Silence is quietness, and if someone is quiet they may be **timid**. The first syllable of **tim**id is the same as the first syllable in **Tim**othy, so these verses are in some book of Timothy.

Verse 13 states that Adam was first **(1st)** formed, so they are in the book of **1st** Timothy.

Adam and **Eve** are both mentioned in these verses: **2** people, so they are in chapter **2**.

No. 3
*Now the Spirit **(the Spirit)** speaketh expressly, that in the latter times **(times)** some shall depart from the faith **(DEPART FROM THE FAITH)**, giving heed to seducing spirits, and doctrines of devils;*
Speaking lies in hypocrisy; having their conscience seared with a hot iron;
Forbidding to marry, [and commanding] to abstain from meats, which God hath created to be received with thanksgiving of them which believe and know the truth.
For every creature of God [is] good, and nothing to be refused, if it be received with thanksgiving:
For it is sanctified by the word of God and prayer.
If thou put the brethren in remembrance of these things, thou shalt be a good minister of Jesus Christ, nourished up in the words of faith and of good doctrine, whereunto thou hast attained.
1st Timothy 4:1-6.

The first three letters of **tim**e are the same as the first three letters of **Tim**othy, so these verses are in some book of Timothy.

Verse one speaks of seducing spirits (plural). It also speaks of the Spirit (singular). Singular is **1**, so these verses are in the book of **1**st Timothy.

DEPART FROM THE FAITH – **4** words so they are in chapter **4**.

No. 4
*For the love of money (**money**) is the root of all evil: which while some coveted after, they have erred from the faith (**THEY HAVE ERRED FROM THE FAITH**), and pierced themselves through with many sorrows.* Ist Timothy 6:10.

The name Timothy means **'honouring God.'** For the purpose of association, think of **honouring God with our money**, so this verse is in some book of Timothy.

Also for the purpose of association, think that we must not put money **1st** in our lives, so this verse is in the book of **1st** Timothy.

THEY HAVE ERRED FROM THE FAITH – **6** words, so this verse is in chapter **6.**

No. 5
*Which in his times he shall shew, [who is] the blessed and only Potentate (**only Potentate**), the King of kings, and Lord of lords;*
1st Timothy 6:15.

The name Timothy means **'honouring God.'** For the purpose of association, think of **honouring your Potentate**, so this verse is in some book of Timothy.

Also for the purpose of forming an association, think of the **Potentate** as being **1st** in importance, so this verse is in the book of **1st** Timothy.

JESUS CHRIST IS THE ONLY POTENTATE – **6** words, so it is in chapter **6.**

2ND TIMOTHY

No. 1
I suggest that you memorize the following two verses.

Be not thou therefore ashamed of the testimony of our Lord, nor of me his prisoner: but be thou partaker of the afflictions of the gospel according to the power of God;
*Who hath saved (**SAVED**) us, and called (**CALLED**) [us] with an holy calling, not according to our works (**not according to our works**), but according to his own purpose and grace (**but according to his own purpose and grace**), which was given us in Christ Jesus before the world began (**before the world began**),* 2nd Timothy 1:8-9.

For the purpose of association, think of '**before the world began**' as before **time** began. The first three letters of **time** are the same as the first three letters of **Tim**othy, so these verses are in some book of Timothy.

SAVED CALLED - **2** words, so they are in the book of **2nd** Timothy.

(1) *not according to our works,*
(2) *but according to his own purpose and grace,*

2 statements, so these verses are in chapter **2**.

No. 2
*Study (**Study**) to shew thyself approved unto God, a workman (workman) that needeth not to be ashamed, rightly dividing (**RIGHTLY DIVIDING**) the word of truth.* 2nd Timothy 2:15.

A **workman** is employed during his life**time**. Letters five, six and seven of life**time** are the same as the first three letters of **Tim**othy, so this verse is in some book of Timothy.

(1) Study
(2) Rightly divide the word of truth

2 things that are to be done, so it is in the book of **2**nd Timothy.

RIGHTLY DIVIDING. For the purpose of association, think of these **2** words as being the most important words in the verse, so this verse is in chapter **2**.

No. 3
But continue thou in the things which thou hast learned **(continue thou in the things which thou hast learned)** *and hast been assured of, knowing of whom thou hast learned [them];*
And that from a child thou hast known the holy scriptures, which are able to make thee wise unto salvation through faith which is in Christ Jesus.
All scripture [is] given by inspiration of God **(INSPIRATION OF GOD)**, *and [is] profitable for doctrine, for reproof, for correction, for instruction* **(instruction)** *in righteousness:*
That the man of God may be perfect, throughly furnished unto all good works. 2nd Timothy 3:14-17.

2nd Timothy 3:16 is the only place in the New Testament where the word **instruction** is used. For the purpose of association think of **Paul instructing Timothy**, so these verses are in some book of Timothy.

Also for the purpose of association, when you read the words *'continue thou in the things which thou hast learned,'* think that you have **learned some things** and they could be in the book of **1st** Timothy. Now you are going to **continue** in the things which you have learned as you **continue** reading **2nd Timothy**, so these verses are in the book of **2nd** Timothy.

INSPIRATION OF GOD – **3** words, so they are in chapter **3**.

No. 4
*Preach the word (**Preach the word**); be instant in season (**BE INSTANT IN SEASON**), out of season; reprove, rebuke, exhort with all longsuffering and doctrine.*
*For the time (**TIME**) will come when they will not endure sound doctrine (**when they will not endure sound doctrine**); but after their own lusts shall they heap to themselves teachers, having itching ears;*
*And they shall turn away [their] ears from the truth (**truth**), and shall be turned unto fables.* 2nd Timothy 4:2-4.

For the purpose of association think of Paul instructing Timothy to **preach the word**, so these verses are in some book of Timothy.

(1) The preaching of Truth.
(2) The rejection of Truth.

2 happenings, so they are in the book of **2**nd Timothy.

BE INSTANT IN SEASON – **4** words, so these verses are in chapter **4**.

Or we could say that the **TIME** (**4** letters) has come in our day *when they will not endure sound doctrine*, so they are in chapter **4**.

TITUS

No. 1
I suggest that you memorize the following verses.

For the grace of God that bringeth salvation hath appeared to all men,
Teaching us that, denying ungodliness and worldly lusts, we should live soberly, righteously, and godly, in this present world;
*Looking for that blessed hope (**Looking for that blessed hope**), and the glorious appearing of the great God (**great God**) and our Saviour Jesus Christ;*

'Thy word have I hid in mine heart.'

Who gave himself for us, that he might redeem us from all iniquity, and purify unto himself a peculiar people, zealous of good works. Titus 2:11-14.

The name Titus can mean **defender**. For the purpose of association, think that the **great God** is our **defender**, so these verses are in the book of Titus. We know that these verses are in the New Testament because Jesus Christ is mentioned.

There is only one other place in the New Testament where the words **great God** are used, and that is Revelation 19:17. *And I saw an angel standing in the sun; and he cried with a loud voice, saying to all the fowls that fly in the midst of heaven, Come and gather yourselves together unto the supper of the great God* **(great God)**;

I presume most people would know that this verse is in the book of Revelation.

Looking for that blessed hope etc. Think of **looking** physically with your **2** eyes, so these verses are in chapter **2**.

PHILEMON

No. 1

I **(Paul)** *beseech thee for my son Onesimus, whom I have begotten in my bonds:*

Which in time past was to thee unprofitable, but now profitable to thee and to me:

Whom I have sent again: thou therefore receive him, that is, mine own bowels:

Whom I would have retained with me, that in thy stead he might have ministered unto me in the bonds of the gospel

But without thy mind would I do nothing; that thy benefit should not be as it were of necessity, but willingly.

For perhaps he therefore departed for a season, that thou shouldest

238

receive him for ever;

Not now as a servant, but above a servant, a brother beloved, specially to me, but how much more unto thee, both in the flesh, and in the Lord?

If thou count me therefore a partner, receive him as myself.

If he hath wronged thee, or oweth [thee] ought, put that on (on) mine account; Philemon 1:10-18.

Paul the apostle is writing here so we know this verse is in the New Testament. Philem**on** is the only book in the New Testament that ends with **on**, so these verses are in the book of Philemon.

Philemon has one chapter.

HEBREWS

No. 1

God, who at sundry times and in divers manners spake in time past unto the fathers (fathers) by the prophets,

Hath in these last days spoken unto us by [his] Son (spoken unto us by [his] Son), whom he hath appointed heir of all things, by whom also he made the worlds;

Who being the brightness of [his] glory, and the express image of his person, and upholding all things by the word of his power, when he had by himself purged our sins, sat down on the right hand of the Majesty on high; Hebrews 1:1-3.

The **Hebrews**/Jews knew that God spoke unto the **fathers** by the prophets, so these verses are in the book of **Hebrews**.

spoken unto us by his Son – **1** person, so they are in chapter **1**.

No. 2
*But unto the Son [he saith], Thy throne, O God, [is] for ever and ever: a sceptre **(sceptre)** of righteousness [is] the sceptre **(sceptre)** of thy kingdom.* Hebrews 1:8.

We read in Esther 5:2 the following words: *And it was so, when the king saw Esther the queen standing in the court, [that] she obtained favour in his sight: and the king held out to Esther the golden scepter **(sceptre)** that [was] in his hand. So Esther drew near, and touched the top of the scepter **(sceptre)**.*

Queen Esther was a **Hebrew**/Jew, so this verse is in the book of **Hebrews**.

God just said these words to **1** person - His Son, so it is in chapter **1**.

No. 3
Therefore we ought to give the more earnest heed to the things which we have heard, lest at any time we should let [them] slip.
*For if the word spoken **(spoken)** by angels was stedfast, and every transgression and disobedience received a just recompence of reward;*
*How shall we **(we)** escape, if we neglect so great salvation; which at the first began to be spoken **(spoken)** by the Lord, and was confirmed unto us by them that heard [him];* Hebrews 2:1-3.

The following is what Matthew Henry the great 17th century Bible commentator had to say about verse 2: Here observe, (1.) How the **law** is described: it was the *word spoken by angels, and declared to be stedfast.* For the purpose of association, think that the **law** was given to the Jews/ **Hebrews**, so these verses are in the book of **Hebrews**.

(**1**) *For if the word **spoken** by the angels etc.*
(**2**) *which at the first began to be **spoken** by the Lord etc.*

spoken is mentioned **2** times, so they are in chapter **2**.

No. 4
For verily he took not on [him the nature of] angels; but he took on [him] the seed of Abraham.

Wherefore in all things it behoved him (Jesus) *to be made like unto [his] brethren, that he might be a merciful **(merciful)** and faithful **(faithful)** high priest **(high priest)** in things [pertaining] to God, to make reconciliation for the sins of the people.*

For in that he himself hath suffered being tempted, he is able to succour them that are tempted. Hebrews 2:16-18.

The **Hebrews**/Jews were familiar with the term 'high priest,' so these verses are in **Hebrews**.

The term **'high priest'** is mentioned in the gospels and in the book of Acts but never in connection with a sacrifice.

(1) merciful high priest
(2) faithful high priest

2 descriptions of our Great High Priest, so these verses are in chapter **2**.

No. 5
*Wherefore (as the Holy Ghost saith, To day if ye will hear his voice, Harden not your hearts, as in the provocation, in the day of temptation in the wilderness **(in the wilderness)**:*

When your fathers tempted me, proved me, and saw my works forty years.

Wherefore I was grieved with that generation, and said, They do alway err in [their] heart; and they have not known my ways.

So I sware in my wrath, They shall not enter into my rest.)

*Take heed, brethren, lest there be in any of you an evil heart of unbelief,in departing from the living God **(THE LIVING GOD)**.* Hebrews 3:7-12.

Verses 7-11 are about the Israelites **in the wilderness**. For the purpose of association, think that the **Hebrew** Bible recorded the wilderness experience, so these verses are in the book of **Hebrews**.

THE LIVING GOD – **3** words, so they are in chapter **3**.

No. 6
*For the word of God **(THE WORD OF GOD)** [is] quick, and powerful, and sharper than any twoedged sword, piercing even to the dividing **(dividing)** asunder of soul and spirit, and of the joints and marrow, and [is] a discerner of the thoughts and intents of the heart.* Hebrews 4:12.

In **Exodus** 14:16 we read about Moses **dividing** the Red sea. *But lift thou up thy rod, and stretch out thine hand over the sea, and divide **(divide)** it: and the children of Israel shall go on dry [ground] through the midst of the sea.*

The book of **Exodus** is part of the **Hebrew** Scriptures, so this verse is in the book of **Hebrews**.

This verse is all about **THE WORD OF GOD** – **4** words, so it is in chapter **4**.
Or – **WORD** – **4** letters.

No. 7
I suggest that you memorize the following three verses.

*Seeing then that we have a great high priest **(A GREAT HIGH PRIEST)**, that is passed into the heavens, Jesus the Son of God, let us hold fast [our] profession.*
*For we have not an high priest **(high priest)** which cannot be touched with the feeling of our infirmities; but was in all points tempted like as [we are, yet] without sin.*
*Let us therefore come boldly unto the throne of grace, that we may obtain mercy, and find grace to help in time of need **(NEED)**.*
Hebrews 4:14-16.

The **Hebrews**/Jews were familiar with the term **'high priest,'** so these verses are in the book of **Hebrews**.

The term **'high priest'** is mentioned in the gospels and in the book of Acts but it is never referring to Jesus.

Verse 16 refers to our time of **NEED** – **4** letters, so these verses are in chapter **4**.

Or – Verse 14 refers to **A GREAT HIGH PRIEST** – **4** words.

No. 8
Though he were a Son **(THOUGH HE WERE A SON)**, *yet learned he obedience by the things which he suffered;*
And being made perfect, he became the author **(author)** *of eternal salvation unto all them that obey him;* Hebrews 5:8-9.

If you look at verse nine you will see the word **author**. This is the Greek word archegos and it is defined as one that takes the lead, and thus affords an example: a predecessor in a matter, or a pioneer.

We are certain that Jesus is the author and finisher of our faith, but for the purpose of association, think that **Abraham** is our example, predecessor and **pioneer in faith** and he was a **Hebrew**, so these verses are in the book of **Hebrews**.

THOUGH HE WERE A SON – **5** words, so they are in chapter **5**.

No. 9
But this [man] **(THIS [MAN])**, *because he continueth ever, hath an unchangeable priesthood* **(priesthood)**.
Wherefore he is able also to save them to the uttermost that come unto God by him, seeing he ever liveth to make intercession for them. Hebrews 7:24-25.

The **Hebrews**/Jews are familiar with the term **'priesthood,'** so these verses are in the book of **Hebrews**.

The word **'priesthood'** is mentioned in the book of 1st Peter chapter 2, but it refers to believers and not the priesthood of Jesus.

THIS MAN – **7** letters, so these verses are in chapter **7**.

No. 10
For such an high priest became us, [who is] holy, harmless, unde-filed, separate from sinners, and made higher than the heavens;
Who needeth not daily, as those high priests, to offer up sacrifice, first for his own sins, and then for the people's: for this he did once

(DID ONCE), when he offered up himself.
For the law maketh men high priests which have infirmity; but the word of the oath, which was since the law, [maketh] the Son, who is consecrated for evermore. Hebrews 7:26-28.

The **Hebrews**/Jews are familiar with the term **'high priest,'** so these verses are in the book of **Hebrews**.

The term **'high priest'** is mentioned in the gospels and in the book of Acts, but never in connection with a sacrifice.

DID ONCE – **7** letters, so these verses are in chapter **7**.

No. 11
For this [is] the covenant (COVENANT) that I will make with the house of Israel (house of Israel) after those days, saith the Lord; I will put my laws into their mind, and write them in their hearts: and I will be to them a God, and they shall be to me a people: Hebrews 8:10.

For the purpose of association, think that The **Hebrews**/Jews **were the house of Israel**, so this verse is in the book of **Hebrews**.

COVENANT – **8** letters, so it is in chapter **8**.

No. 12
But Christ being come an high priest (high priest) of good things to come, by a greater and more perfect tabernacle, not made with hands, that is to say, not of this building;
Neither by the blood of goats and calves, but by his own blood he entered in once into the holy place, (HOLY PLACE), having obtained eternal redemption [for us]. Hebrews 9:11-12.

The **Hebrews**/Jews were familiar with the term **'high priest'** so these verses are in the book of **Hebrews**.

The term **'high priest'** is mentioned in the gospels and in the book of Acts, but never in connection with a sacrifice.

HOLY PLACE – 9 letters, so these verses are in chapter **9**.

No. 13
For Christ is not entered into the holy places made with hands, [which are] the figures of the true; but into heaven itself, now to appear in the presence of God for us:
*Nor yet that he should offer himself often, as the high priest (**high priest**) entereth into the holy place every year with blood of others;*
For then must he often have suffered since the foundation of the world: but now once in the end of the world hath he appeared to put away sin by the sacrifice of himself.
*And as it is appointed unto men once to die (**ONCE TO DIE**), but after this the judgment (**judgment**):*
So Christ was once offered to bear the sins of many; and unto them that look for him shall he appear the second time without sin unto salvation. Hebrews 9:24-28.

The **Hebrews**/Jews were familiar with the **high priest entering into the holy place**, so these verses are in the book of **Hebrews**.

9 is the number of judgment, so they are in chapter **9**.

Or - **ONCE TO DIE – 9** letters.

No. 14
*Then said I, Lo (**Lo**), I come (in the volume of the book it is written of me,) (**in the volume of the book it is written of me,**) to do thy will, O God. Hebrews 10:7.*

In the volume of the book it is written of me. The **Hebrew** Bible is all about Jesus, so this verse is in the book of **Hebrews**.

If ***Lo*** is written with a lower case **l** and a capital **O** (**lO**) it looks similar to **10**, so it is in chapter **10**.

The parallel verses are in Psalm 40:7-8. *Then said I, Lo, I come: in the volume of the book [it is] written of me,*
I delight to do thy will, O my God: yea, thy law [is] within my heart.

No. 15

*And every priest standeth daily ministering and offering oftentimes (**OFTENTIMES**) the same sacrifices, which can never take away sins:*
*But this man, after he had offered one sacrifice for sins for ever (**AFTER HE HAD OFFERED ONE SACRIFICE FOR SIN FOR EVER**), sat down on the right hand of God;* Hebrews 10:11-12.

The **Hebrews**/Jews offered sacrifices, so these verses are in the book of **Hebrews**.

AFTER HE HAD OFFERED ONE SACRIFICE FOR SIN FOR EVER – 10 words, so they are in chapter **10**.

Or: **OFTENTIMES – 10** letters.

No. 16

*[It is] a fearful thing to fall into the hands (**HANDS**) of the living God (**living God**).* Hebrews 10:31.

The term **'living God'** is used frequently in the New Testament, but the term **'the hands of the living God'** is only used in the book of **Hebrews**. The **Hebrews**/Jews were well used to hearing about the **living God**, so this verse is in the book of Hebrews.

For the purpose of association, think that the **HANDS** have **10** fingers, so it is in chapter **10**.

No. 17

*But without faith [it is] impossible to please [him]: for he that cometh to God must believe (**MUST BELIEVE**) that he is (**he is**), and [that] he is a rewarder of them that diligently seek him.* Hebrews 11:6.

The **Hebrews** /Jews **believed** that **'God is'** so this verse is in the book of **Hebrews**.

MUST BELIEVE – 11 letters, so it is in chapter **11**.

246

No. 18

Wherefore seeing we also are compassed about with so great a cloud of witnesses, let us lay aside every weight, and the sin which doth so easily beset [us], and let us run with patience the race that is set before us,

*Looking unto Jesus the auther **(author)** and finisher of [our] faith; who for the joy that was set before him endured the cross, despising the shame, and is set down at the right hand of the throne of God.* Hebrews 12:1-2.

These two verses need to be read as a whole in order to understand what is being said. If you look at verse two you will see the word **author**. This is the Greek word archegos and it is defined as one that takes the lead, and thus affords an example: a **predecessor** in a matter, or a pioneer.

Jesus is the author and finisher of our faith and he was the author and finisher of Abraham's faith.

And the scripture, foreseeing that God would justify the heathen through faith, preached before the gospel unto Abraham, [saying], In thee shall all nations be blessed. Galations 3:8.

Abraham is portrayed in Scripture as the great **predecessor** of faith and he was a **Hebrew**, so these verses are in the book of **Hebrews**.

(1) We are compassed about with a cloud of witnesses.
(2) We are to lay aside every weight.
(3) And the sin which easily besets us.
(4) We are to run with patience.
(5) There is a race before us.
(6) We are to look unto Jesus.
(7) He is the author of our faith.
(8) He is the finisher of our faith.
(9) There was joy set before Jesus.
(10) He endured the cross.
(11) He despised the shame.
(12) He is set down at the right hand of God.

The above verses are in chapter **12**.

No. 19

*For consider (**consider**) him (**Jesus**) that endured (**endured**) such contradiction of sinners against himself, lest ye be wearied and faint in your minds.* Hebrews 12:3.

The **Hebrews**/Jews didn't accept Jesus as the Messiah. For the purpose of association, think that they need to **consider** Jesus, so this verse is in the book of **Hebrews**.

JESUS ENDURED – **12** letters, so it is in chapter **12**.

No. 20

*Follow peace with all [men], and holiness (**HOLINESS**), without which no man shall see the Lord (**LORD**):* Hebrews 12:14.

The **Hebrews**/Jews think they are holy enough in themselves, but of course we know that is not so. **Holiness** comes from the **Lord** and the Hebrews/Jews need to learn this. *Follow peace with all men, and holiness, without which **no man** shall see the Lord:* **no man**– Hebrew, or the rest of us, so this verse is in the book of Hebrews.

HOLINESS LORD - **12** letters, so it is in chapter **12**.

No. 21

*Jesus Christ the same (**same**) yesterday, and to day, and for ever.* Hebrews 13:8.

Jesus Christ is the **same** glorious person in the Old Testament (**Hebrew** Bible) as He is in the New Testament, so this verse is in the book of **Hebrews**.

7 is the number of **spiritual perfection**, and **6** is the number of **man**. Jesus is **perfection** (**7**) and also **man** (**6**), **7+6 =13**, so this verse is in chapter **13**.

Or - **ALWAYS THE SAME** – **13** letters.

No. 22
*Now the God of peace, that brought again from the dead our Lord Jesus, that great shepherd **(GREAT SHEPHERD)** of the sheep, through the blood of the everlasting covenant **(everlasting covenant)**,*
  Make you perfect in every good work to do his will, working in you that which is wellpleasing in his sight, through Jesus Christ; to whom [be] glory for ever and ever. Amen. Hebrews 13:20-21.

Memorize that the book of Hebrews is the only place in the New Testament where the words **'everlasting covenant'** are used.

The words **'everlasting covenant'** are used fourteen times in the Old Testament and the **Hebrews**/Jews were familiar with this term, so these verses are in the book of **Hebrews**.

GREAT SHEPHERD – **13** letters, so they are in chapter **13**.

JAMES

No. 1
*But let him **(him)** ask in faith, nothing wavering. For he that wavereth is like a wave **(wave)** of the sea **(sea)** driven with the wind **(wind)** and tossed.* James 1:6.

Some environmentalists think that **wind** farms drive birds away. The first letter of James is **J** and there is a bird called a **Jay**, so associate the Jaybird with wind, and you will remember that this verse is in the book of James.

For the purpose of association, think that **him, wave, sea** and **wind** are all singular words, and singular means **1**, so this verse is in chapter **1**.

No. 2
*But be ye doers (**doers**) of the word, and not hearers only, deceiving your own selves.* James 1:22

Jam is the first three letters of **Jam**es. For the purpose of association, think that if you want to make **jam** then you must 'do' (you must be a **doer**), or there will not be a finished product, so this verse is in the book of James.

A believer's **1**st priority should be to **do** what God's word commands, so this verse is in chapter **1**.

No. 3
*For as the body without the spirit (**the body without the spirit**) is dead, so faith without works is dead also.* James 2:26.

The first letter of James is **J** and there is a bird called a **Jay**.
For the purpose of association, think of the **spirit** or soul taking flight like a **Jay**bird when it leaves the **body**, so this verse is in the book of James.

I appreciate that the Bible mentions spirit, soul and body, and the Word of God pierces even to the dividing asunder of soul and spirit.

And the very God of peace sanctify you wholly; and [I pray God] your whole spirit and soul and body be preserved blameless unto the coming of our Lord Jesus Christ. 1st Thessalonians 5:23.

For the word of God [is] quick, and powerful, and sharper than any twoedged sword, piercing even to the dividing asunder of soul and spirit, and of the joints and marrow, and [is] a discerner of the thoughts and intents of the heart. Hebrews 4:12.

(1) body
(2) spirit

2 parts of man, so it is in chapter **2**.

No. 4

Even so the tongue is a little member, and boasteth great things. Behold, how great a matter a little fire kindleth!

And the tongue [is] a fire, a world of iniquity: so is the tongue among our members, that it defileth the whole body, and setteth on fire the course of nature; and it is set on fire of hell.

For every kind of beasts, and of birds, and of serpents, and of things in the sea, is tamed, and hath been tamed of mankind:

But the tongue can no man tame **(But the tongue can no man tame)**; *[it is] an unruly evil* **([it is] an unruly evil)**, *full of deadly poison* **(full of deadly poison)**. James 3:5-8.

We can lick **jam** with our tongues, and **jam** is the first three letters of **Jam**es, so these verses are in the book of James.

Verse 8 says:
(1) *But the tongue can no man tame;*
(2) *it is an unruly evil,*
(3) *full of deadly poison.*
3 descriptions of the tongue, so they are in chapter **3**.

No. 5

Go to now, ye that say, To day or to morrow we will go into such a city, and continue there a year, and buy and sell **(sell)**, *and get gain:*

Whereas ye know not what [shall be] on the morrow. For what [is] your life? It is even a vapour, that appeareth for a little time, and then vanisheth away.

For that ye [ought] to say, If the Lord will **(IF THE LORD WILL)**, *we shall live, and do this, or that.* James 4:13-15.

Jam is the first three letters of **Jam**es. For the purpose of association, think of **selling** jam, so these verses are in the book of James.

IF THE LORD WILL – 4 words, so they are in chapter **4**.

1ST PETER

No. 1

*Blessed [be] the God **(God)** and Father of our Lord Jesus Christ, which according to his abundant mercy hath begotten us again unto a lively hope by the resurrection of Jesus Christ from the dead,*

To an inheritance incorruptible, and undefiled, and that fadeth not away, reserved in heaven for you,

Who are kept by the power of God through faith unto salvation ready to be revealed in the last time.

Wherein ye greatly rejoice, though now for a season, if need be, ye are in heaviness through manifold temptations:

*That the trial of your faith **(trial of your faith)**, being much more precious than of gold that perisheth, though it be tried with fire, might be found unto praise and honour and glory at the appearing of Jesus Christ:*

Whom having not seen, ye love; in whom, though now ye see [him] not, yet believing, ye rejoice with joy unspeakable and full of glory:

Receiving the end of your faith, [even] the salvation of [your] souls.

Of which salvation the prophets have inquired and searched diligently, who prophesied of the grace [that should come] unto you:

Searching what, or what manner of time the Spirit of Christ which was in them did signify, when it testified beforehand the sufferings of Christ, and the glory that should follow.

Unto whom it was revealed, that not unto themselves, but unto us they did minister the things, which are now reported unto you by them that have preached the gospel unto you with the Holy Ghost sent down from heaven; which things the angels desire to look into.

1st Peter 1:3-12.

Verse seven speaks of the **trial of your faith**. For the purpose of association, think that Peter's faith was tried, so these verses are in some book of Peter.

N.B. I am not saying that Peter was the only one who had his faith tried. We all know what it is like to have our faith tried. I am merely forming an association.

For the purpose of association, think that **God** is mentioned **1st** in these verses, so they are in the book of **1st** Peter.

Jesus is mentioned after God the Father and He is **1** with God the Father, so these verses are in chapter **1**.

No. 2
*Forasmuch as ye know that ye were not redeemed with corruptible (**corruptible**) things, [as] silver and gold, from your vain conversation [received] by tradition (**tradition**) from your fathers;*
*But with the precious blood of Christ (**the precious blood of Christ**), as of a lamb without blemish and without spot:*
Who verily was foreordained before the foundation of the world, but was manifest in these last times for you,
Who by him do believe in God, that raised him up from the dead, and gave him glory; that your faith and hope might be in God.
1st Peter 1:18-21.

When **Peter's** faith was tried concerning knowing Jesus he failed in the presence of man who is **corruptible**. Romans 1:23. *And changed the glory of the uncorruptible God into an image made like to corruptible (**corruptible**) man, and to birds, and fourfooted beasts, and creeping things.* These verses are in some book of **Peter**.

N.B. I am not saying that Peter was the only one who failed in the presence of corruptible man, we are all guilty of the fear of man. I am merely forming an association.

Think of **tradition** as being **1st**, so these verses are in the book of **1st** Peter.

There is only **1** thing that redeems us, and that is **the precious blood of Christ**, so they are in chapter **1**

No. 3

I suggest that you memorize the following verses.

Wherefore gird up the loins of your mind, be sober, and hope to the end for the grace that is to be brought unto you at the revelation of Jesus Christ;
As obedient children, not fashioning yourselves according to the former lusts in your ignorance:
But as he which hath called you is holy, so be ye holy in all manner of conversation;
*Because it is written, Be ye holy (**holy**), for I (**I**) am holy.*
1st Peter 1:13-16

For the purpose of association, think that Peter was the one who denied Jesus and yet he was able to be **holy**, so these verses are in some book of Peter.

Holiness should be the **1st** priority for believers, so they are in the book of **1st** Peter.

The last phrase says for I am holy. **I** is similar in appearance to **1**, so the above verses are in chapter **1**.

No. 4

Wherefore laying aside all malice, and all guile, and hypocrisies, and envies, and all evil speakings,
As newborn babes, desire the sincere milk of the word, that ye may grow thereby:
If so be ye have tasted that the Lord [is] gracious.
To whom coming, [as unto] a living stone, disallowed indeed of men, but chosen of God, [and] precious,
*Ye also, as lively (**lively**) stones, are built up a spiritual house (**a spiritual house**), an holy priesthood (**an holy priesthood**), to offer up spiritual sacrifices, acceptable to God by Jesus Christ.* 1st Peter 2:1-5.

One day Jesus told Simon Peter that he would be called Cephas. *And he brought him to Jesus. And when Jesus beheld him, he said, Thou art Simon the son of Jona: thou shalt be called Cephas, which is by interpretation, A stone (**stone**).* John 1:42.

Remember that Jesus told Simon (the apostle Peter) that he would be called Cephas, which by interpretation means **stone**. The Greek word for Peter is Petros and means **stone**. We read of lively stones in these verses, so they are in some book of Peter.

Verse five says 'lively stones' and the first letter of lively is similar in appearance to **1**, so the above verses are in the book of 1st Peter.

We are told in verse five that believers are:
(1) **a spiritual house,**
(2) **an holy priesthood,**

2 things, so these verses are in chapter **2**.

No. 5
*Unto you therefore which believe ([HE]) [he is] precious (**precious**): but unto them which be disobedient, the stone (**1 stone**) which the builders disallowed, the same is made the head of the corner,*
1st Peter 2:7.

For the purpose of association, think that Jesus would be most **precious** to Peter as he was the one who denied Him and needed His forgiveness, so this verse is in some book of Peter.

N.B. I am not saying that Peter was worse than the rest of us. We are all sinners and stand in need of forgiveness. I am merely forming an association.

1 stone, so this verse is in the book of **1**st Peter.

HE is precious. When saying this sentence accent the word '**HE.**'

HE – **2** letters, so this verse is in chapter **2**.

I am aware that the associations given for this verse could also apply to 2nd Peter chapter 1. So to help you remember that it is **1st** Peter chapter 2, and not 2nd Peter chapter 1, think of the parallel verse in Psalm 118:22. *The stone (**stone**) [which] the builders refused is become the head [stone] of the corner.* This verse is in the Old

Testament and that was before Jesus was born, so for the purpose of association think that the **stone** was **1st**, so it is **1st** Peter.

No. 6
For what glory [is it], if, when ye be buffeted for your faults, ye shall take it patiently? but if, when ye do well, and suffer [for it], ye take it patiently, this [is] acceptable with God.
*For even hereunto were ye called (**called**): because Christ also suffered for us, leaving us an example, that ye should follow his steps (**that ye should follow his steps**):*
*Who did no sin (**NO SIN**), neither was guile found in his mouth (**Who did no sin, neither was guile found in his mouth**):*
1st Peter 2:20-22.

Verse 22: ***Who did no sin, neither was guile found in his mouth:***

For the purpose of association, think that there was **guile in the mouth** of Peter when he denied the Lord, so these verses are in some book of Peter.

And he denied it again. And a little after, they that stood by said again to Peter, Surely thou art [one] of them: for thou art a Galilaean, and thy speech agreeth [thereto].
*But he began to curse and to swear, [saying], I know not this man of whom ye speak (**I know not this man of whom ye speak**).*
Mark 14:70-71.

For the purpose of association, think that Jesus goes **1st**, and we **follow his steps,** so these verses are in the book of **1st** Peter.

NO SIN – 2 words, so they are in chapter **2**.

No. 7
*Casting (**casting**) all your care upon him (**JESUS**); for he careth for you.* 1st Peter 5:7.

For the purpose of association, think that Peter was a fisherman and was accustomed to **casting** nets into the sea, so this verse is in some book of Peter.

In this verse we are advised to **cast** our cares on Jesus, and He is number **1** in every sense of the word, so it is in the book of **1**st Peter.

For the purpose of association, think that those who have been saved by grace will cast their cares on Jesus. **5** is the number of grace, so this verse is in chapter **5**.

Or **JESUS – 5** letters.

No. 8

*Be sober, be vigilant **(be vigilant)**; because your adversary the devil **(DEVIL)**, as a roaring lion, walketh about, seeking whom he may devour:*
Whom resist stedfast in the faith, knowing that the same afflictions are accomplished in your brethren that are in the world.
1st Peter 5:8-9.

Be vigilant. For the purpose of association, think of Peter as desiring to give this advice because he failed to be vigilant, so these verses are in some book of Peter.
And he denied it again.
And a little after, they that stood by said again to Peter, Surely thou art [one] of them: for thou art a Galilaean, and thy speech agreeth [thereto].
But he began to curse and to swear, [saying], I know not this man of whom ye speak. Mark 14:70-71

N.B. I am not saying that Peter was the only one who needed to be vigilant. We all need to be vigilant because the devil is still a roaring lion. I am merely forming an association.

Think that the **1st** thing Peter would desire to do would be to warn us to be sober and vigilant, so the above verses are in the book of **1st** Peter.

DEVIL – 5 letters, so they are in chapter **5**

2ND PETER

No. 1
*Wherefore the rather, brethren **(brethren)**, give diligence **(diligence)** to make your calling and election sure: for if ye do these things, ye shall never fall:* 2nd Peter 1:10.

For the purpose of association, think that Peter would be the one to warn about diligence because he failed to be diligent in prayer and denied his Lord. *And he* (Jesus) *cometh unto the disciples, and findeth them asleep, and saith unto Peter, What, could ye not watch with me one hour?*
Watch and pray, that ye enter not into temptation: the spirit indeed [is] willing, but the flesh [is] weak. Matthew 26:40-41.

N.B. I am not saying that Peter was the only one who needed to be diligent. We all need to be diligent. I am merely forming an association.

The word '**brethren**' is a plural word. For the purpose of association, think that 1 is singular and 2 is plural, so the above verse is in the book of **2nd** Peter.

For the purpose of association, think that making our calling and election sure is number **1** in importance, so this verse is in chapter **1**.

No. 2
Knowing this first, that no prophecy of the scripture is of any private interpretation.
*For the prophecy came not in old time by the will of man: but holy men of God **(holy men of God)** spake [as they were] moved by the Holy Ghost **(Holy Ghost)**.* 2nd Peter 1:20-21.

Peter denied his Lord. For the purpose of association, think that he became a **holy man** in spite of his denials. So these verses are in some book of Peter.

(1) holy men of God
(2) Holy Ghost

2 agents, so they are in the book of **2nd** Peter.

1 Spirit directing the men, so these verses are in chapter 1.

I am aware that these verses could be in the book of 1st Peter chapter 2. When we write 2nd Peter 1:20-21 2nd Peter is before 1:20-21, so to help you to remember that they are in 2nd Peter chapter 1 think that the **holy men of God** in the Old testament were moved by the **Holy Ghost** before Peter was born, so the association **holy men of God** and **Holy Ghost** comes first and therefore refers to the book of 2nd Peter.

1ST JOHN

No. 1

That which was from the beginning, which we have heard, which we have seen with our eyes, which we have looked upon, and our hands have handled, of the Word (Word) of life;

(For the life was manifested, and we have seen [it], and bear witness, and shew unto you that eternal life, which was with the Father, and was manifested unto us;)

That which we have seen and heard declare we unto you, that ye also may have fellowship with us: and truly our fellowship [is] with the Father, and with his Son Jesus Christ.

And these things write we unto you, that your joy may be full.

This then is the message which we have heard of him, and declare unto you, that God is light, and in him is no darkness at all.

If we say that we have fellowship with him, and walk in darkness, we lie, and do not the truth:

But if we walk in the light, as he is in the light, we have fellowship

one with another, and the blood of Jesus Christ his Son cleanseth us from all sin.
If we say that we have no sin, we deceive ourselves, and the truth is not in us.
If we confess our sins, he is faithful and just to forgive us [our] sins, and to cleanse us from all unrighteousness.
If we say that we have not sinned, we make him a liar, and his word is not in us. 1st John chapter 1.

The beginning of these verses is similar to what we read in John's gospel chapter **1**, so they are in the book of **1**st John chapter **1**.

Notice the capital **W** for **W**ord.

No. 2
*My little children (**LITTLE CHILDREN**), these things write I unto you, that ye sin not. And if any man sin, we have an advocate (**advocate**) with the Father, Jesus Christ the righteous:* 1st John 2:1.

The words '**little children**' as referring to the disciples, are used once by the Lord Jesus in the gospel of John 13:33, and once by Paul when writing to the Galatians 4:19.

In the book of **1st John** the words '**little children**' are used nine times, so for the purpose of association, think of the book of **1st John** as the '**little children**' book.

The above verse contains the word '**advocate**,' and advocate can be defined as one that pleads in another's behalf. So again for the purpose of association, think that **children** need someone to plead on their behalf, so this verse is in the book of **1st John.**

LITTLE CHILDREN – **2** words, so it is in chapter **2**.

No. 3
*Love not the world (**love not the world**), neither the things [that are] in the world (**neither the things that are in the world**). If any man love the world, the love of the Father is not in him.* 1st John 2:15.

260

It is widely believed that **John** was the apostle whom Jesus loved. For the purpose of association, think of Jesus loving John and John loving Jesus and not the **world**. So this verse is in some book of John.

Also, for the purpose of association, always think as you read this verse I must not love the world but I must love Jesus. If we love Jesus and not the world then He is **1st** in our lives, so this verse is in the book of **1st** John.

(1) *Love not the world,* (it is not our final home).
(2) *neither the things that are in the world.*

We are told **2** times to have no love for the world, so this verse is in chapter **2**.

No. 4
*Whosoever is born **(born)** of God **(BORN OF GOD)** doth not commit sin; for his seed remaineth in him: and he cannot sin, because he is born of God.* 1st John 3:9.

When you read this verse think of what is recorded in John 1:12-13. *But as many as received him, to them gave he power to become the sons of God, [even] to them that believe on his name:*
*Which were born **(Which were born)**, not of blood, nor of the will of the flesh, nor of the will of man, but of God **(of God)**.* So the above verse is in some book of John.

Born: For the purpose of association, think that the **1st** thing that has to happen to us before we can function in this world is that we have to be born, so this verse is in the book of **1st** John.

BORN OF GOD – **3** words so it is in chapter **3**.

No. 5
*And he that keepeth his commandments **(keepeth his command-ments)** dwelleth in him, and he in him. And hereby we know that he abideth in us **(ABIDETH IN US)**, by the Spirit **(Spirit)** which he hath given us.* 1st John 3:24.

It is widely believed that John was the apostle whom Jesus loved. For the purpose of association, think of John **keeping His commandments** because He loved him, so this verse is in some book of John.

When you read this verse think of 1st John 4:1. *Beloved, believe not every spirit, but try the spirits whether they are of God: because many false prophets are gone out into the world.*

There is only **1 Holy Spirit**, so this verse is in the book of **1**st John.

ABIDETH IN US – **3** words so it is in chapter **3**.

No. 6
*Beloved, believe not every spirit (**BELIEVE NOT EVERY SPIRIT**), but try the spirits whether they are of God: because many false prophets are gone out into the world.* 1st John 4:1.

It is in John's gospel that we read about Jesus telling His disciples that He will send the **Spirit of truth** (see below).

In this verse we are warned to *believe not every spirit, but try the spirits whether they are of God:*

For the purpose of association, think that John would be the best person to tell us to try the **spirits** as he has already told us that Jesus will send the **Spirit of truth**. So this verse is in some book of John.

When you read this verse think immediately that there is only **1** Spirit of truth, so it is in the book of **1**st John.

BELIEVE NOT EVERY SPIRIT – **4** words, so this verse is in chapter **4**.

And I will pray the Father, and he shall give you another Comforter, that he may abide with you for ever;
*[Even] the Spirit of truth (**Spirit of truth**); whom the world cannot receive, because it seeth him not, neither knoweth him: but ye know him; for he dwelleth with you, and shall be in you.* John 14:16-17.

But when the Comforter is come, whom I will send unto you from the Father, [even] the Spirit of truth (Spirit of truth), which proceedeth from the Father, he shall testify of me: John 15:26.

Howbeit when he, the Spirit of truth (Spirit of truth), is come, he will guide you into all truth: for he shall not speak of himself; but whatsoever he shall hear, [that] shall he speak: and he will shew you things to come. John 16:13.

I suggest that you memorize 1st John chapter 4 so that you know which verses are in it.

No. 7
There is no fear in love (love); but perfect love (love) casteth out fear: because fear hath torment. He that feareth is not made perfect in love (love). 1st John 4:18.

It is widely believed that **John** was the apostle whom Jesus **loved**.

For the purpose of association, think that this verse would be in some book of John because it mentions the word **love** three times.

This verse is in what we could call the 'love chapter', i.e. **1st John chapter 4**. There are **21** verses in this chapter and the word love is mentioned **19** times. If you want to remember which chapter is the love chapter, think love and four. These two words each have four letters and the second letter is **o**.

No. 8
For whatsoever is born of God (WHATSOEVER IS BORN OF GOD) overcometh the world: and this is the victory that overcometh the world, [even] our faith.
Who is he that overcometh the world, but he that believeth that Jesus is the Son of God? 1st John 5:4-5.
When you read these verses think immediately of **John** 1:13: *Which were born (Which were born), not of blood, nor of the will of the flesh, nor of the will of man, but of God (of God).* The above verses are in some book of John.

For the purpose of association, think that being **born** is the **1st** thing that happens to us either physically or spiritually, so these verses are in the book of **1st** John.

WHATSOEVER IS BORN OF GOD – **5** words, so they are in chapter **5**.

I suggest that you memorize 1st John chapter 5 so that you know which verses are in it.

No. 9
*He that hath the Son hath life; [and] he that hath not the Son of God (**Son of God**) hath not life (**hath not life**).* 1st John 5:12.

Remember I stated at the beginning of this book that Jesus was portrayed as the **Son of God** in the gospel of **John**, so this verse is in some book of John.

For the purpose of association, think that there is only **1** Son of God, so it is in the book of **1st** John.

NO LIFE WITHOUT THE SON – **5** words, so this verse is in chapter **5**.

2ND JOHN

No. 1
And now I beseech thee, lady, not as though I wrote a new commandment unto thee, but that which we had from the beginning, that we love one another.
And this is love, that we walk after his commandments. This is the commandment, That, as ye have heard from the beginning, ye should walk in it.
*For many deceivers are entered into the world, who confess not that Jesus Christ is come in the flesh (**For many deceivers are entered into the world, who confess not that Jesus Christ is come in the flesh**).*

*This is a deceiver (**DECEIVER**) and an antichrist (**ANTICHRIST**).*
   Look to yourselves, that we lose not those things which we have wrought, but that we receive a full reward.
   Whosoever transgresseth, and abideth not in the doctrine of Christ, hath not God. He that abideth in the doctrine of Christ, he hath both the Father and the Son.
   If there come any unto you, and bring not this doctrine, receive him not into [your] house, neither bid him God speed:
   For he that biddeth him God speed is partaker of his evil deeds.
   2nd John 1:5-11.

When you read verse seven think immediately of what we read in **John** 1:14. And the Word was made flesh (***And the Word was made flesh),*** *and dwelt among us, (and we beheld his glory, the glory as of the only begotten of the Father,) full of grace and truth.*

For the purpose of association, think of the book of **John** as being the book that mentions the Lord's flesh frequently, so the above verses are in some book of **John**.

DECEIVER ANTICHRIST – 2 words, so they are in the book of **2**nd John.

There is only 1 chapter in 2nd John.

3RD JOHN

No. 1
*I wrote unto the church: but Diotrephes (Dio**tre**phes), who loveth to have the preeminence among them, receiveth us not.*
   Wherefore, if I come, I will remember his deeds which he doeth, prating against us with malicious words: and not content therewith, neither doth he himself receive the brethren, and forbiddeth them that would, and casteth [them] out of the church. 3rd John 1:9-10.

John is the only person who wrote **3** epistles and letters 4, 5 and 6 in Dio**tre**phes sounds similar to **3**, so these verses are in **3**rd John.
There is only one chapter in 3rd John.

JUDE

No. 1
Beloved, when I gave all diligence to write unto you of the common salvation, it was needful for me to write unto you, and exhort [you] that ye should earnestly contend for the faith which was once delivered unto the saints.

For there are certain men crept in unawares, who were before of old ordained to this condemnation, ungodly men, turning the grace of our God into lasciviousness, and denying the only Lord God, and our Lord Jesus Christ. Jude 1:3-4.

Just memorize that these verses are in the book of Jude. Jude has only one chapter.

No. 2
*And the angels which kept not their first estate, but left their own habitation, he hath reserved in everlasting chains under darkness unto the **jud**gment of the great day.* **Jud**e 1:6.

This verse is about the judgment of the fallen angels, and when we read of judgment in the Bible it is usually human beings who are being referred to. As this is a different judgment, then for the purpose of association, think that the first three letters of **jud**gment are the same as the first three letters of **Jud**e, so this verse is in the book of Jude. Jude has only 1 chapter.

The only other place in Scripture where we read of the **judgment** of the fallen angels is in 2nd Peter 2:4. *For if God spared not the angels that sinned, but cast [them] down to hell, and delivered [them] into chains **(chains)** of darkness, to be reserved unto judgment **(judgment)**;*

It is easy to remember that this verse is in **Peter**. Just think of him being in **chains** in the prison.

And when Herod would have brought him forth, the same night Peter was sleeping between two soldiers, bound with two chains (chains): and the keepers before the door kept the prison. Acts 12:6.

I know that Paul was in chains too, but when he writes his epistles he doesn't name them **'Paul'.**

When reading about angels think plural. **1** is singular and **2** is plural, so this verse is in **2**nd Peter.

When reading about chains think plural, **1** is singular and **2** is plural, so this verse is in chapter **2**.

The Lord Jesus referred to the devil and his angels in Matthew 25:41, but the word **judgment** is not mentioned. *Then shall he say also unto them on the left hand, Depart from me, ye cursed, into everlasting fire, prepared for the devil and his angels:* Matthew 25:41.

REVELATION

No. 1
I (I) am Alpha and Omega, the beginning and the ending (ending), saith the Lord, which is, and which was, and which is to come, the Almighty. Revelation 1:8.

The last book of the Bible is Revelation. Think of Revelation as the **ending**, so this verse is in Revelation.

The 'I' at the beginning of the verse looks similar to **1**, so it is in chapter **1**.

No. 2
Unto the angel of the church of Ephesus write; These things saith he that holdeth the seven stars in his right hand, who walketh in the midst of the seven golden candlesticks;

I know thy works, and thy labour, and thy patience, and how thou canst not bear them which are evil: and thou hast tried them which say they are apostles, and are not, and hast found them liars:

And hast borne, and hast patience, and for my name's sake hast laboured, and hast not fainted.

Nevertheless I have [somewhat] against thee, because thou hast left thy first love. Revelation 2:1-4.

In these verses the Lord Jesus is **reveal**ing truths about the church at Ephesus, so they are in the book of **Revelation**.

The remainder of chapter **2** and all of chapter **3** record truths about the other six churches. **2+3=5. 5** is the number of grace and it is because of God's grace that there are churches. The above verses are in chapter **2** because the church at Ephesus is the first one mentioned.

If you would like to memorize the seven churches mentioned in Revelation then try this simple association.

Ephesus	Every
Smyrna	Saint
Pergamos	Praises
Thyatira	The
Sardis	Saviour (of)
Philadelphia	Peace
Laodicea	Love

To help you remember that Philadelphia comes before Laodicea think that Jesus was called the Prince of **Peace** in the book of Isaiah before He came to demonstrate His **love** for us.

No. 3
The four and twenty elders fall down before him **(FALL DOWN BEFORE HIM)** *that sat on the throne, and worship him that liveth for ever and ever, and cast their crowns before the throne* **(and cast their crowns before the throne)***, saying,*

268

Thou art worthy, O Lord, to receive glory and honour and power: for thou hast created all things, and for thy pleasure they are and were created. Revelation 4:10-11.

This is the only place in the Bible where we read *'and cast their crowns before the throne.'* I imagine most people would realize that these verses are in the book of Revelation.

FALL DOWN BEFORE HIM – **4** words, so they are in chapter **4**.

There is only one other place in the Bible where we read the words **'fall down before him'** and that is in Psalm 72:11.
Yea, all kings shall fall down before him *(fall down before him)*; all nations shall serve him.*

No. 4
And they sung a new song (THEY SUNG A NEW SONG), saying, Thou art worthy to take the book, and to open the seals thereof: for thou wast slain, and hast redeemed us to God by thy blood out of every kindred, and tongue, and people, and nation;
And hast made us unto our God kings and priests: and we shall reign on the earth. Revelation 5:9-10.

I presume most people would be aware that these verses are in the book of Revelation.

THEY SUNG A NEW SONG – **5** words, so they are in chapter **5**.

No. 5
And I beheld, and I heard the voice of many angels (THE VOICE OF MANY ANGELS) round about the throne and the beasts and the elders: and the number of them was ten thousand times ten thousand, and thousands of thousands;
Saying with a loud voice, worthy is the Lamb that was slain to receive power, and riches, and wisdom, and strength, and honour, and glory, and blessing. Revelation 5:11-12.

I imagine most people would know that these verses are in the book of Revelation.

THE VOICE OF MANY ANGELS – 5 words, so they are in chapter **5**.

This is the only place in the Bible where the words *'the voice of many angels'* occurs.

No. 6
And I beheld when he had opened the sixth (6th) seal, and, lo, there was a great earthquake; and the sun became black as sackcloth of hair, and the moon became as blood;
And the stars of heaven fell unto the earth, even as a fig tree casteth her untimely figs, when she is shaken of a mighty wind.
And the heaven departed as a scroll when it is rolled together; and every mountain and island were moved out of their places.
And the kings of the earth, and the great men, and the rich men, and the chief captains, and the mighty men, and every bondman, and every free man, hid themselves in the dens and in the rocks of the mountains;
And said to the mountains and rocks, Fall on us, and hide us from the face of him that sitteth on the throne, and from the wrath of the Lamb:
For the great day of his wrath is come; and who shall be able to stand? Revelation 6:12-17.

I imagine most people would realize that these verses are in the book of Revelation.

Verse twelve tells us the **6th** seal was opened, so they are in chapter **6**.

No. 7
Saying, Amen: Blessing, and glory, and wisdom, and thanksgiving, and honour, and power, and might, [be] unto our God forever and ever. Amen.
And one of the elders answered, saying unto me, What are these which are arrayed (ARRAYED) in white robes? and whence came they?
And I said unto him, Sir, thou knowest. And he said to me, These are they which came out of great tribulation, and have washed their

robes, and made them white in the blood of the Lamb.

Therefore are they before the throne of God, and serve him day and night in his temple: and he that sitteth on the throne shall dwell among them.

They shall hunger no more, neither thirst any more; neither shall the sun light on them, nor any heat.

For the Lamb which is in the midst of the throne shall feed them, and shall lead them unto living fountains of waters: and God shall wipe away all tears from their eyes. Revelation 7:12-17.

I imagine most people would know that these verses are in the book of Revelation.

ARRAYED – **7** letters, so they are in chapter **7**.

No. 8

And the seventh angel sounded; and there were great voices in heaven, saying, The kingdoms of this world are become [the kingdoms] of our Lord, and of his Christ; and he shall reign for ever and ever.

And the four and twenty elders, which sat before God on their seats, fell upon their faces, and worshipped God,

*Saying, We give thee thanks, O Lord God Almighty, which art, and wast, and art to come; because thou hast taken to thee thy great power, and hast reigned (**THOU HAST TAKEN TO THEE THY GREAT POWER AND HAST REIGNED**).*

And the nations were angry, and thy wrath is come, and the time of the dead, that they should be judged, and that thou shouldest give reward unto thy servants the prophets, and to the saints, and them that fear thy name, small and great; and shouldest destroy them which destroy the earth. Revelation 11:15-18.

I presume most people would know that these verses are in the book of Revelation.

THOU HAST TAKEN TO THEE THY GREAT POWER AND HAST REIGNED – **11** words, so they are in chapter **11**.

No. 9

And there was war in heaven: Michael and his angels fought against the dragon; and the dragon fought and his angels,

And prevailed not; neither was their place found any more in heaven. (AND PREVAILED NOT; NEITHER WAS THEIR PLACE FOUND ANY MORE IN HEAVEN).

And the great dragon was cast out, that old serpent, called the Devil, and Satan, which deceiveth the whole world: he was cast out into the earth, and his angels were cast out with him.

And I heard a loud voice saying in heaven, Now is come salvation, and strength, and the kingdom of our God, and the power of his Christ: for the accuser of our brethren is cast down, which accused them before our God day and night.

And they overcame him by the blood of the Lamb, and by the word of their testimony; and they loved not their lives unto the death.
Revelation 12:7-11

I imagine most people would know that these verses are in the book of Revelation.

AND PREVAILED NOT; NEITHER WAS THEIR PLACE FOUND ANY MORE IN HEAVEN – **12** words, so they are in chapter **12**.

No. 10

Here is wisdom. Let him that hath understanding count the number of the beast: for it is the number of a man; and his number [is] Six hundred threescore [[and] six (FOR IT IS THE NUMBER OF A MAN; AND HIS NUMBER [IS] 666). Revelation 13:18.

I imagine most people would be aware that this verse is in the book of Revelation.

FOR IT IS THE NUMBER OF A MAN; AND HIS NUMBER IS 666 – **12** words and **1** group of numbers, so it is in chapter **13**.

No. 11

And whosoever was not found written in the book of life was cast into the lake of fire. Revelation 20:15.

If one is not already familiar with this verse, and does not know there is such a verse in the Bible it will certainly be a **revelation** to them, so this verse is in the book of Revelation.

On learning about this verse one would want to know **when** this would happen. The first syllable of **twen**ty rhymes with **when**, so this verse is in chapter **20**.

No. 12
I am Alpha and Omega, the beginning and the end, the first and the last (last). Revelation 22:13.

I presume most people would know that this verse is in the book of Revelation.

If you have memorized the number of chapters in the book of Revelation then you will know that the **last** chapter is **22**.

This is the end of this book, but hopefully not the end of forming associations. There are probably so many more verses in the Bible that you will want to form associations for. Enjoy the privilege which is ours i.e. having a copy of God's precious word to study.

My e-mail address is mgbarr96@gmail.com

Looking forward to hearing from you.